DRAWN TO THE LIGHT

Revelations of Knowledge of the Inner Meaning of Life

DRAWN

to the

LIGHT

Revelations of Knowledge of the Inner Meaning of Life

ELLA EVERS-MEINARDI

PORTLAND•OREGON
INKWATERPRESS.COM

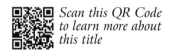
*Scan this QR Code
to learn more about
this title*

Library of Congress Control Number: 2018948051

Publisher: Inkwater Press | www.inkwaterpress.com

Paperback ISBN-13 978-1-62901-552-1 | ISBN-10 1-62901-552-0
Kindle ISBN-13 978-1-62901-553-8 | ISBN-10 1-62901-553-9

1 3 5 7 9 10 8 6 4 2

Table of Contents

Dedication and Acknowledgments ix

Introduction xi

PART I • XV

TURNING POINT

A Broken Triangle 1, *Funeral Arrangements* 10, *Eternal Goodbyes* 12, *Funeral* 13, *The Diamond Light* 16, *Giving Birth* 20, *Christmas 1973* 22, *An Unusual Sentence* 23, *Rays of Light and Inquiry* 27

PART II • 31

EARLY YEARS

My Childhood 33, *Vicissitudes of War* 35, *Liberation and Trauma* 38, *Revelation of Truth* 42, *Harmen* 45, *Marriage* 46, *South America* 48, *Caribbean Island* 49, *Revealing My Spiritual Side* 53

PART III • 57

WIDENING HORIZONS

New Lights of Understanding 59, *Meeting an Artist* 61,
An Important Dream 64, *A New Marriage* 69, *Two
Husbands* 72, *Loyalty* 75, *Reiki* 79, *Huna Initiation* 82, *A
Beacon of Light* 85

PART IV • 87

DWESHA AND RAGA

Breakdown 89, *An Ancient Prayer Revealed* 93, *A Vision* 95,
To the Coast 97, *The Beloved and I Are One* 99, *Fire
Initiation in Montana* 102, *Meeting Earlyne* 106

PART V • 109

DRAWN TO THE EASTERN LIGHT

Touched by Divine Love 111, *Hearing About Sai Baba* 113,
Lightning Strikes 117, *Pilgrimage* 120, *Ashram Life* 125,
Ponderings on the Path 130, *Parents* 132, *Puttaparthi
1989* 136, *Interview* 140

PART VI • 145

PRACTICING THE TEACHINGS

Russians 147, *Graduation Time* 150, *When Silence
Speaks* 152, *Destiny for David* 156, *Reflections* 162, *Hypnotic
Spell* 167, *Shirdi Sai Baba* 171, *Book of Bhrighu* 174

PART VII • 177

PATHWAY OF KUNDALINI

Kundalini Returns 179, *Help Offered* 184, *Guided to
the Third Eye Book* 186, *An Invitation to India* 191,
Dr. Goel 195, *Classroom in Paradise* 199, *The Guru
Watches* 205, *Receiving Divine Grace* 209, *Meditation Camp*

in Bhigaan 211, *A Different Look at Paradise* 216, *Vision of the Divine Guru* 224, *Mahashivaratri in Bhigaan* 226, *My Father* 230, *Kundalini Movements* 234, *Merging with My Guru's Guru* 237

PART VIII • 241

STUMBLING BLOCKS

Obstacles on the Path 243, *Back to Guruji's Ashram* 246, *Screams in Kundalini* 251, *Kundalini and Sex* 254, *Going Home to Turmoil* 257, *A Glimpse of Light* 262, *Saying Goodbye* 265, *Meeting Ammachi* 268, *Major Change and Challenge* 270, *The Guru Lives* 273, *Guruji's Statue* 275, *Blessings for Writing* 279

PART IX • 285

FROM FORM TO FORMLESS GOD

Mahashivaratri 2000 287, *Doubts* 294, *Personal Pain* 299, *"Not Now"* 305, *Resurrection* 308, *Our Sai World Crashes* 312, *Taking a Stand* 317, *The Sai Baba Cult* 320, *Analysis of Sai-Miracles* 324, *Aftermath* 329, *Transition* 332

EPILOGUE

Esoteric Knowledge 345, *My Journey* 348

Appendix 353
Glossary 357
Bibliography 363

Dedication and Acknowledgments

This book is dedicated to my deeply beloved husband Harmen Evers, whose untimely death propelled me to search for the true meaning of life. It is also dedicated to my parents, with a special Dutch *"Dank U wel"* ("thank you") to my mother for having been my first spiritual teacher. My deep heartfelt thanks go to my late husband Jon Sutton, who always encouraged me to explore all possibilities in life.

This book is also written in memory of and gratitude to Gurudev Shri Siddheshwar Baba Maharaj, also known as Shri Guruji or Dr. B.S. Goel. His initiations and teachings of the *Kundalini* pathway are forever immeasurable.

Special thanks of gratitude go to my dearest friend, healer, counselor and mystic, Ton Borgesius, who helped me move through many obstacles on my life's journey to the light.

I also thank my adult children, David and Femke, for keeping me ever alert to consider different points of view and to practice tolerance. I am especially grateful to David, who gave me the support I needed when caught between the languages of Dutch and English.

My deepest gratitude goes to my friend Ada Waalboer of The Netherlands for spending hours of her time reading my text and its many revisions and giving valuable inspirational critique. I am eternally in her debt.

I believe she and other friends and family were truly sent by God at the exact time needed, and to all I give thanks. Their help has added profound insight and spiritual joy to my life.

Finally, a special "thank you" goes to Craig Sommers, the attorney who helped me see my way through the myriad of problems I was facing following the death of my husband. Resolving those problems freed me to start a life of spiritual exploration and to answer the burning questions I had about death, dying and the reason why we live.

Not all names mentioned in my story are real. I used fictitious names only when I could not obtain permission.

*I offer this book to my innermost
Guru who has been drawing me to His beaconing
Light in which I seek my refuge.*

Introduction

IN YOUR LIGHT – Rumi
"I know you're tired but come, this is the way...

In your light, I learn how to love.
In your beauty, how to make poems
You dance inside my chest where no-one sees you,
but sometimes I do, and that sight becomes this art." – Rumi

The light attracts all that lives. We could never see the light if the darkness did not reveal it. We have come to Earth to play out our destinies as souls, a play between darkness and light. Most of us intuitively know this to be true, especially when we move on in our lives. We are all drawn to the light, revealing "knowledge and truth" to us about who we are and what God is...

Everyone has a story to tell. My story began in the dark days of occupation in WWII when I lived on the frontline in my hometown Nijmegen in The Netherlands. My Sunday school teacher during the war taught me at a very early age that God is light, that we can get nearer to him when we think of him and smile those inner clouds away when we are sad. I went through early life with my secret smile on the inside, my early inner truth. After the war, I became a reflective child suffering from post-traumatic stress disorder. While meditating at the age of twelve, life, as I had known it, exploded into an all-knowing awareness and the entire universe stood revealed before me. The experience touched my being so completely that I went through an inner personality change in which my psychological scars of pain and fear of the war vanished for good. I felt stronger, but kept the revelation hidden deep inside me, because I had no words to describe what had happened to me.

Despite the experience, I grew up as a normal teenager, went to school, and became a librarian. I married at a young age and with my husband moved from The Netherlands to Suriname, then Curaçao and later on to the United States of America.

Within ten months of our moving to California, a hit-and-run car killed my young husband while he was biking home. Shocked to the core of my being and nine months' pregnant with our second child, I slowly began to wonder where my husband had gone, asking, "Is there an afterlife?" Later on I also asked the questions: "Why do we live, why do we die, and what is this life about?" I did not know that these were the questions that mankind has always pondered...

The death of my husband was a turning point in my life. New mystical openings immediately happened and my life took a new direction. My spiritual journey back to what I had known at the age of twelve began...

Drawn to the Light is written for those who also wonder deeply about the true meaning of life and who will keep searching despite the enormous efforts it takes to find the truth. I know that when a spiritual aspirant seriously and with full focus sets out to find the essence of who we actually are, sudden shifts in consciousness may spontaneously occur. I call these shifts revelations as they happen when the veil covering our limited vision lifts and higher realms of consciousness become visible, bringing the light of knowledge within our reach.

I am aware that many of my readers have had many profound experiences, and I am glad to know for certain that I am not alone in this... Like most, I am an ordinary seeker with a heartfelt longing and strong aspiration to become one with the light of eternal knowing, called Cosmic Consciousness.

My book begins in Western thought until the road opens to embrace the treasures found in ancient Indian thought. I point out that God is with us under many names and forms, as described in various religious and mystical texts. I illustrate that He actually appears in our lives, as He did in mine, during childhood and adulthood, in times of crisis, in times when we think of Him, and in times when we least expect it. In my story, He revealed himself through many divine images and visions. God, as the source of all appearances, ultimately points to that formless Consciousness itself. I feel quite privileged to have touched upon that source of all knowledge.

Drawn to the Light shows that the divine light will lead the practitioner through visual and auditory images, the "seeing" and the "hearing" clairvoyant and clairaudient, until the seeker has an expansion in understanding the divine truth. It is like a seedling growing naturally into a large tree to take in a wider view. For a seeker this new perspective begins to encompass other forms and other teachers of that same light, that same truth. A seeker will come to understand that God is the same everywhere, namely in all names, all forms, and in all practices of sincere worship.

God is the substratum in all things, and through deep meditation the light of God inside us is found. Some people, like myself, have seen this light spontaneously. This can happen as we are opening beyond the known dimensions into that greater awareness impossible to describe in words.

Since time immemorial, humankind has known the possibility

of contact with this infinite cosmic energy. Connecting with it is like finding the highway straight to the luminous heart of God.

Drawn to the Light is also written for seekers who want to know about *Kundalini* awakening, and those who are experiencing *Kundalini's* sacred rise, grace and pitfalls and who need help and more information regarding this cosmic power. *Kundalini*, also called the cosmic serpent, is known to be no other than the divine *Shakti*, the energy of fire, which, once awakened, will help finalize the goal of all spiritual life: the understanding of *tat tvam asi* (translation: *That* thou art) found in the text of the Chandogya Upanishad VI, 8:7.

I want my reader to know that I will use the terms God, the light of God, higher Consciousness, Self, the Cosmic Christ, Cosmic Consciousness, the divine Mother, the Absolute, the Eternal, *Shakti, Shakti-Kundalini, Atman, Rishi*, the Real, Brahman, Beloved, He, Lord, *That*, divine light, truth and light intermittently, as all depict that one source from which all things flow into existence.

The purpose of this book is simple. It is to take you on my journey and inspire you where to look and how to find that light of God that is drawing all of humanity to His glorious light that surpasses all understanding.

TRUTH IS ONE; THE SAGES SPEAK OF IT IN DIFFERENT WAYS (Rig Veda)

PART I

Turning Point

Chapter One

A Broken Triangle

I was nine months' pregnant. The preceding months had been a time of wondrous feelings of gladness and anticipation. A new child was to be born. The whole world would change. The baby, alive and well, was making itself known by pushing its tiny feet and hands against the womb, bulging my already fully stretched abdomen.

I had told my four-year-old son over and over again about the great event of the coming birth of our new baby. "Oh, December will be a glorious month," I often joyfully proclaimed.

We had come to the United States following an invitation for my husband to become an assistant vice president of one of the world's largest financial institutions.

Harmen, my husband, our son David, and I had only been in Marin County for ten months. We had left a tropical island in the Caribbean, Curaçao, where Harmen was the economist for the central banking system. In San Anselmo, we had bought our dream house, a custom-built luxurious three-level wood-framed home with views over the rolling hills of California. While living in foreign countries for years, Harmen, David, and I had become a very close-knit family.

It was November 23, 1973. Harmen and I got up around six in

the morning, drowsy, still wanting to sleep more. "I had a night-mare," Harmen said. "So did I," I replied, adding, "Let's not talk about it. Dreams deal with our fears, they are not real." In my dream that night I had seen Harmen together with his father, who had died eight years before. It gave me a feeling of foreboding, which I didn't want to relay to my husband just before he set off for work. While Harmen was getting dressed to go to his work at the bank in San Francisco, I ran down the stairs to prepare break-fast. As always, I was in a rush to get Harmen out the door in time to catch his commuter bus at six-thirty in the morning.

After eating his toast with a fried egg in a hurry, Harmen, already dressed in his raincoat, stood up. He looked very serious, his face pale, and he was in deep thought. A light shone from his gray-blue eyes through his dark-rimmed glasses. With one shoulder up and the other down, he made a statement. "Ella," he said, "as soon as the baby is born I want to buy life insurance, so that if anything should happen to me there will be enough money for our new child to attend college." I believe that what he said was in response to his nightmare. Touched by his thought-fulness, I told him how warm these sincere thoughts of love and caring towards our unborn child made me feel.

As Harmen was leaving the house that morning, I went back to bed to give my unborn child and myself a chance to rest again. David was still sleeping. "No need to wake him up." His nursery school was closed since it was the Friday after Thanksgiving. A few hours later David and I got up slowly and took our time to get ready for the day. I decided that we would spend part of the day looking for a special card to announce the birth of the baby. Harmen had asked me to take care of everything regarding the birth and all other things pertaining to the family household. He had no time to concern himself about these things, as all his time and thoughts were taken up by the banking business.

The day was gray and cloudy with drizzles of rain barely wet-ting the pavement. After a few hours of driving around Marin County, I became tired and realized that few stores were open the day after Thanksgiving. I gave up my search, and little David and I returned home empty-handed. At home, David curled up on the sofa in our cozy family room to watch *Sesame Street,* while I began preparations for dinner in the adjacent kitchen.

Then the telephone rang. An impersonal, almost hostile voice was telling me that my husband must pick up his bike from the bike shop that night, or else he could not reclaim it, because it had been in the shop too long. Harmen had bought a European-style bicycle to bike around the area on the weekends. After a month, he had taken it back to the bicycle shop for a small new-bike adjustment service. There had not been any time for him to pick it up. The rains had started and even thoughts of biking had been fading.

The commanding voice on the phone stirred my soul in a strange way. It felt as if an icicle had penetrated my heart for a second. I hung up pondering much...and continued cooking dinner – potatoes, green beans with meatballs and a Dutch meat sauce. Dinner was almost ready when the doorbell rang. It was Harmen. I could see the happiness in his eyes when he shouted jokingly, "Where is the baby?" I put my arms lovingly around him. "Of course still in here," patting my stomach, "otherwise, you know I would have phoned you!"

We were, the three of us, a unique triangle of Dutch culture. Harmen was our hero, the focus of our attention. He was glad to come home every day to his special world. Speaking his native tongue relaxed him from the stress he felt at the bank, where he had to speak American English at a professional level. Harmen went upstairs to take a shower and David and I came along to share our experiences of the day. This was our daily routine of reconnecting and celebrating our togetherness. "Harmen, the bike shop called. They really want you to pick up your bike," I said, while Harmen put on his leisure clothes.

I went downstairs, set the table, finished cooking and called, "Dinner is ready!" David and Harmen came running down the stairs and we sat down to eat. The dining area was completely private, bordered by forests that continued on to our hilltop, where a horse ranch was located. The sounds of whinnying horses had often reminded us of the drama of the battle of good vs. bad guys in the movies of the American Wild West.

The evening was getting dark. I switched on the lamp over our dining table. Harmen and David enjoyed this typical Dutch winter dinner very much. David loved it so much that some of Harmen's string beans even ended up on David's plate.

All of a sudden, after he finished dinner, Harmen stood up and said, "Ella, would you please take me to the bike shop. I must go now." He put on his jacket to leave. "Help me, Ella, please help me, take me *now*, without delay!"

I was alarmed, because Harmen appeared tense in a strange way. I paused for a moment and replied, "Let us take David with us, or better yet, call a baby sitter so we could go out for a cup of coffee besides picking up your bike."

"No, Ella, put David in bed now. Don't put his pajamas on, but put him in bed as he is. Please, please, I beg you to take me this very moment!"

I walked to the kitchen and then back to the dining area, saying, "But a car could hit you from behind. Wait until tomorrow when it is light."

"Please, Ella, take me, take me... I must go now!"

I wanted him to stay home, because there was some sense of fear in me for his safety, but the thought raced through my mind that I was not his mother and that he had the freedom to make his own decisions to go or not to go when or where he wanted. So I put David in bed and said to him, "Mamma will be right back; it will just be a few minutes to take Pappa to the bike shop."

During our short drive in the car, I sat behind the steering wheel, my right arm affectionately wrapped around Harmen's shoulder. I tried to relax him by stroking him softly. When we arrived at the bike shop, I asked, "Shall I wait for you?"

"No, take a right turn at the street next to the bike shop, turn around, go straight home and take care of David."

I did what he said reluctantly. Something did not feel right. After I turned around, I followed a strong impulse to stop the car in front of the bicycle shop. From across the street I looked at my husband, clearly visible under the lights of the shop. I saw him talking with a clerk. I waved, and waved again my goodbye. I think he did not see me. Very slowly and with much hesitation, I drove away.

At home I rushed upstairs to check on David, but he was already fast asleep. I felt like cleaning up the house since I had not had the chance to do so during the day. I worked to make the house beautiful and shiny. I washed all Harmen's shirts, hanging them to dry on plastic hangers in the laundry room. I washed the pants that were part of my pregnancy outfits. When everything was perfect, I sat down and rested. It was nine o'clock. I wondered when Harmen would be back. I remembered he had asked me to sew a zipper in his work pants. I decided to really make him happy and fix the pants. It was around ten in the evening when I again began to wonder where he could be. It was a special shopping night in San Rafael, but the stores were only open until nine.

Harmen had told me over and over again that he intended to buy a special gift for me to commemorate the birth of the baby and that he could hardly wait until the baby was born. He had been asking me what I wanted and emphasized, "It has to be something very beautiful. Whatever you really want, you shall have." Even though I had said, "Please wait till the baby is born," I knew that it was very much on his mind to purchase this special gift in advance. "Maybe he is shopping for the gift he had been talking about so much," I thought and yet at the same time I realized again that the stores were definitely all closed by now. Something must have happened. I wanted to call some of my new friends to tell them that I was worried, but since it was already late, I restrained myself and waited...

I tried to make myself comfortable on the sofa. I picked up *U.S. News and World Report* from the magazine stack and began to read. The main article with a cover page photo of John F. Kennedy had been written to observe the 10-year anniversary of his assassination. The article spoke about Bobby Kennedy as well, and the tragic fact that his surviving widow was pregnant at the time of his assassination. This story struck me, and all of a sudden I had that deep inner sense that this might be my fate as well. I began to panic, my thoughts racing. "Stop thinking such thoughts," I told myself. I quieted myself down as much as I could and waited, but my heart was throbbing wildly.

The house was in perfect stillness when I heard footsteps on the outdoor stairway leading to the front door. "Was it finally Harmen?" Our little dachshund Daphne did not move, nor did she bark. She just stood there as if nailed to the ground. "How strange," I thought. I was in my underpants barely covered by my maternity blouse. My clean slacks were hanging to dry in the laundry room.

The doorbell rang. Daphne remained quiet and motionless. Through the window next to our front door I looked through the bamboo beaded curtain and saw three men standing on the front porch, in utter silence. A thought flashed through my mind, "Three unknown men at my door at 11:00 P.M. at night, this cannot be right. What should I do?" I ran to the laundry room and hastily put on my pants. I took a deep breath and slowly walked back to the front door and lifted the bamboo beads up away from the window. I gestured to the three men through the glass window: "Who are you?"

One of the men wore a Sheriff's star. Only from having watched Wild West movies did I understand what this meant and consequently I opened the door. "Are you Mrs. Evers?" they asked.

"Yes," I said. And then in a whisper, "Is my husband dead?"

A moment of great suspense followed, an eternity of silence. Time stood still and my mind froze. Their reply came, "Yes, your husband is dead."

Little do I remember of the sequence of events that took place after the three men sat down in my living room. They told me that a car had hit Harmen from behind and sped away. I was informed that such a hit-and-run was a serious crime in California. "When your husband was found and transported to Marin General Hospital he was already dead on arrival." I hardly could take it in.

I was given some of Harmen's belongings, his wallet with two dollars in it and a ticket from the bike shop. They put his golden ring depicting Viracocha, the Inca creator God, into my hands and said, "This is one of your husband's rings. We are sorry it took so long to find your husband's identity. He was finally identified through the ticket of the bike shop he carried in his wallet. Your husband died five minutes past eight." That was about ten minutes after I had dropped him off at the bike shop... "We cannot give you more of his belongings. Everything went to the crime laboratory. We tried to take your husband's wedding ring off, but this was impossible."

"I know," I said, "my husband wants to keep his wedding ring on."

I was not surprised at this. Harmen had told me over the twelve years of our marriage that when he died he wanted to be buried with his wedding ring on. Up to this point, I had remained reasonably calm. Then I stood up and an indescribable pain of loss began to take hold of me. I remember pacing up and down the living room again and again, saying, "But I am pregnant, he cannot be dead, I am pregnant, he cannot be dead." Then I called for him: "HARMEN...HARMEN...HARMEN!" The sound of the words reverberated throughout the house. Only that sound of his name was all there was.

David heard my cry and came rushing down the stairs from his bedroom still dressed in his corduroy pants and his white cotton shirt with dark blue kitty cats. *"Mamma, wat is er gebeurd?"* "Mamma, what has happened?"

I took my son into my arms while squatting at his level to look into his eyes. "Remember I took Pappa to the bike store? A car came and hit him from behind. It was so bad that his body could no longer live. Then God took Pappa up to heaven. He cannot come home to us again. God will take care of Pappa and I will take care of you!"

The world around me disappeared and only David and I remained in it. Our triangle was broken forever. My world as I knew it had shattered. At that moment of realizing that Harmen was gone forever, a hidden aspect of enormous strength and determination inside of me awakened. In this new state, I began to take charge of the situation and make phone calls to The Netherlands to bring the sad news to our nearest relatives, my parents and my brother-in-law Theo, who was to inform Harmen's mother in person.

David and I would never be the same again. I was the only one in charge now, the only decision-maker in a completely different culture of which I had no knowledge as yet. While on the phone I was unaware that the officers were leaving and that other people were entering my house. No one spoke while I made the phone calls. But for my voice, there was complete silence in the house. Then I wondered whether my unborn baby could be in real danger because of the overwhelming shock to my whole system. With an immense desire to protect the life of the baby, I called my gynecologist and informed him of my husband's passing. I asked, "What can I do to keep the baby safe?"

My doctor assured me, "Nothing can happen to the baby. It is full-grown and ready to be born. I will prescribe sleeping pills so that you at least can sleep."

Then thoughts of my husband's body alone in the funeral home began to haunt me and I phoned to find out if someone would be there at all times during the night. I would certainly have gone in person and stayed with my husband's body if I had not been so very pregnant and if my son had not needed me. The funeral home official assured me there was someone with the body.

We had been attending the Lutheran Church in nearby Fairfax and I decided it was best to immediately call our minister to ask for spiritual help. Unfortunately, it was his weekend off. I proceeded to phone his back-up and implored him to say the appropriate prayers for my husband. This minister did not seem to understand why I felt this was important and he did not properly respond to my dire needs as one would expect of a man of the cloth to do. Contrary to my Dutch religious upbringing it was crystal-clear to me that prayers were crucial for Harmen at this time. I wanted to send out prayers to urgently beseech God to open heaven's door to receive my husband's soul.

As I began to pay attention to my surroundings, I noticed that some of my neighbors whom I had known only for a few months started to file into our living room. Some of them might have been in the house for a while. I had been completely unaware of their presence. It must have been after midnight. I sat down on the sofa.

I got a glimpse of Ellen Forristal, my spunky high-spirited Dutch-Jewish neighbor, her dignified face shrouded in sobering silence. I could not connect...and felt as far away as if living in another world. I remember Ray, a high school teacher from up our hill, holding my hands, urging me to cry. "But if I cry, it is only for myself and not for Harmen! What can I do for Harmen?" was what I needed to know.

That night and many nights to follow were the darkest of my life. The light had left and I had become a person with only a working brain handling the family affairs almost mechanically with a sense of enormous responsibility in response to what I thought Harmen would have wanted me to do. I no longer could feel anything. I was in total shock.

In this time of utter despair I was unaware that this turning point in my life would shift my life's attention in a completely different direction. The events that followed the death of Harmen reawakened my deeper being and provided the basis of my spiritual journey to come. This would lead to the experience of sudden revelations of spiritual knowledge and an understanding of the connection between this world and the next.

Chapter Two
Funeral Arrangements

The next day, the bank's vice president accompanied by his wife and an assistant vice president came to my house to assist me with the funeral arrangements and contracts. "Mrs. Evers, we will never forget Dr. Evers," Harmen's boss said, seemingly shocked. "Let this be the day to always remember him. A year from now we will meet here again in his memory!"

"Helmut," I said, "Within the year, all of you will have forgotten my husband completely." I had made a prophetic statement and the truth of it became apparent in the very near future.

In my mind I had no doubt that these men ultimately would not be my friends. Harmen had often spoken about some unbelievable intrigues and political maneuverings at the bank, where power struggles took place devoid of much humanity. Shaken as his colleagues may have appeared at that moment, I knew their sympathy would be of short duration. Even though I was in a high state of distress, intuitively I was acutely aware not to expect any help from these bankers in the long run.

All of my life I had been frightened by the sight of funeral homes that I had seen in The Netherlands, where they displayed caskets in their front windows, and now I found myself with the banker colleagues in such a place in Marin County called "Chapel of the Hills." The building was of a Spanish stucco style with a red tiled roof. Flowerbeds and a small palm tree bordered a well-kept green lawn in the front. Inside, silence and semi-darkness set the appropriate tone for my state of mind. When I had to select a casket for my husband, something broke in me. I felt love flowing from the depth of my heart, making me choose the best and most beautiful silver-blue metallic case in which to rest Harmen's remains. Nothing spooked me, as I spontaneously put my arms in the gauze-like lining of the coffin to fill it with all the feelings I held for my husband. Energy of infinite love began pouring through my whole being into the coffin.

Back in the office of the funeral home, I asked, "Can I now see my husband?"

The funeral director replied, "Mrs. Evers, it is really better for you to remember him as he was."

I nevertheless insisted that I simply had to see him, but then in the next moment, I hesitated as I thought of my pregnancy and the potential harm that might happen to the baby from the shock. I decided that the bankers should view Harmen's body first. I asked them, "Please see him for me, and report back to me how bad this really is and…"

The funeral director interrupted me and said, "The body is not in any state to be viewed."

"When," I asked, "can the body of my husband be seen?"

"Next week Tuesday," came the reply.

"Very well, I am making my commitment now that I will come to say goodbye to my husband on Tuesday, because I am his wife!" Looking the man straight in the eyes, I asked, "Are you the one who will deal with my husband's body doing those things that need to be done?" When the answer was affirmative, I kept looking into the man's eyes and said, "I am sure that you deal with a lot of bodies and that you cannot always bring your whole being into this kind of work, I mean your heart and spirit. I understand that this could burn you out quickly. But I am asking you today, that when you deal with my husband's body, to feel compassion, because this is a different case. Here is a man that may be dead, but is not dead yet, because he is very alive inside of me," and I pointed to my unborn baby.

My look into the man's eyes was long and penetrating and I knew that his soul understood my intent to have him lovingly deal with the remains of my husband.

Chapter Three

Eternal Goodbyes

The next Tuesday, I drove to the funeral home accompanied by my parents and my brother-in-law, who had arrived from The Netherlands the day before. Even though my family had come to help and support me, I felt completely alone and could not connect with them emotionally. It seemed that even though they were present, they lived in a different sphere and I could not go there. In my state of mind their world of being was far away and there was no possibility for them to be able to reach to where I was. I was completely lost and yet I could think.

We were ushered into a small room where Harmen's body lay in an open coffin. My first reaction to seeing him was immeasurable shock and disbelief. I stammered, "What have they done to you?" while noticing that Harmen's thick blond eyelashes had been replaced with black ones. The small bouquet of red roses I had sent some days ago to be with him lay dried out in brownish color on his coffin. As I looked at my husband dressed in his best pinstriped dark business suit, all the love I had ever felt swept over me. In that moment I understood that greater love of the Christ and knew that this love had the immense power to call the dead back to life. I understood what Jesus had said, that love does lift and move mountains. While I felt this enormous power of love flowing, I fought with my conscience. I wanted to call my husband back from the dead and almost knew I could do it. Then a thought entered my mind that this was blasphemy and that even though I thought I could, I should not do it, because I was not the Christ and I did not know God's plan. In that moment I surrendered to the will of God and spoke my final eternal goodbyes. I placed Harmen's psalm book into his hands opened at a most beautiful hymn, but suddenly it fell away and closed. Bewildered, I put the silk red bookmark to where the hymn could be found and laid the closed book under his folded hands. "He will find it," I said.

More thoughts of farewell now came to me and I said, "I will see you in *your* tomorrow."

I heard Theo, who was standing behind me, say, "I promise that I will take care of at least one of the children should this be needed." I silently responded to him, thinking, "Never, never will the children be separated!" It was my soul's pledge to my husband.

Chapter Four

Funeral

So far I had been able to sleep only two hours a night even after taking the prescribed sleeping pills. Most nights, I walked around the house or sat at Harmen's desk with vague hopes that I would somehow be able to connect with him. Occasionally, I would stroll downstairs, sometimes looking at my parents asleep in the family room and Theo fast asleep on the sofa in our living room. To me, the house seemed veiled in a darkness of which I was a major part. Our dream house certainly had taken on a total new reality.

It was November the twenty-eighth, the day of Harmen's funeral. I got dressed early in the morning in the long black formal maternity dress I had bought the day before in the same store where Harmen and I had bought my pregnancy outfits with the joy of expecting our baby. The sorrow I felt while fitting these clothes of mourning was immense. Not able to take in more emotional pain, my heart began to block the feelings, leaving its space hollow and empty. In my mind I knew that Harmen wanted me to dress in style and I would do anything that would have pleased him. I knew I had to be his representative facing the bankers and other people that day. With this strong sense of obligation and determination I stood, dressed in my black pregnancy dress, looking out the window.

The time was around six-fifteen in the morning. The large windows allowed me to see the green rolling hills awakening in the first morning light. How weary and odd it felt standing there, alone, fully dressed for the funeral. It was like a dream, nothing felt real. No one was up yet in the house.

While I kept staring out of the window, I slowly became aware that the dogs in the neighborhood were howling. They sounded like a pack of wolves. I was not surprised at this... I sensed intuitively that the dogs were responding to my husband's spirit walking through our neighborhood. Harmen had told me that when he walked to the main road every morning at six-fifteen, many of the neighborhood dogs would come to greet him. Harmen had gotten to know these dogs well, and they had become his early morning friends. Sometimes they even accompanied him to the Golden Gate Transit bus stop at Butterfield Road. I imagined now that the dogs could see him in spirit form and were bemoaning his death. It felt very eerie. "Do you hear what I hear?" I asked my mother after she got up. She nodded affirmatively. The dogs continued to howl for a long time.

Later that morning we left for Chapel of the Hills. In the funeral chapel, Harmen's casket, surrounded by flowers, was standing on an elevated platform. The president of the bank sent a large wreath made up of white carnations and dark-red anthuriums. I was ushered to sit down in the front row facing the casket. I do not remember who else was there. Our son, David, was at a friend's house, because I felt he was too young to attend his father's funeral.

Harmen and I had discussed death years before and we both believed that small children should never be forced to attend a close relative's funeral. This opinion was based on a movie we had seen called *The Three Faces of Eve*, in which severe psychological damage was done to Eve because her mother had forced her to say goodbye to her dead grandmother.

People were filing into the chapel. Catholic friends and acquaintances kneeled at the casket to say some prayers. It touched my heart deeply, because I sensed that prayers would be beneficial to Harmen's soul. I felt overcome with gratitude. When the organ began to play the melody of Bach's *Sonaten und Partiten für Violine allein*, Harmen's favorite, it was as if the sounds were coming directly from heaven above. I began to lose myself. I was thinking: "All this is for Harmen," and even told my parents and Theo, "Please, do not weep, for this is Harmen's memorial service, the last thing we can ever give to him. Think only of him!"

I had asked the San Anselmo flower shop to replicate from a photo the bouquet that Harmen had given me on our wedding day. Now Harmen's favorite flowers, red roses and white carnations, were resting on top of the silver-blue steel casket.

At my request, the minister of our church spoke about how Jesus during his crucifixion promised one of the criminals crucified beside him, and who showed faith in him, "Truly, I say to you, today you will be with me in Paradise." My hope was that the New Testament promise was meant for all men of faith. It was my personal plea for Harmen, "to be with Him in Paradise."

After the service, I noticed that the casket was being placed in the hearse. I quickly decided to sit next to the driver in the front seat to be near my husband's body on the way to Mount Tamalpais Cemetery. Our pastor saw me and felt compelled to sit down beside me. I did not know at that point where my parents and my brother-in-law were. I was completely alone, alone with my husband. There was nothing else. Squeezed between the body of the minister and the driver on our way to the burial grounds, I talked about the many good deeds Harmen had done, especially his work for the Lions Club and the blind organization in Curaçao, as if I needed to defend him before God.

I sensed Harmen's presence all around and was absorbed in my deep love for him. Upon our arrival at the cemetery, Harmen's boss, close colleagues and neighbors got ready to carry the casket from the hearse to the open grave. Even though I was in my last month of pregnancy, I moved towards them and took the end handle of

Harmen's casket in my left hand and laid my right hand on top of the casket in a gesture to caress the body inside. I felt the baby making its presence known. I was performing as if in a trance.

Again the minister spoke and invited me to say a few words as well. Standing next to the casket, I prayed aloud *het Onze Vader* (the Lord's Prayer). Then I was asked to say my final goodbyes. In a flash of inner knowledge about the importance of freeing my husband's soul, I moved closer to the casket to perform a special ritual that I had never seen or heard of before. A higher force guided me... I asked the funeral-home representative the location of my husband's heart. He pointed it out to me. I placed my hands on the casket where Harmen's heart lay inside the coffin. I felt god-like light flowing through my heart and hands into my husband's heart. I was completely unaware there were other people present.

After a few more words by the minister, I left the cemetery in the car of one of Harmen's colleagues. The actual burial would take place in our absence. When we passed over the hill behind the grave, I looked back to cast my last glance of farewell toward my husband's casket. The sky was deep blue and the sun cascaded its golden rays on the silver-blue colors, illuminating it. After we crossed the hills back to Sir Francis Drake Boulevard, I looked up to Mount Tamalpais, our favorite mountain, and noticed a small white cloud appearing as if from nowhere. Slowly, it rose up along the mountainside till it passed the top of the mountain, where it disappeared into the celestial zenith. I imagined it was my husband's soul ascending into the heavens.

Chapter Five
The Diamond Light

At night, I kept wandering through the house lost in complete darkness. During the day, my parents and brother-in-law tried to help me in any way they could think of. I appreciated all they did, but at the same time understood how their world was still intact while the world I knew had shattered to pieces. Unable to connect with them, I withdrew into a world of my own that I still needed to come to terms with.

A week after the funeral, I just could not sit home any longer without doing something about the heinous crime committed against Harmen. In my mind it was important to find his killer, the driver of the hit-and-run car. According to the information from the police, this person was still at large.

"I need to get personally involved," I thought. All of a sudden, like a bolt of lightning out of the blue sky, an article I had read in the Caribbean newspaper when I lived in Curaçao came back to mind. It was the story of a Dutch psychic who lived in the Hollywood area in California. His name was Peter Hurkos. Peter was famous for solving police cases. I felt that I should talk with Mr. Hurkos and ask him to help find the person who killed Harmen. A Dutch banker Harmen and I knew had recently moved to Los Angeles and offered his assistance to call the local Hurkos telephone number. He soon discovered that Peter Hurkos was doing business as a company and that it was impossible to talk to Peter personally without paying a significant amount of money up front. "Ella, I feel that the best thing for you is to call the Hurkos Company yourself and plead your own case."

I mulled things over for a couple of days. The more I reflected, the more I felt I needed to make contact with the chief of police first to get some form of approval before going ahead with my ideas. One morning, I set out for the San Anselmo Police Department determined to at least offer my ideas to solve the hit-and-run case. I walked into the police station and identified myself. They knew who I was… I asked to see the chief, Mr. Raymond Buchignani, and was taken to his office at once. As I sat down, I said to him, "I have come to offer help in a perhaps rather unorthodox way, one that my own deceased husband might not have favored." I continued, "Please, hear me out…and if you conclude that I

17

am a bit of a crazy woman, feel free to state it, because I certainly will understand that!" I began telling the chief about the extraordinary clairvoyance of Peter Hurkos and asked him what he thought about having help from psychics like him.

The chief, without any hesitation, replied, "We welcome them. They have assisted us with clues and solutions in many of our cases, numerous times." I felt relieved and continued my narration of Peter Hurkos's amazing life. After I had finished, Mr. Buchignani said, looking at me seriously, "Mrs. Evers, here is my desk, here is my telephone, they are all yours. Make any call you need to make. Contact Mr. Hurkos." There I was in my maternity clothes, nine months' pregnant, sitting behind the desk of the Chief of Police of San Anselmo attempting to find justice. I made the phone call to Los Angeles, but soon found that the Dutch banker had been correct. Without paying money in advance, it did not seem possible to even discuss the reason for my call. Disappointed, but not defeated, I left the police station. While slowly driving home I wondered what my next step should be.

At home I felt drawn to go straight up to Harmen's study to phone the Hurkos Company once more. This time another secretary came on the line. Before I could say anything, she too told me: "You have to pay at least $5,000.00 to start a case with Mr. Hurkos!" I pleaded with her and explained that Mr. Hurkos was my compatriot from The Hague in The Netherlands, but she coolly interrupted and said, "To speak with Mr. Peter Hurkos, you first need to pay $500." I reacted by saying: "Please, may I at least speak with Mrs. Hurkos?" To my utter surprise this wish was fulfilled and I got Mrs. Hurkos on the line. I described how the image of the photo of her and her husband published in the Antillean newspaper from years back had come to me a few days after my husband's funeral. I told her that Harmen and I were from the same country and town as her husband Peter. I added how my life was in financial disarray and that I had yet to give birth to my second child. "I have no money coming in and benefits do not seem to be forthcoming soon." I pleaded intensely, trying with all my might to persuade her to have her husband help find the criminal: "It is not only to bring the criminal to justice, but also to find out if there is any type of insurance coverage to help us financially!" I told Mrs. Hurkos that the police chief had indicated that he was very interested to work with her, to no avail...and suddenly realizing that help was not forthcoming in this manner, I hung up and ran downstairs to tell my parents what had transpired. My mind went blank for a moment when I heard my mother saying, "Oh, what dreadful people. All they can think about is money."

I stepped outside the family room into the brown-tiled hallway and closed my eyes, mentally recalling the face of Peter Hurkos as I remembered him standing with his wife beside a swimming pool under a row of tall palm trees. Not asking for anything, I spoke to the vision in my mind, and said, "You are not a bad man. You are a *good* man, a *very good* man!"

To my astonishment, my forehead opened and a great illuminating light of intense clarity and beauty appeared between my two eyebrows out of nowhere. I just stood there amazed and overtaken by this diamond-like resplendent light, an eternal moment in which I experienced a state of heightened awareness, never questioning or wondering why this was happening. I simply knew that I was connecting with Mr. Hurkos on a soul level. I do not know how long I stood in that hallway, but I was shaken back to my outer senses when the telephone rang. I ran upstairs to Harmen's study to pick up the phone. I was not surprised that it was Mrs. Hurkos. She said that she had talked to her husband and that he offered to help me for free. "It will be your Christmas present," Mr. Hurkos had said.

Mrs. Hurkos asked me to mail pictures of Harmen and some other items that had belonged to him. About a month later, I received a letter from Peter Hurkos informing me that he had not been able to receive impressions as to who the killer might be. I was advised that by doing a thorough search "on location" of the scene of the crime, he could perhaps better sense the whereabouts of the killer. This time that would not be possible without a consulting fee. I decided not to hire him, as it was clear to me that I should not spend large funds during such uncertain times.

My whole focus had been on finding the killer, but instead I received an utmost blessing of the opening of my forehead and the revelation of the presence of the brilliant diamond-white light. At that time, I had no knowledge yet what the experience of this light would mean for my life. I did not know that the place between the two eyebrows is called the "third eye," or the "eye of God," in eastern thought. It would take a long journey to learn that this diamond light is also described in the east as:

> The diamond light proceeding from the heart of the Divine Consciousness that brings the opening of the Divine Consciousness wherever it goes.
>
> From: The Mother of the Sri Aurobindo Ashram, Pondicherry, India.

This brilliant light, revealed to me while focusing on the pure goodness of Peter Hurkos, would never leave me. It would appear time and time again in my new life without Harmen. I became drawn to it. This light became my secret companion.

Chapter Six

Giving Birth

My labor pains started early on the evening of December eighth. I called Sue, my teacher in natural childbirth. In the week before Harmen's death, I had just finished her eight-week class on the Bradley method of birthing in which a husband assists his wife through specific breathing techniques to facilitate the birth to occur naturally. Sue generously promised to take over Harmen's role and also offered to drive me to the hospital as soon as I had to go...

The next morning after I described how often the contractions followed each other, Sue decided it was that time. With labor pains in full swing, I packed some personal items and the new baby clothes in an overnight bag. When Sue arrived to pick me up in her VW bus, I stood at the front door with the overnight bag in one hand and my typewriter in the other. I explained to Sue, "My life is business from now on."

I had stepped into the shoes of my late husband. I had to be father, breadwinner and mother at the same time. I promised myself to accomplish these new tasks to the utmost of my abilities. Strong and determined on one side, I also felt great sadness, anguish and much inner pain when I arrived at Marin General Hospital where Harmen, only fifteen days before, had arrived by ambulance and was pronounced "dead."

I was taken into the labor room. It was like living through a dream from which I hoped to wake up and find Harmen at my side. The contractions intensified and I felt that the baby was ready to be born. The water broke... A nurse rushed me to the delivery room just in time. During those moments, knowing full well that the birth was at hand, I closed my eyes. Sue screamed, "Ella, open your eyes, the baby is coming." Then I saw the baby like a miniature form of my husband exiting from my body. I saw Harmen's face in the face of my child.

"A daughter!" the doctor declared.

"She looks just like her father, just like her father!" To see his face again now in the face of my child was a most touching miracle. Holding my daughter, I looked at her, Harmen's last precious gift, so promising and alive. In fact, this was the present he had been talking about just a few weeks ago.

A pediatrician examined the baby and pronounced her healthy. With my baby in my arms, a kind nurse wheeled us into the maternity ward. She asked, "Which room would you prefer?" I said, "I want a room as close to Mount Tamalpais Cemetery as possible." She brought me into a room viewing the hills beyond which Harmen's grave was located. I felt the love for my husband and my daughter merging, giving me a sense of completeness. I called my family, who were anxiously waiting at home to hear from me. In that moment, I looked at myself as if from afar and heard myself saying, "...and her names are Femke Flora Reina." It was Sunday morning, the ninth of December.

Chapter Seven
Christmas 1973

Christmas came. An even deeper darkness began to close in on me. On Christmas Eve I called David to my side. The living room was unlit. I lit a small candle, took the Bible out of the bookcase and began to read the old story of the birth of the holy child from the New Testament. It was our family tradition. It was up to me now to continue this spiritual ritual I had started twelve years ago when I married Harmen. I put my arm around David's shoulders, pulling him close in a loving embrace. I felt that only he and I understood the darkness and the desolation of that moment.

The story of angels appearing in golden rays of light accompanied by heavenly music to announce the glorious birth of the Christ child to the shepherds, as well as the brilliant star guiding the wise men to the place of his birth, had always held a deep fascination for me. It always connected me with a sacred place deep within me. Now I was attempting to give David a touch of that miraculous Light of God that I knew could appear even in the midst of darkness with angels singing.

But I did not feel that real joy of old this first Christmas without Harmen. The light of that small candle flickering in the darkness gave me nevertheless a glimpse of hope that eventually even the smallest of light could create a new dawn. I sensed the presence of my parents somewhere at a distance, but they were not part of what was happening. The baby, unaware of the loss of her father, lay asleep, safely covered in her brand new white wicker bassinet richly adorned with lace coverings. This was the month of December, of which I had so joyfully proclaimed, "It will be a glorious month!" a very short while ago.

Chapter Eight

An Unusual Sentence

One morning in February, I heard a knock on the back door. I opened and saw it was the chief of police, Mr. Raymond Buchignani, and his deputy. "Mrs. Evers," the chief said, "We are here to tell you that we have arrested the man who killed your husband. You are the first to know since you have worked so hard to help us."

I invited the two men to sit down in my living room. The chief of police further reported, "The man who killed your husband was found through our secret witness program, but for the time being he can only be held on charges involving a forged driver's license. Through the secret witness program, a witness will come forward to testify that this man is the hit-and-run killer. The arrested man is a known individual to the police and has been jailed before, for thefts amongst other things." Sadly, the news could not bring Harmen back, but I nevertheless felt some sense of relief as well as immense gratitude to the local police that they had apprehended his killer.

Two days later I read in the newspaper that the hit-and-run man, while awaiting his court appearance, had assaulted a sheriff, leading to additional charges against him. I pondered often whether I should pay a visit to this man in his prison cell. I wanted so badly to reach this man on a deeper level to tell him about the devastating effects of his crime on our small family so that it would never happen again. In reality, I never could bring myself to actualize these thoughts. But I strongly sensed I should not hate the man, because I believed that holding thoughts of hate would hurt us more than him. I decided it was best to let the justice system take care of punishing his crime.

I received a phone call from the district attorney, who said, "Mrs. Evers, I need your help... I assume that you are the only one in California who knew Drs. Evers well and who could answer questions that may come up regarding his person. I would like you to testify in the hit-and-run case of your husband. Will you help us?" It did not take me long to accept that invitation to stand with the district attorney.

It was the second week of a three-week trial in Marin County's Superior Court when I sat down in the witness stand and was asked to swear on the Bible and speak the truth. My own attorney, Craig Sommers, was sitting outside the courtroom with David and baby Femke. I was nervous. I had never testified in court before. I glanced over to the face of the accused sitting with his attorney on the right side of the courtroom as seen from the witness stand. It was quite a shock to come face to face with the man who killed my husband. I gave him a blank stare. The defendant had taken the Fifth Amendment, which meant that he could not be asked any questions in the courtroom.

I trembled when the assistant district attorney showed an enlarged picture of Harmen to identify him as my husband and as the man who had been killed. That picture of Harmen so alive connected me with a world gone forever. I regained my mental strength when it dawned on me that I represented Harmen, who could not speak for himself. It gave me the courage I needed. I wanted to make sure that Harmen's truth was correctly addressed when the defense attorney, desperate to find something for his client, asked, "How competent a biker was your husband, and how much had he been biking in this country since his new bike had been in the bike-shop for quite some time?" Fortunately, I recalled that before buying his bike Harmen had been borrowing a bike from our neighbors while they were on their summer vacation. For verification I had to give their address to the court.

The defense attorney went further and asked, "Did your husband use a bike in Curaçao, where you lived before coming here?"

My answer was "No, my husband did not bike in Curaçao." I knew that the daily strong trade winds kicking up sand and dust had not been conducive for bicycling. The defense, sensing at this point an advantage, continued, inquiring of other times Harmen might have used a bike. Extremely alert as to what was happening, I cut in, saying: "People born in The Netherlands are all good bikers."

How true this was. In my days in The Netherlands, the bike was considered one of the most practical modes of transportation. We were born on bikes, as it were, and use them much like Mongolians use their horses. Per capita there are perhaps more bikes in The Netherlands than any other place in the world. These were the thoughts that ran through my mind. I made sure the court and jury understood this when I added, "Biking is part of the Dutch culture and my husband certainly knew how to use his bike." My alertness gave me a powerful feeling that I was not useless in the court proceedings and that I contributed something that was needed. I knew I had stood tall and strong for Harmen despite the fact that speaking from the witness stand was so frighteningly new to me.

After my participation, I no longer followed the case as it progressed through the court. One morning a reporter from the local newspaper surprised me with a telephone call and asked, "Have you heard the sentence of the hit-and-run man?" I said that I had not. The reporter continued, "The sentence against the defendant is set for five years in prison on charges of manslaughter. The man also has to pay $100 each month for a period of three years into a trust account for the benefit of your baby daughter to accumulate money to pay for her college." The reporter wanted to know the baby's name for the story he was writing.

I was amazed. Femke was the only one mentioned to be a beneficiary. I suddenly recalled how Harmen on the morning of his death had mentioned that he had had a nightmare, and afterward said, "Ella, as soon as the baby is born I want to buy life insurance, so that if anything should happen to me there will be enough money for our new child to attend college." I wondered deep down in my heart if the judge had been aware, on a different level, that a college account was already in place for David. "Could it be possible that the judge had been influenced by Harmen's spirit?"

It took me several months to get the courage to see the judge to check with him the validity of such intuitive feelings. Mr. Craig Sommers had already mentioned that, as far as he was concerned, the sentence was not written according to California law. One afternoon I could no longer bear the uncertainty and decided to visit Judge Best. Upon entering the judge's chambers, I stood for a split second spellbound when I noticed some very familiar items on his desk. It was odd, but Harmen also had those same items displayed in his study: the bell of the Kiwanis, the Lions Club membership, as well as the Rotary Club recognition of appreciation.

For a moment, I stood there...lost in a past that was gone. I quickly had to pull myself out of this reverie and face the judge. "Why?" I asked, "Why, in the trial against my husband's killer, did you sentence with a stipulation for the defendant to pay money into a trust for my daughter's college fund?"

The judge went silent for a while and when he spoke, he said, "I simply do not know." He added, "It is an unusual sentence. I have never sentenced in the same manner before and would probably never do it again." He continued, "It may well have been your husband's spirit influencing me to write in that special condition."

I left, convinced that it was indeed Harmen who had influenced the judge. What the judge did not know was that less than a year ago, we had been discussing the violent murder of a family in our area. Harmen had said, "Especially in cases where the breadwinner of a family is killed, a criminal should be held responsible and pay at least for college tuition."

Chapter Nine

Rays of Light and Inquiry

How well I remembered the summer before the baby was born. Harmen and I were sitting in the living room, talking. Some serious thoughts were on my mind and I said, "Harmen, now that I am pregnant again, I feel so vulnerable and dependent on you. What would happen to me if you were not here? I think I couldn't handle that. It makes me feel weak just thinking about it."

Harmen's reply was, "No, you are not weak, you will be able to take care of things. I know that for certain."

A few months after Harmen's death these thoughts of my husband came back through my mother-in-law, who called from The Netherlands. She confessed how, while visiting us in Curaçao, she strongly came to believe that I had too much say in matters regarding her son's banking business. She let me know that she had warned her son to not allow me to advise him all the time on his business as only he, certainly in her mind, was the expert banker. But now, my mother-in-law came to share with me how my husband had then responded to her. He had said, "Mother, Ella has a superb feel for business. I often ask her opinion. She has a logical mind mixed with a great intuition. I do rely on her a lot as she usually comes up with some excellent ideas."

In her concern for me my mother-in-law just wanted to set things straight by letting me know highly Harmen had thought about my ideas of handling business affairs. I was amazed, realizing how much courage it must have taken her to phone me to confess what she had said behind my back three years earlier. I was touched and felt as if Harmen himself had called, telling me again, "Yes, you can do it!" The fact that he believed me to be a strong person gave me that much needed strength.

One day a repairman came to my house to service our washing machine. After he finished the job I made him a cup of coffee and he sat down at our breakfast table. Out of the blue, he began talking about his life. He told me how he had lost his wife and how he had learned to cope and take care of his two children. He proudly showed me their pictures, which he carried in his wallet. They were very young. I had not said anything about myself. I just listened to this man and after he left I felt less alone in my experience, as I realized that others had gone through similar life trials. The message again was: "Yes, you can do it."

I used to get my gasoline at the Red Hill Shopping Center nearby, just as I had done when Harmen was alive. One morning, the owner of the station who pumped my gas said, "I am always watching you whenever you come here to get gasoline. I know what happened to you. I know what you are going through." He paused, and added, "You're doing all right." The manner in which he said this made me aware that some people did know and did care. These occurrences were like little rays of light that brightened my days.

Most of the time we were by ourselves, the three of us. During the day, David attended nursery school while I went shopping with baby Femke. On one occasion, I was in the supermarket carrying Femke in my arms. When I took my groceries through the checkout stand, the clerk said with a big smile, looking at my baby, "What a beautiful baby."

I tried to smile back, but felt as if something exploded inside me. I wanted to burst our screaming and shouting for the whole universe to hear, "But this baby does not have a father!" The pain of the injustice that had been done to the children and me threw me into the abyss of loss and despair. "Why did my children not deserve to have their father, and why did I not deserve to have my husband? Why...why?"

Harmen's death made me think a lot of the fleetingness of life. Soon I began to ask questions that rose from the depth of my being, the same ones I had been pondering when I was a child in post-war Holland: "Who am I? From where have I come? Where am I going? What is life all about?" This time I added, "Where is Harmen, where has he gone?"

Much later, I came to understand that these are the essential questions that man has always posed and that a need to find the answers lives in every one of us.

PART II

Early Years

Chapter Ten

My Childhood

I was born in Nijmegen, located south of the River Waal. It is the oldest city in The Netherlands, dating back to 5 B.C., the days of the Roman Empire, when it was called Ulpia Noviomagus Batavorum. I was but a tiny baby when, on the tenth of May 1940, the Germans invaded my country. They bombed airfields and bridges, followed by parachute droppings of troops and equipment. The Blitzkrieg style war was at first met with more resistance than Hitler anticipated, and to force the country into surrender the Germans bombed and flattened the city center of Rotterdam, causing many casualties. They threatened to level other major cities with famous cathedrals, castles and other historical treasures. The Dutch defense was ill equipped to stand against the overwhelming military might of the invaders. After five days of heroic fighting the Dutch capitulated. A five-year Nazi occupation had begun, which would leave a permanent mark on my country as it did on me.

The historian, Dr. L. de Jong, in his book *The Occupation*, recounts the story of a Dutch clergyman, the well-known Dr. J.J. Buskus. This minister tells how after the bombardment of Rotterdam, on May 14, 1940, he drove his car to the city-center to see if his church was still standing and to check what may have happened to his council members. He saw the streets ablaze with roaring fires. The center of the city looked entirely desolate, but for one single man completely oblivious to his surroundings, standing alone with both fists clenched shouting to himself and for the world to hear, "I will not take this, I will not take this."

The protest of this lonely voice is symbolic of the genuine Dutch spirit speaking: a voice outraged against the terror that was taking place. That spark of consciousness in this single man later re-emerged as the voice of the Dutch resistance movement. It was in February 1941 when that same spirit expressed itself in the organizing of a general labor strike in Amsterdam to show the Germans that the Dutch would not stand for the cruel oppression of their Jewish compatriots. The Germans, in response, brutally oppressed the Amsterdam effort with horrific reprisals against innocent people. Fear of the occupier became rampant, yet that tiny voice of consciousness could never be entirely extinguished.

My parents loathed the Nazis and hated living under the boots of the occupier, but at the same time felt quite anxious about the peril the Germans represented and what this meant to our family.

My first memory of the war is of a troop of German soldiers marching through my street at seven o'clock in the morning. I must have been two years old. I can still see myself hanging out the attic window and watching them march, while they sang, *"Auf der Heide blüht ein kleines Blümelein, und das heißt Erika!"* (On the heather fields blooms a small flower, and her name is Erika). They marched to the tune, stamping their military boots heavily on the ground. I often had followed groups of neighborhood children running after these marching soldiers, teasingly thumbing our noses behind their backs. I was too young to know the real danger. Other children did know, but as children are, challenging danger became the new game.

Trying to be like the other kids, I was, that morning, making derogatory faces at the marching soldiers, when my mother caught me. She gave me a severe reprimand and urged me never

ever to do that again. The intense fear in her voice shook my being. I was only a small child, but simply had to know and understand the threat the Germans posed; this knowing, however caused anxiety in me.

When the Germans invaded the country, the Dutch royal family and government fled to England. A government in exile was established in London. As the Queen was of the House of Orange, orange became a forbidden color during the occupation years.

One summer afternoon, I was drinking some artificial orange juice in the garden of my parents' friends. I realized that my sloppy way of drinking was turning my mouth orange. Frightened, I asked my mother, "Will the Germans see it?"

Chapter Eleven

Vicissitudes of War

My family book dates back to the fifteen hundreds. Recordings show that many had been ministers of the Protestant Church in a time span of more than four hundred years. Even though it was wartime and I was only three years of age, it may come as no surprise that my mother found it necessary to send me off to Sunday school in the nearby elementary-school building.

My teacher was a lovely woman and what she taught made a life-long impression on me. She said, "God is like the sun, always shining with a bright embracing light that warms the soul." She added, "Sometimes clouds may appear and hide God from our sight." I will never forget that beautiful smile on my Sunday school teacher's face when she further proclaimed, "All you have to do is to smile with all your heart and all your soul, and then the clouds will evaporate and you will know God." Her metaphor gave me at a young age a glimpse of the truth I would later be seeking. When I felt sad and alone, I practiced smiling and this practice gave me a sense of joy.

My mother was another early spiritual teacher who taught me how to pray during the early war years. First, she taught an easy child's prayer and later on she said, "You are smart enough to learn *het Onze Vader* (the Lord's Prayer)." Soon thereafter, she left the choice to say or not say prayers before sleeping entirely to me. She hardly spoke of God ever again. My mother gave me the religious freedom to develop in my own way. The Lord's Prayer and seeing God as Light, from then on, became part of the essence of my being and my strength.

I became aware of whispering conversations in my family regarding my father's brother. The Germans had arrested him. Uncle Herman had been working for the Dutch Resistance Movement. His task was to circulate an underground newspaper called *Het Parool (The Truth)*. *Het Parool* carried the news of the Queen and our government in exile including the true movements of armies, air attacks and sea battles with true figures, different from the war-serving news found in the German-controlled media. During a *razzia* (raid by the SS) of a location in The Hague, the Germans found a notebook listing several underground workers, which included my uncle's name. After a short imprisonment in the so-called Oranje-Hotel (Hotel Orange) in Scheveningen, the underground workers were put on transport to concentration camp Vugt.

As young as I was, I could feel an intense nervous tension hanging over my family like a dark cloud. I just knew something was amiss. On my third birthday, December 1942, my sister and I were left with friends to spend our first night away from home. My parents traveled to Utrecht to be near my uncle, as he would stand trial in a German-held secret "mock" court. The sentence was: *Zum Tode verurteilt*, in other words, death by firing squad.

On February 5, 1943, shots sounded near the airport of Soesterberg, ending the lives of thirteen courageous men, the voices of Dutch resistance. My uncle, among them, was twenty-nine years old. My father was ordered to pick up Uncle Herman's belongings from the Ortz Kommandant in Amersfoort. When my father arrived home, he opened the suitcase and found his brother's prisoner's clothes and lots of scraps of linen apparently used to bandage his wounds and sores, and a secret tiny book describing the tortures he endured. The linens reeked of filth, blood and gore and I still remember how the pungent stench suddenly filled up our house.

I was so young and did not understand the tragedy of the event until later. But nevertheless during childhood and even more so during adulthood, Uncle Herman's execution haunted me on occasion. My thoughts would dwell on my uncle's last moments. I wondered how he took it and what thoughts may have come to him when facing the firing squad. I also pondered what happens after our bodies die. Uncle Herman became a silent inner hero, as he had demonstrated courage to stand up against evil. I often wondered if I too would find such strength of character when this was called for in my own life.

Later in that so terrifying year for my family, the war began to intensify. Nijmegen is near the German border and we watched hundreds of thousands of the Allied planes flying over on their way to bomb targets in Germany. Except for foggy days these planes filled the skies every day and night.

On February 22, 1944, Allies' planes missed their objective, believing they were flying over Germany, and by that error the inner city of Nijmegen was bombed. The city was burning and I saw the sun completely disappear behind thick black billowing clouds of smoke and fire. I watched as I was standing on our rooftop with my mother and sister. It all felt extremely eerie.

Besides the bombardment, the population had to deal with severe food shortages. An illegal black market existed where food sold for exorbitant prices. One day, my mother came home with one egg that she had bought on the black market. I had never seen an egg before. She soft boiled the egg for my baby brother, who was a toddler. There was no money to buy more than one egg. I was four years old when I saw my mother spoon-feeding this mysterious food into my brother's mouth. I stared at the shape and colors and smelled the aroma. I felt hungry and wanted desperately to have a bite of this miraculous food. I kept silent as I was well trained by my parents to endure things one cannot change. I just stared in agony as baby Herman, in my mother's lap, would spit out bits and pieces of this precious egg and how my mother carefully spooned it back into his mouth. I watched...and felt a flow of saliva dribbling from my mouth. Strangely, my mother apparently had no idea of my intense longing for this food. I sat glaring at the egg, feeling the insatiable pain of my empty stomach. The experience left me with such a trauma that even today I have not totally given up eating eggs, while I am in all other aspects a strict vegetarian!

Chapter Twelve

Liberation and Trauma

One day in April 1944 my mother woke up and said to my father, "I had a remarkable dream. She recounted:

> We [the family] were standing in front of the house watching many planes flying over the Goffert [the name of the park in front of our house]. All of a sudden the whole blue sky filled up with parachutes. There was no cloud in the sky and I could see these parachutes very clearly as they came down. After watching the whole scene we went inside. The doorbell rang... I opened the door and saw two young men standing there. They said, "The parachute troops have landed on the Konijnenpad and they are asking for bread." I went to the kitchen and made several sandwiches with sugar, the only

food in the house, wrapped them in paper, and gave it to the young men. They put the package in a bag and left.

My mother's dream occurred months before D-Day (June 6, 1944), the invasion of the Allies in Normandy, France. My parents took my mother's dream to be just a pipe dream as it was far-fetched to believe that our liberators would ask for food from our already meager rations.

But on the seventeenth of September 1944, my mother's dream came true in the exact way she had dreamed it. After the Allies landed by parachute, our lives changed significantly as the war intensified. We lived right in the middle of it. The troops moved back and forth. One night my mother and father decided that we should flee, because the danger of losing our lives seemed imminent. We left our house with many neighbors following. Several times, my sister and I had to crawl over the ground to avoid the bullets flying overhead. Tanks and trucks with infantry troops were everywhere. I remember a big American military man with white arm cuffs directing traffic. All civilians were directed to a nearby castle where we spent the night. When we woke the next morning, my parents were told by the military to return home.

The Goffert Park in front of our house had become a tent camp for Allied troops. My mother, who spoke English fluently, realized that the military needed additional housing and addressed some officers who were talking across the street. She offered to share our large house with the some of the troops. The officers happily accepted her kindness and consequently our house became the home for several young soldiers from England. An army cookhouse was set up just a few houses down the street. Our new roommates would secretly bring my mother leftovers from the cookhouse, which otherwise would have been thrown away. Ecstatic to be able to prepare our food with fried bacon from the military kitchen, my mother creatively set to work to cook dinners with the protein we desperately needed.

Every day and every night, German planes came overhead to attack the Allies. The Allies had searchlights with which to spot them and then shoot them down. Planes came tumbling down from the sky engulfed in roaring fires. One time such a burning plane almost hit our house. In the morning we found pieces of the plane in our yard. In front of our house stood a big cannon. One morning, my father, sister and I were standing next to this cannon that was ready for firing at the German planes. A soldier gave us pieces of cotton for our ears to protect our eardrums. The cannon blasts were so loud and the air pressure so enormous that I fell over from the impact. The constant air pressure blew out the large windows in our house. The hinges of the doors came loose, but my parents did not care, as long as we pulled through unharmed.

The cellar underneath the house became our hideout from air raids till our family permanently moved in for several months on end. It was a relatively small space with brick walls and a large pipe of the sewer system in plain sight. My mother covered the cement floor with our mattresses, sheets and blankets. Our family of five slept in close proximity to one another. My parents hoped that the cellar would provide some safety from grenades, knowing full well that bombs could flatten the whole house and bury us alive. The war became so intense that we had to stay in the cellar night and day fully dressed, including coats and shoes, in order to be ready to flee at a minute's notice. When the air raids began I sang my Sunday school songs and smiled just as my Sunday school teacher had taught me. It gave me a sense of protection.

Hitler decided that the Germans must at all cost win Nijmegen back from the Allies, and my city became the front line. Enduring the shelling of our city became our new way of life.

Christmas that year was the most memorable of my whole childhood. Our English friends cut a fir tree from the Goffert Park. The huge tree was cut several times till it fit in the door entrance. Our family and the English soldiers decorated the giant tree with all the shiny ornaments and tinsel from pre-war times. On Christmas Eve we sat around the Christmas tree, lit with real white candles, its branches reaching to the ceiling. We sang English

Christmas carols. Under the tree lay an array of gifts for my family: cans of soup, cans with plum pudding, cans of cheese, bread, coffee, tea and chocolate bars. I was totally unaware that bombs were falling on the city while I dreamily sat entranced looking at the Christmas tree candles that were burning as if a mysterious wand had touched them to light up in fascinating colorful auras.

On the fifth of May 1945, all occupied parts of The Netherlands were finally liberated and peace was declared. The Dutch, freed from oppression, were overcome by exuberant joy. I was five when the whole country seemed to be in a dance of happiness. There were bands and music fanfares in every town. Young couples, old couples and new lovers took to the streets to celebrate and dance. I remember enthusiastically waving my red, white, and blue Dutch flag and proudly wearing an orange paper hat. Queen Wilhelmina returned from exile and traveled the country to make a personal appearance to her people. An overwhelming feeling of unity and love for the royal family was tangible everywhere.

The joy was short-lived. The country lay in ruins. There was still a severe lack of food. Few arrived back from concentration and forced labor camps in Germany. A time of reflection began, which included the counting of the dead. Many families mourned. My family mourned again the death of my uncle, after his body was dug up from the mass grave on the heather fields near Soesterberg. Now the stress of five years of occupation became evident in constant conversations between people who had survived the horrors. No one could let go of the past war years. Today this would be diagnosed as post-traumatic stress disorder. The war had left its mark on every one. Many people also suffered from post-traumatic psychosomatic diseases and diseases caused by years of malnutrition. My mother was one of them. She suffered migraine headaches and other illnesses and could not leave her bed. My father hired a housekeeper to take care of the household.

Chapter Thirteen
Revelation of Truth

My father, the head of the bookkeeping department of a large oil company, was assigned to a new post in The Hague, a large city in western Holland. In August 1948, the time came to leave Nijmegen for good. There was still an enormous housing shortage, and my parents were fortunate to find a two-bedroom flat for our family of five in the south end of the city.

I had a hard time adjusting to living in The Hague. War memories lingered in my mind. I worried about our vulnerability if a new war would start, because the flat had no cellar to flee to. I was around nine when I secretly began to collect aluminum foil to cover our windows against radiation, in case of an atomic attack, in some vague child-like hope this would help.

My mother's health remained weak due to the war years and she suffered other illnesses for which surgeries were required. Finally, when diagnosed with pleurisy, she was sent away to a sanatorium. My mother's state of health, and the constant over-wrought concern of my father whether my mom was going to live or die, began to take its toll on me.

I began to wonder what life was all about. The mood in our house was dark. My father had to hire and fire housekeepers to take care of my sister, brother and me for the time he was away at his office. The hired pseudo-mothers cooked foods I did not like and had manners I did not understand. I missed the warmth of my mother's presence. My father took care of us on the week-ends. After my mother returned home, I began to suffer from abdominal pain. My parents were concerned and took me from one doctor to the next, but none could diagnose the cause of my mysterious pain. I was a sensitive child constantly pondering all sorts of things especially war, death and disease. When Jantje, a young playmate, died during the war, my friend Ans and I used to decorate his grave in the cemetery behind the Catholic Church in the Groene Straat. It made me contemplate death quite a bit, as I wanted to know Jantje's whereabouts. I began to have dreams in which I was a skeleton in a grave, and this frightened me.

My parents had a book entitled *Het Grijze Kind (The Grey Child)* by Theo Thijssen, which had a story of a child who knew things at a very young age. I thought that I too was such a grey child. I sensed there was some greater knowledge inside myself that I could tap into. I remember sitting in front of the window of our flat when I was twelve, staring out, but not taking in what I saw outside, rather looking inward. From time to time I would close my eyes and connect with a deeper me. In these types of what I now call meditative states, I would ask repeatedly, "Where do I come from? Why do I live? Where am I going? What is between two thoughts?" One day when I drew my awareness deeply within myself with a one-pointed focus, my surroundings, body and mind completely disappeared and I entered into an indescribable moment of total awareness, bringing about immeasurable joy. All knowledge of the whole universe and its meaning stood revealed within me, and I realized that I, too, was that knowledge.

I do not know where this happened and how long I remained in that state. I remember just being one with this knowledge (divine truth). I understood who I really was. There was nothing more to do. Time may have gone by or stood still when the revelation of full knowledge overtook me. When some notion of time reappeared, my mind posed the question: "Why live this life now that I know?" Ready to dissolve in this all-knowing consciousness, I felt sure I could just leave my body and life story behind, right then and there, and remain at one with the supreme knowledge. But then an ethereal impression came upon my mind forming words and I heard, "There is a reason for your life and you have to live it!"

At that moment, the feeling of being in a boundless state of all-knowingness left me and I again became aware of my physical body and personal surroundings. That night I wrote in my diary: "I am only twelve years old and I know." I realized that my parents were not my real parents, as my first relationship was to an eternal Self, my eternal parent. I realized that "I" was my own Self. I had to honor and obey my birth parents, but my true guidance would come from that source, that all-knowingness I experienced, which I later understood to be the same as the infinite Light.

I felt as if a heavy burden had been lifted from my shoulders, freeing and allowing me to become the person I was meant to be. I was no longer bound to my parents. Their fears and limitations no longer had an effect on me. Something inside of me was broken and I felt strong and new. My abdominal pains disappeared completely.

Despite this intense life-changing experience, I soon became a typical teenager. I kept the experience to myself and never told anyone. It was my most personal sacred secret.

I was fortunate that my father's employer owned a large private estate on the shore of a lake, where employees and their families could swim, sail, canoe and partake in a variety of other sports. I became fond of biking to this park-like land called Te Werve and getting into a canoe to paddle around the lake after school. I loved the outdoors. With my canoe, I often just ended up floating around the lake in a meditative state in an effort to reconnect again to who I really was.

Another unusual event took place when I was seventeen. My mother, sister and I were sitting in the front room of our flat. My sister was teasing my mother in a way that I did not like. While I was listening, I said out of the blue, "Do you know what love is?" At that exact moment indescribable beautiful words, teachings on higher love, flowed from my mouth. I was speaking words that were not my own, words far beyond my understanding of love at that time. Words kept flowing and I felt completely overtaken by what came through. Even though I could not retain or understand the exact words, the level from which they came affected me, causing another shift within. I felt beautiful and uplifted and listened in awe... I can still feel the sacredness of these words even now. My mother and sister were just sitting there, staring at me. I do not think they understood what was happening. I knew that for a short while I had been lifted to a higher plane of consciousness, a plane of infinite love where all is beauty and harmony.

Chapter Fourteen

Harmen

I loved to dance, but dance parties at our school were rare. Our principal was concerned that students would bring alcohol or go on to other parties afterwards where anything could happen for which he might be blamed. Mr. De Haas was indeed old-fashioned. I knew he favored me and so I tried to win him over by begging him to have our dance, but he refused.

A student in my class named Rudy had a solution. He lived in a high-rise bank building in the center of The Hague across from a large church building named Grote or Sint-Jacobskerk. On the top floor of the bank was an empty attic. Rudy's father, the manager of this building, told his son, "You can use the attic to have dance parties for your school friends. Decorate the attic in any way you like." My HBS (special super high school) friends and I got together and decorated the empty walls with colorful paintings including a whole jazz orchestra. During my last HBS year, my friends and I often met for partying at our attic-space in the bank building.

One evening a month after graduation, Rudy called me for a dance at the attic. I arrived early and had a cup of tea with Rudy's parents. Then the door opened and Rudy's cousin, a law student, appeared with his friend Harmen. I had never seen them before. Harmen and I began a conversation. He talked at length about the topics I also cared about, politics, economics and literature, and seemed to be very well read. He appeared to have a profound knowledge of Dutch poetry. I was thrilled meeting him as I recognized a part of myself in him, a feeling I never experienced before. After sharing many topics of interest, Harmen proposed to leave the attic party. Instead of dancing with the high school crowd we walked around the center of The Hague, talking about things in life that concerned us. It was a beautiful warm summer night in 1958.

I knew I had found my kindred spirit in Harmen. He must have felt the same way and soon we began to see each other on the weekends. We both liked making trips to the countryside, traveling on Harmen's Vespa scooter. We enjoyed parks, beaches and the dunes, but also visiting exhibitions in various museums. We read European literature and discussed writers and their stories and enjoyed seeing wonderful movies. Harmen and I were very compatible. For the first time in my life I felt I met someone I understood and who also understood who I was.

Harmen was an economics student at the University in Rotterdam at that time and I was a beginning student of history at the School for Languages and Literature in The Hague. It took Harmen until the late fall of the next year to ask me to marry him. There had never been any doubt in my mind. We were meant for each other.

The day after my engagement, on the train to my job in Sassenheim, I had the joyous feeling that my everyday co-travelers all spotted my sparkling new engagement ring. This ring symbolized the sweet connection to the man I adored. I beamed with perfect joy. It was then that Harmen became the center of all my thoughts.

Chapter Fifteen

Marriage

There was still a tremendous housing shortage in The Netherlands and when Harmen's employer, a large electronics firm, could provide us with a beautiful flat in a village called Rijswijk, we jumped at this chance and got married. It was September 1, 1961. I was twenty-one years old.

Our civil ceremony took place at City Hall in Voorburg, a suburb of The Hague, from where Harmen and I and our small wedding party proceeded to the Vrijzinnige Kerk (Non-Orthodox Protestant Church) to be married. The happiness I felt to be married to Harmen was immeasurable. It was the fulfillment of all I could ever have dreamed. Our new home in Rijswijk had a view of the lake of Te Werve where I had spent my teen years swimming, canoeing and sailing.

Shortly before my marriage I switched from studying history to studying for a library degree so that I could apply for a new job position to earn a living. I was appointed as a staff member of the Union Catalogue at the Royal Library in The Hague. Within two years of living in Rijswijk, Harmen was transferred to a new position at the main office of his company in the southern part of the country. After a home search for more than half a year, Harmen's new company offered us a three-level brick house in a quiet little village called Geldrop. We loved putting lots of effort into decorating our new house. Our new surroundings were to be in a modern style of vivid colors and smart designs in draperies, carpets and furniture. Looking back, I realize how fortunate I was that Harmen and I had exactly the same taste and ideals. We played this out to our hearts' content. After the house decorating was finished, I began study with a private teacher of English to work toward a teaching degree. On the weekends Harmen, our new puppy dachshund Daphne and I would take long walks on the wonderful trails through surrounding forests and heather fields. It was an almost dreamy existence.

Chapter Sixteen
South America

After Harmen received his Doctorandus degree in International Economics we were finally free to follow the spirit of adventure to go abroad and obtain a wider vision of the world. Harmen applied for bank positions in several countries, and when an interesting post at the Central Bank of Suriname in South America was offered to him, he accepted the invitation to become the head of its Economic Research Department.

In September 1966, many of our close relatives met us at the Amsterdam airport, Schiphol, to wish us bon voyage. Sad to leave The Netherlands, but at the same time excited to begin a new chapter in our lives far away from the western world we knew, we boarded our first flight by air.

Paramaribo, the capital of Suriname, lay on the Suriname River, a large brown muddy river. In downtown Paramaribo old-fashioned colonial style wooden houses with large screened front porches and beautiful tall palm trees lined the streets. The climate was hot and humid. We had arrived in the tropical rain forests of the Amazon region.

We spent our first month in the Kersten Hotel in the center of town. With the bank's assistance we found a suitable house to rent. It was a whitewashed concrete bungalow, trimmed with turquoise green along a corrugated gray metal roof. We had a lovely porch with green colored posts that held up part of the roof over a marble terrace floor. Each side of the veranda had built-in flower boxes filled with tropical plants. After siesta time the veranda routinely became our favorite spot. In the tropics this is the time of leisure before the early dusk sets in, a time to talk and sip cold afternoon drinks. From the porch Harmen and I watched Daphne, our rambunctious dachshund, chasing snakes, lizards and frogs, or wildly digging holes to pursue the hunt without much success.

Life began at early dawn and at seven sharp, I dropped

Harmen off at the Central Bank to continue on to the Kersten stores to buy groceries. By the time I came back home my wonderful maid usually had already arrived with bags of vegetables she had bought at the local markets. Eugenie was a hard-working beautiful Creole woman who took care of most domestic work. I was free to read, write letters overseas, and meet friends at the social club where we could eat, swim and play tennis. After living a year in this tropical land, I accepted a position to work as a librarian at the Cultural Center of Suriname.

In our third year in Suriname I became pregnant, which we thought would be unattainable for us. Expecting our first child meant total change, making us feel excited and a bit anxious about our emerging responsibilities. The pregnancy went well and I delivered our son David safely in the General Hospital of Paramaribo.

Chapter Seventeen

Caribbean Island

Harmen and I wanted to enhance our financial security to adequately provide for our baby son. As this was not possible by staying in Suriname, Harmen applied for a new bank post on the island Curaçao in the Caribbean. Within weeks, he received a reply that he was chosen to fill the position of head of the Economic Research Department.

Curaçao was then still part of a group of six islands called The Netherlands Antilles. We explored the island during a two-week vacation before David was born. Pleasantly surprised to find western foods, clothing and toys on the island in a more varied supply than in Suriname, we felt drawn to make the move to this tropical vacation island we had fallen in love with.

After a month sabbatical in The Netherlands, I arrived in

Curaçao on December 26, 1969, with baby David and our dog Daphne on a KLM (Royal Dutch Airlines) plane decorated with Christmas greens and shiny ornaments, as it was the second day of Christmas for the Dutch. Harmen, who had left our country two weeks earlier in hopes of finding proper housing, was standing on the rooftop terrace of the airport arrival hall waving his enthusiastic welcome to us with both arms.

As it was difficult to find rental housing, we decided to buy a small bungalow in a new subdivision in a rather isolated part of the island. The desert climate, both hot and dry, was known for its northeast trade winds blowing fine sand through doorways and windows. The hills were mostly covered with tall cactuses and creepers. I designed a landscape for our newly built house and hired a crew of superb Portuguese gardeners to set up the new landscaping. As the island did not have fresh water sources, the gardeners had to build craters around the newly planted vegetation, Curaçao style, to keep the rather expensive distilled seawater from escaping. The intense light of the tropical sun combined with daily watering made our pink, white and red oleanders, varied-color bougainvillea and deep red hibiscus grow inches a day.

I enrolled in a course to study Papiamento, the local language of the Antilles. One evening, I invited a classmate to practice with me while Harmen took off in his Triumph Spitfire to visit a friend. After my guest left, I sat on our porch enjoying the stillness and comfortable temperature. Around eleven, a police car appeared. Two officers came to the front gate and one of them said, "Your husband has been in a dreadful accident. You need to come to the hospital at once."

The two men guided me to St. Elizabeth's Hospital on the island's west coast, where they accompanied me into the emergency operating room. Harmen lay stretched out on the operating table. A surgeon was drilling a hole through his knee. Shocked, I asked, "Is my husband under anesthesia?"

"Not necessary," the main surgeon replied. "He is going in and out of consciousness."

Harmen's thighbone had been broken, leaving a gaping deep wound in the upper leg. He also suffered a multiply fractured jaw and facial cuts and bruises. The situation was clearly serious. As I watched, Harmen remained in a state of unconsciousness; whenever he came to, he appeared delirious, not knowing fully who or where he was.

By six o'clock in the morning I went home to check on David. When I was sure the maid was taking care of him I left for the bank to deliver bank documents from Harmen's brief-case, which the police had retrieved from his wrecked sports car. I saw the bank president and when I put my hand forward to shake hands I was shocked to notice that my hands were blood-stained. I opened the case, and found wet bloodstained papers lying amongst shattered pieces of glass from the windshield. I do not know what happened further. I was in such a state... The next thing I remember is that I went back to the hospital where I talked to the head nurse, who said, "Your husband's leg wound is extremely serious and could cause danger to his life."

"But," I said, "when my husband is out of danger, how long does he have to stay in the hospital?"

"Until Christmas or longer," she answered in an assured manner. It was the last day of May and December seemed far away. I was speechless for a moment believing she must be joking, but this was not the case.

Harmen hung in traction for the next four months. I deco-rated his room with paintings from home, moved in a playpen for David and stored diapers in the closet. I spent most of my time at the hospital and often functioned as a back-up nurse. David would come along during the daytime hours.

Aside from us, Harmen did not have many visitors. Mr. Henri Beerkema, Harmen's secretary, and his twenty-six-year-old wife, Eva, would show up occasionally. Eva was expecting their first child and was in the sixth month of her pregnancy. She had a keen interest in little David, who was playing in the playpen in Harmen's hospital room. I shared my young mother experiences with Eva and showed her how to fold the cloth diapers we used on the island. One weekend, I heard from a bank colleague that Eva had been admitted to the hospital with breathing problems. The next Monday I went to the flower shop to order her a bouquet. I called the hospital and asked, "Where do I send flowers for Mrs. Beerkema, which room is she in?"

Out of the blue the hospital operator stated, "Mrs. Beerkema's corpse has been moved to the morgue."

I was flabbergasted and sank for a moment into shock and disbelief. "How was this possible? I had just seen her. She was so alive awaiting her baby!"

I rushed to the hospital to tell Harmen the sad news. I knew I needed to initiate some actions to help Henri, which my husband could not do from his hospital bed. I got on the phone with the bankers to seek their help. As I witnessed myself pleading for their compassion, I felt my own spiritual heart opening for the first time. Later at the funeral, I stood next to Henri in the scorching tropical sun while the bodies of mother and baby were placed in an above-ground grave that was being built in our presence. But for the sounds of the setting and cementing of one stone on top of the other, I stood there for hours in silence and again felt such compassion that it surprised me. It made me finally understand what is meant by the term unconditional love, the ever-present love that flows from the heart of God. I was unspeakably touched by this drama of sadness, in essence so contradictory to life's expectations, which welcome babies and applaud mothers who give birth. As Harmen's accident had already called us to see the deeper meaning of life, the death of Eva and her baby made us value life even more.

Four months passed by. They finally removed the pin from Harmen's knee and the weights for the traction. Harmen could neither walk nor stand, but I emphatically insisted against hospital advice to take him home by ambulance. Our dog Daphne waited for hours on the porch as if she knew he was coming. Harmen arrived late in the afternoon and was carried in on a stretcher to a movable bed placed on the porch. How surprised he was to find a new garden around the house, lusciously grown tall during his absence, which he now could enjoy. His injured leg could not move, and he explained to me, "It feels like a solid log." To bring life back to the atrophied muscles, he had to practice prescribed physical exercises on a daily basis. He never complained, but I knew that these exercises were very painful. With tremendous determination he slowly regained enough strength in his leg to learn to stand and walk again at exactly that same time as David took his first baby steps. After eight months, he was ready to resume his responsibilities at the bank.

Harmen was in many ways a changed man, and my care for him ignited such deep love that he swore he would never travel anywhere in the world without taking David and me along. For the next few years the three of us traveled extensively for banking business and vacations until Harmen's next appointment came about: an international banking position in the United States.

Chapter Eighteen

Revealing My Spiritual Side

We had been in San Anselmo, California, for about ten months. Little did we suspect that the final week of our marriage had arrived. All we knew was that our second child was soon to be born. While focusing on the great event of the birth, Harmen fell off his commuter bus in San Francisco and suffered a mild concussion. He had to take bed rest for a week. When he was about to return to the office, the wife of a close colleague at the bank called me. Ling announced, "Ella, I have to tell you that some major changes are taking place at the bank. This is all happening while your husband is on sick leave. I am not allowed to give you any details. This call is a warning for your husband and you must swear not to tell him anything about my phone call to you." I immediately promised Ling I would not tell anything, because shocked as I was, I wanted to hear more. Ling continued, "My Christian prayer group and I are praying for Harmen. His health and life are on the line, but our prayers may well save him." After having said that, she hung up. "What in God's name is Ling trying to tell me?" I thought, greatly concerned. All I could fathom was that a power struggle was brewing at the bank. Then I remembered a dream I had earlier that year.

My dream:

> I am with Harmen inside a large stone building. We are moving rapidly through long dimly lit hallways. I am holding my husband by the hand. Frantically looking for the exit and with feelings of extreme urgency, I am trying to find a way to escape the building. I notice to my horror that all windows are cemented in and all doorways are solidly blocked. Panic sets in… I turn into another hallway and surprisingly find granite steps leading downwards to the outside. "That must be the way," I think, escorting Harmen down the stone steps. At the bottom of the stairs I find a funeral procession waiting…an open hearse draped in black and pulled by several black horses covered with long black cloaks. The scene reminded me of an old-fashioned royal funeral, like the picture I had seen in my parents' photo album. The horses and the hearse block the exit completely. In a final and determined effort to get through, I bend down, still holding Harmen by the hand, to have us crawl underneath the horses' bellies. I feel the horses' bodies above us and we are almost on the outside when their bodies join together like the pieces of a jigsaw puzzle, trapping us. I wake up…

The dream puzzled me, but now my intuition was telling me that the large stone building could well represent the bank from which there appeared to be no escape. I became frightened as to what kind of situation awaited my husband when he would return to International. Colleagues were clearly digging his grave, symbolized by the funeral procession waiting at the only exit from the bank building.

My head was spinning and I broke down and said to my husband: "Harmen, Ling called and made me swear not to tell you anything about her phone call. I am extremely alarmed and find what she said disconcerting as well as impossible to understand." I gave him the peculiar information that in and of itself did not tell anything specific. I warned him to play things carefully at the bank in the coming weeks. Harmen immediately understood the seriousness of this call. When he returned to work the next morning, he was determined to find out what was happening behind his back. From the bank, he phoned me several times a day with updates on what he had uncovered so far. An immense power struggle for the position of vice president was at hand and it felt like a matter of life and death.

Harmen said, "Ella, I must fight and win."

"What for?" I said, and then added, "Do not do this for me. I am very pleased as to where we are now. Do not take any risks for my sake."

Harmen then answered, "I think I must do this for myself to prove I have the capacity to win."

Trained as an intelligence officer in the Dutch air force, Harmen was taught to scrutinize and analyze complex situations. But his close colleague, who had served in American Intelligence in Taiwan, found out. Ling phoned again, scolding and telling me that her husband had attempted to strangle her, as he deduced from Harmen's moves that she had talked to me.

Due to the stress, as well as the uncertainty it created regarding my husband's position at the bank, we began deep conversations about the meaning of life, often expressing how close we felt. We made new plans for our family's future, including our baby that was soon to be born.

All the days of my marriage I had prayed the Lord's Prayer before sleeping, surrendering all of me to the will of God. "Thy Will be done..." was what I lived by. Harmen did not know about my spiritual side, which I kept hidden from everyone since the divine revelation when I was a child of twelve. During my last week with him, I finally revealed my secret, and fully explained my spiritual side to him. I also disclosed that I had prayed for him while he took his examinations at the university. I described how, while in deep prayer, I visualized the light of knowledge pouring into his mind as I circled the building he was in. I was surprised to hear that he had known it all along. He said that he felt the presence of the power of a higher intelligence during his examination.

The power struggle at the bank did not get resolved that week. The exit out of the dilemma remained blocked when the black horses, symbolizing death as well as the horsepower of the hit-and-run Cadillac, formed one block from which, despite my good efforts, escape was not possible...

PART III

Widening
Horizons

Chapter Nineteen

New Lights of Understanding

Being dead does not mean nonexistence. There is another place where spirits go, which is in a different dimension than ours. Jesus in the New Testament says, "In my Father's house are many mansions." Metaphorically he is telling us that after this life each of us goes to one of God's many "mansions." These spiritual dimensions cannot be experienced by our limited senses.

When I looked at Harmen's face as he lay in his casket at the funeral home, I became instantly aware of his living presence. I was in a state of shock, which allowed me to go beyond the normal senses of sight, hearing, touch, taste and smell. In a heightened state of awareness I said to him, "I will see you in your tomorrow." I knew that I had yet to live a long life, while Harmen now in the other world time-frame of his new dimension would see me soon, perhaps even in his tomorrow.

Years later I was not surprised to read in *Destiny of Souls* by Dr. Michael Newton that one year in the heavenly worlds corresponds with approximately fifty years of life on Earth. I immediately understood these differences of time-frames when I felt Harmen's presence at the funeral home. I was intuitively perceptive of a truth not known to men in general.

Shortly after Harmen's passing I hoped to find more concrete answers about the hereafter from the minister of my church. My minister, who came to check how I was doing, did not answer any of my urgent questions. Instead he said, "Mrs. Evers, it is time for you to let go of your husband and go on with your new life."

I felt painfully let down by such remarks. Despite his opinion, I knew I simply had to talk about Harmen. I had to express my continuing love and concern for him, otherwise how could I live through this tragedy? Not only did I still have my love for Harmen, but I also cared to know what was happening to him. My recurring thoughts were: "Where is Harmen? Where did he go? Is he alive? Is he well?" I desperately was longing to know and understand the heavenly worlds beyond.

After the funeral my parents left to get back to their lives in The Netherlands. When I finally found myself alone with the two children in my new situation, I pondered again the meaning of death and dying. At night when the children were asleep I often sat in the living room in my husband's favorite chair imagining his spirit coming and visiting me, and hoping I would be able to see him, but no matter how hard I tried nothing of the sort ever happened.

Many people in Marin County had read about my husband's hit-and-run death in the newspapers. A woman I did not know who was touched by our tragedy spontaneously phoned and offered the help of the minister of her church to sort things out, spiritually speaking. I accepted, as I longed with all my heart to speak to a minister who might answer some of my most pressing questions. The minister kindly offered to come to my house. I was delighted. The minister of my own church had let me down, but nevertheless I still believed ministers to be the experts on having knowledge of God and the hereafter.

The first question I posed was, "Where do the dead go?"

The minister declared before I even could continue, "Your husband is in a beautiful place."

"But where is that place?" is what I wanted to know.

The minister answered, "Suppose your husband liked playing

golf while here on Earth, I can assure you that playing golf is what he is doing where he is now."

I replied with pain in my heart, "I will tell you what my husband really wanted while here on Earth. He wanted to be with me and nothing else."

I painfully concluded that it was fruitless to ever talk again about death and the hereafter with any man or woman of the cloth.

Chapter Twenty
Meeting an Artist

Well over a year had gone by since Harmen's death and it still felt as if a knife was stuck deep in my heart. I was in grief. I knew I had to move on for the sake of the children as well as my own. Important decisions had to be made. Even though Marin County in California was a beautiful place to live, I had not integrated enough into American culture and society to feel that sense of home I needed. Harmen had represented my Dutch culture and upbringing, and without him I wondered where I belonged. I experienced feelings of extreme loneliness and felt uncertain in which world the children and I should live. Since I still had family and friends in The Netherlands, it ultimately seemed logical to make plans to move back there. After lots of concentrated efforts I managed to sell our San Anselmo home. Caring friends offered their mother-in-law apartment for rent as a temporary place till I was ready for the next step. Jim and Pat Cowley lived in the upstairs house and were most congenial. Most of our furniture was put in harbor storage in San Francisco ready for overseas shipment.

I needed time to pay attention to some complicated financial questions before leaving the country. Nothing seemed easy. Our family life moved forward as well as was possible under the new circumstances. David attended kindergarten while Femke and I stayed home in our small apartment on top of the hill near our former house. Femke had grown into a healthy, good-natured and beautiful toddler. She brought joy to our life, but I felt unbearable sadness not to have a father for her.

Anton and Ursula Woltering, our former neighbors in San Anselmo, had moved to Sonoma. Ursula called and said, "Ella, why don't you come over here with the children and spend an afternoon with us before leaving for Holland?"

The invitation was music to my ears and I gratefully accepted. I liked Ursula, who was from Germany. She had a deeper understanding of death and its dreadful aftermath because of her WWII experience on the other side of our border. We arrived late and I realized it was already Femke's naptime. As a punctual mother I insisted that Femke should have her nap.

Ursula said, "Use one of our bedrooms and join us after she falls asleep!" Femke had a long nap and woke up around dinnertime. Ursula asked, "Why don't you all stay for supper?" I enthusiastically accepted. It felt so warm, homey and complete to be with a family where the father was present.

Shortly before dinner a man named Jon Sutton arrived. Jon was an artist who had been commissioned by my friends to create a tapestry for the wall of their house under construction. Jon had been driving for nine hours all the way down from Oregon, where he had his permanent residence. He had called Anton and explained that he could not find the location of their new house. Anton responded by saying, "Come, have dinner with us first, then afterward I will take you there!"

There were nine of us for supper that night. The atmosphere was very joyful. Jon, with much gusto, played the piano and sang songs from a musical he had composed. Afterwards we got into lively discussions about astrology and Jon looked up the various stellar configurations of our births in his astrology book. He further colorfully described, in his artistic manner of speaking, the beautiful acres of land he owned in Oregon, a state I had never heard of before. Mesmerized I listened.

I had been collecting souvenirs to bring to The Netherlands and was hoping to find a large photograph of Mount Tamalpais, the mystical high towering mountain I had come to love so much. "Do you know any good art photographers?" I asked Jon, explaining I wanted a photo of Mount Tam.

Jon said, "I happen to know the best photographers in Marin County and will find something good for you." I gave him my phone number without hesitation, thinking that I would find a good picture if I asked enough people. In all honesty I never thought to hear from Jon again.

A few months later I received a phone call. After I said, "Hello?" I heard a voice saying, "Jon Sutton here!" My reply was: "What, who?" I had totally forgotten the name.

"I couldn't find a photo of Mount Tamalpais for you, so I decided to paint a watercolor instead. Can I come over for coffee and show it?"

Later that morning I saw Jon coming up the steep long driveway carrying the artwork under his arm. After he arrived he sat down in my little apartment and unfolded the painting. His work immediately impressed me, but I hardly dared to say it. The businesswoman's voice inside my head took hold of me, propelling me to say, "Let's talk about price first!" I reasoned that if I praised the painting too much, the price would certainly go up.

How surprised I was when Jon said, "Any person who likes Mount Tamalpais that much should have it. It is a present for you." I was deeply touched.

We had coffee and a piece of my best sherry cake. As soon as Jon left I rushed to my neighbors upstairs. With the watercolor tightly tucked under my arm I rang the doorbell. Pat came to the door. Before she could say anything, I said, while lifting the protective cover off the painting, "I received a present, a present from heaven!"

I could not believe that anyone would give me something so beautiful for free. I was so happy about it that I took it with me that afternoon to show it to a man friend I had recently met.

Again I remarked, "I got a present from heaven," while showing this man Jon's watercolor.

After Jon returned to Oregon, I began to receive letters from him. Often he included a poem exclusively written for me. One letter came with a suggestion of marriage. I was not interested. The other man I met was also talking about marriage. It was extremely confusing to me. I already had blueprints of the house I was to purchase in The Netherlands and had my admission papers for attending law school in Nijmegen. All my plans were in place to move back to my home country in just a couple of months. Our airline tickets had just come in the mail.

Then Jon revisited California. He often appeared on our doorstep and on occasion he would cook delicious and interesting American-style meals for our small family. He took us on hikes and we visited the San Francisco zoo with him. His presence provided a warm sense of family spirit.

The worst pain I felt deep in my heart was never to see Harmen's face again, that trusted face I had known so long. I had looked everywhere in hopes of finding someone who might even slightly resemble him. My other suitor looked like Harmen. He was also a businessman, but he was not Harmen. It was eerie. Looking at him made me remember that face I missed so enormously.

Chapter Twenty-one

An Important Dream

A decisive person, I could not bear having the attention of two men while I was ready to move back to my home country. One night, I could not tolerate it any longer. I thought, "Here are two men who want to marry me. I am a widow with two children. What am I to do? Should I pay any attention to these possibilities or not?" I decided to ask God.

The children were already fast asleep when I put my favorite Bible under my bed pillow. I lay down on my bed and as I started to pray a small picture my Bible teacher in elementary school had given me appeared in my inner vision. It was a colored rendering of Jacob wrestling with an angel with large wings, which in the holy Bible, Genesis 32, verse 24, is depicted as a man, which is God himself in reality. In the Hebrew translation Jacob is fighting with God himself (New International Version: www.biblegateway.com):

> And Jacob was left alone; and a man wrestled with him until the breaking of the day. When the man saw that he did not prevail against Jacob, he touched the hollow of his thigh; and Jacob's thigh was put out of joint as he wrestled with him. Then he said, "Let me go, for the day is breaking." But Jacob said, "I will not let you go, unless you bless me." And he said to him, "What is your name?" And he said, "Jacob." Then he said, "Your name shall no more be called Jacob, but Israel, for you have striven with God and with men, and have prevailed." Then Jacob asked him, "Tell me, I pray, your name." But he said, "Why is it that you asked my name?" And there he blessed him. So Jacob called the name of the place Peni'el, saying, "For I have seen God face to face and yet my life is preserved."

When my Bible teacher narrated the Genesis story, he told us that to receive a blessing from God one has to wrestle with God or his angel, and to not give up till you see him face to face. To me this meant to pray with all my heart, soul and might.

Tuning into the biblical Jacob, I began to pray with all the fervor I had in me, ready to fight with the angel until God gave me the answer I needed. I was twisting and turning while I prayed on and on and felt myself sinking deeper into unknown realms. While I kept turning and turning around in my bed beseeching God to speak to me, I became aware of my own being on a soul level. As I went deeper and deeper yet into the core of my being, I found myself wrestling with the angel of old. How little did I know about prayer in those days, and yet I knew, because knowledge was not new to me. "Had God not revealed the fullness of his knowledge when I was only a child of twelve?" I continued to pray without repose, struggling with the mighty angel, a representation of God's power. I felt myself slipping away from the connection to the world and sleep came...and then in a dream:

> Harmen appears... He is dressed in his white tennis outfit. I do not know he had died when I see him. We begin a conversation through mental telepathy from a place between the two eyebrows in the forehead. I experience instant thought transfer for the first time in my life. As Harmen and I begin talking in this manner, we are reviewing the many aspects of life, back and forth, from him to me and from me to him. Toward the end of the dream, Harmen makes a final statement with enormous clarity, "Ella, if you must make a decision, choose the most humane person."

There the dream ended. Soon I found myself in yet another dream.

> I am present in the middle of a large orchestra. They are playing the *Ninth Symphony* of Beethoven. I hear the choir singing from the "Ode to Joy," *Alle Menschen werden Brüder* (all men become brothers)...

I awoke. The sounds of the orchestra and the choral voices were still around me. I heard it clearly. The choir kept repeating over and over again, *"Alle Menschen werden Brüder..."*

I was one with the orchestral sounds and the voices, experiencing an elevated state of consciousness. After some unknown time had gone by, the sounds slowly faded away and I came back to my normal state of being.

After my soul-talk with Harmen and realizing the depth of beauty of Beethoven's music, I was no longer the same person. The intensity of what had happened shifted something in my innermost being. On a bodily level these transforming experiences had caused my body and bed sheets to be soaked with so much perspiration that I was completely drenched. It was early Sunday morning and the sun was shining into our living room. The children were still fast asleep. I was in a daze wondering, "What did my dream with Harmen and Beethoven's music want to tell me?"

Jon kept visiting and often had me listen to *The War Requiem* by the English composer Benjamin Britten that he was studying at that time. The other man came to visit as well.

As a child I had not received a musical upbringing. Radios were forbidden during the war and when radios reappeared after 1945, I became aware that my father was not fond of listening to music even though my mother was. In high school I only learned the basics of music for one year. I felt inadequate to marry a person like Jon whose heart and mind were set on being a full-time composer of classical music. I believed that I could not sufficiently match Jon's understanding of music and concluded that it would be unfair to marry Jon.

Experiencing the depth of the *Ninth Symphony* of Beethoven changed my opinion. It showed me that I had an understanding of music on an aesthetic and spiritual level. In my dream with Harmen the message was that compassion was the most important consideration in making choices in life. The elements of brotherliness and compassion were also present in the lyrics of the "Ode to Joy," *"Alle Menschen werden Brüder"* in Beethoven's *Ninth Symphony.*

Harmen's last words, "If you must make a decision, choose the most humane person," kept haunting me. The words had been spoken ethereally through his third eye, which I later understood is the place where God resides in man. Of the two men who wanted to marry me I had no doubt that Jon was the most humane. The revelation of the dream and the music made it clear to me that should I remarry, it had to be Jon.

I immediately started to have doubts, as I am also a practical woman. "After all," I thought, "my children and I need to be provided for," and I realized this could be problematic if I married an artist-composer. I still did not seem to be able to make a final decision soon and many weeks went by.

One weekend Jon invited me to see a play at the California high school where he had taught. I love plays, so I agreed to go. It was an enjoyable comedy called *You Can't Take It with You*, by George Kaufman and Moss Hart. After the play ended the high school students lined up to meet Jon, who was their former teacher. They hugged him with obvious delight and he appeared to have been a most popular teacher. After the show Jon and I went to a restaurant to have something to drink. It was then that Jon asked, "Could we be engaged?" I became quiet and in deep thought for a while. Then the dream with Harmen flashed before my eyes and I heard the lyrics of the chorus singing about brotherly love. Spiritually I just knew I could match Jon and I said, "Yes."

The coming weeks, Jon began to introduce me to his San Rafael friends. They were all courteous, interesting and intelligent people and most of them had Jon Sutton tapestries or other artwork of Jon's hanging on their walls. I soon became acquainted and impressed with the many facets of Jon's visual art, all of an artistic fine quality I had not expected.

One Sunday morning Jon took me to his church in Tiburon. We entered a bit late. The congregation was in deep prayer. To my total amazement they were praying one of Jon's poems, which he had written for me. When they finished, Jon stood up in front of the whole congregation and gave an eloquent speech about how he had proposed to me and how I had accepted. "Another hidden talent unveiled," I thought. I simply fell in love with Jon's seemingly endless artistic capacities.

After the sermon and closing prayers, the minister walked directly toward me. He did not introduce himself. All he said was, while looking me straight in the eye, "And of all people, Jon Sutton is the most 'humane person' I know." I was stunned and in that moment I realized the happenings in my life were in perfect divine order. I did not tell Jon my dreams or what the minister said to me until years later.

Chapter Twenty-two

A New Marriage

Saying "yes" to Jon's proposal for marriage held also great significance for David. As my character was shaped by the German occupation in WWII, followed by the liberation and its aftermath of post-traumatic stress, the trauma of Harmen's death similarly affected the forming of David's character at the age of four. The wondrous event of the birth of the baby we had been waiting for became enshrouded in the darkness of the incomprehensibility of death. David, like me, became a wise or grey child beyond what other boys his age could comprehend.

I was concerned when I was told that since his father's death David was in such an apparent state of shock that he was no longer communicating with the fathers of his friends even though his English was quite sufficient. Today I understand how unfathomable the death of his father must have been. Only after Jon appeared in his life as a potential adoptive father figure did David begin to interact again with the other fathers. It did not surprise me. Jon had a joyous and playful attitude and he had always wanted to be a father.

One afternoon, I sat down with little David and explained how Jon had asked me to marry him and that this also meant that he was to become David and Femke's stepdad. I asked David what his thoughts were about having a father again. As young as he was, David had an extraordinary response, provoking a long dialogue. In the end I was relieved when he said positively "yes" to the marriage. Femke was too young to ask, but I had no doubt that she too would have agreed.

In The Netherlands my wedding announcement caused a shock wave of disbelief, especially to my parents, who were waiting for our return. I never felt at ease enough to reveal the dream that prompted my decision for the marriage. I am sure that in their opinion I was making a grave mistake not letting more years go by before thinking about remarriage. But in my sense of time, one hundred years had already gone by, one hundred years of unspeakable sorrow and pain. The experience of death had aged me beyond the understanding of my contemporaries. I wondered if I could ever feel young again.

A year later we traveled to The Netherlands to introduce Jon to my family and friends. The family was still not thrilled and occasionally acted as if I had forgotten Harmen, which was painful to me. My mother-in-law, from whom I expected nothing, understood me completely. She intuitively knew how deep the scars of Harmen's death were and that I yet must have mustered up enormous courage to try for another life, which benefited her grandchildren as well. She did not speak English, but said, after silently observing how Jon dealt with the children, "Ella, Jon is a exceptional human being," reminding me again of what Harmen pointed to in my dream "to choose the most humane person." My mother-in-law became the most ardent supporter of my new marriage and remarkably extended the love for her deceased son to Jon and me. During our stay in The Netherlands and later through letters and a visit, she continually expressed gratitude towards Jon. Her support created a strong bond of love between us that never broke.

Our newly formed family had moved to a beautiful home in Eugene, Oregon. David was starting first grade at an elementary school nicely located amongst green rolling hills and forests, just around the corner. Femke was a constant delight. She had a happy and strong confident personality. I was pleased for us to be a complete family once more.

As I did my best to create a loving atmosphere, I also realized that grief still lingered within me. Jon was keenly aware of it. I was unable to enjoy movies or read novels, which signaled to me how different I was from others my age. I felt as if the hit-and-run car had struck me down too. I was not fully crushed, but also not fully alive. To know that the dead are alive was still enormously important to me. I knew Harmen's body lay in the grave but "where had his spirit gone?" These were my lingering thoughts... Slowly I began to develop some of my own ideas regarding the possibility of an afterlife.

On my thirty-sixth birthday Jon gave me a small book by Dr. Raymond Moody titled *Life after Life*. We were having my birthday breakfast in a restaurant and during the meal I felt so drawn to the title that I could not help but start reading. I read *Life after Life* in one day. All the ideas I had been speculating about were to me indeed believable as they described people, who had clinically died and come back to life to tell what they experienced while out of body and how this experience changed their lives for the better. Reading Moody's many reports started a beginning of new understanding and hope in my life. I was relieved to know that I had not been wishfully imagining other dimensions, but that there are indeed such places where life continues.

A year later I became a realtor. My first clients were Lea and Bill Mirabella, who wanted to move westwards from the East Coast. I sold them a large house and after they settled in, my husband and I were invited to visit. Bill showed me their well-stocked library of esoteric books. I started reading. My first book was *A World Beyond* by Ruth Montgomery. Other books followed, many of them about great English mediums like Ena Twigg. These books delighted me and I could not get enough of them. All the books pointed to the truth of an afterlife. I learned about mediums transmitting messages from the world of the departed spirits. They can help grieving survivors to realize that their loved ones are still alive in spirit form.

One evening Bill and Lea took me to a class in psychometry offered by the minister of the Spiritualist Church, Virginia Hacket, a reputable medium. A minister in a Spiritualist Church is different from Christian churches in so far as their ministry is to make contact with the spirit world. When we walked into Virginia's house I sat down on one of the empty chairs arranged in a semicircle. Virginia, an ordinary-looking older woman, was sitting on a chair with the Bible in her lap. I had heard that she had the ability to hear the voices of spirits that sought to have contact through her. Virginia had her back toward us and was talking to a person on the far side of the room. Suddenly she turned completely around, looked straight at me and said, "Hey, you there! Do you have someone over here?"

Surprised I nodded and said, "Yes, my first husband."

Then a message from Harmen came through so rapidly that I at first could barely understand what was being said. Though bewildered, I managed to focus as Harmen spoke the following words, "When I first entered the other worlds, I was very sad. I did not want to leave you! I have suffered as much as you have, but now things are getting better and I am beginning to understand more." I suddenly heard the medium scream, "Don't do that!" I noticed that an invisible hand pulled her hair upwards. It was Harmen's personal sign, a bit hilarious, but very much in a manner I was so familiar with. He had always had such a sense of humor. Harmen's spirit left and I sat back in my chair in a daze. I did not doubt that Virginia had made contact with Harmen. The experience made a profound impression on me and I hoped that there would be other occasions for such encounters.

Chapter Twenty-three

Two Husbands

I continued reading mystical books, which opened my mind to embrace the existence of the spirit worlds. One morning when I was asleep an invisible hand touched me softly on the lower back and I awoke. I became aware that kisses like a warm breath of love floated over me. These kisses did not seem to touch my skin. My immediate thought was, "These are spiritual kisses." I was not fully awake and did not know whether Jon was in the bed with me, but I assumed he was. I was well aware that Jon was a very spiritual person and my next thought was, "Could he be this spiritual?" There was a sweet serene beauty to these kisses with a love not of this world. I checked with my hand whether Jon was in bed. He was not.

I was still not quite awake when I began to smell my favorite eau de cologne 4711. I picked up my sheet to smell where the scent came from and found that the top sheet exuded the 4711. I rested a bit longer, while half-awake, and not quite understanding what was happening. Our bathroom on the top floor was being remodeled and to take a shower I had to walk down two staircases to the ground floor. Lazily, I decided to linger on in my bed and enjoy the scent of the eau de cologne.

After five minutes I slowly got up, took a towel and proceeded to the downstairs shower. When I turned on the water, the delicate but distinctive aroma of the eau de cologne mingled with the water as it cascaded down on me. Only Harmen had known how fond I was of that scent. He used to sprinkle it on my bed pillow at night. That morning I was not thinking about Harmen, but just enjoyed breathing in the fine fragrance I had not smelled for so long. Enthralled, I fell into a space of pure beauty and ecstasy... Then I heard a voice singing to me, "Fly me to the moon," and

... let me play among the stars
...In other words
Hold my hand
...darlin' kiss me*

I remembered the song as Harmen's favorite, but never knew the lyrics to the song. Before our marriage when he worked for Dutch Intelligence, he did his undercover work in the evenings and at night

---

*   I could not write in the full lyrics because it is copyrighted material, but anyone can find the complete song on the Internet.

in a private villa in Scheveningen. When there was no decoding work at the villa, he would stroll off and listen to the music in a nearby nightclub. He especially loved the performance of Rita Reys of the Cocktail Trio when she sang "Fly Me to the Moon."

That morning I clearly heard all the words while streams of water with eau de cologne 4711 cascaded down on me. I did not think, just experienced. A few minutes later I stepped out of the shower, draped the towel around me and looked in the large mirror across the shower stall. In the mirror I saw the reflection of the most beautiful being I had ever seen. Sparks of star-like light were shining from every pore of my translucent looking face and I realized that I was that being. Much later, after delving even more deeply into books about the spirit worlds, I learned that I had seen my own spirit body.

I ran out of the bathroom and rushed to Jon, who was working in his composer's room on the ground floor, to tell him what had happened. The strange thing was that even though "Fly Me to the Moon" was Harmen's song, I still was not thinking of him. I simply was not thinking at all that morning. I believe that I was in a space between this world and the next. Jon heard my story and all he had to say was, "You are a very lucky woman. You have two husbands."

Half a year later, my friends, the Mirabellas, asked me to go with them to the spiritualist camp in Canby in northern Oregon. I had read in my metaphysical books about direct voice communication and was keenly interested in experiencing such communication with Harmen. At the camp we found a woman-medium who promised to do "direct voice."

I was led into a small room where I sat down with her. Within minutes, she fell into a deep trance state. When the first words came through, she was struggling to get them out. I heard her say, "Ella Me..." but she could not get it right. Of course I completed it for her: "Ella Meinardi." For Americans it is most difficult to pronounce the Dutch "ei." Then the voice said, "I come to you often and kiss you. Are you aware that I kiss you?"

When I said, "Yes," I broke down sobbing. "Please do not cry, do not be sad," the voice said, but I kept on crying from happiness as well as from sorrow. The medium could not continue.

Chapter Twenty-four

Loyalty

Through mediums and direct experiences I knew that Harmen was trying to show me his survival in the other worlds. Beside those experiences, I had recurring dreams of seeing Harmen, which startled me as "I remember that I am also married to Jon." My dream:

> I look at Harmen with great pain in my heart and tell him I remarried. I must tell Jon that Harmen has come back to me. I am confused. I have two husbands. Which one should I live with? I have love for both men and feel extremely torn...

In waking life, on a subconscious level I undoubtedly held a deep desire to have Harmen back. Deep down I also may have been in denial that he really died, which often happens when a healthy young husband who has everything to live for suddenly dies. The fact that he had truly passed away was not yet fully integrated in my subconscious. My hopes and dreams for a future with him had not been completely erased from my mind. The fact is that the mind does not and cannot understand death.

There was yet another reason why I had these persistent dreams. Three months before Harmen's passing I watched a movie on television I could not forget:

> The movie is about a Vietnam veteran captured by the Viet Cong. While living under harsh conditions in his prison

camp, the memory of his wife and infant daughter in the United States keep him alive.

His wife, in the meantime, receives a notification from the Army that her husband is missing in action. Four years go by. By then, the husband is presumed dead. The wife feels that she is free to marry her husband's best friend.

After the marriage, the movie shows the veteran making a risky escape from a prison camp. As he finally reaches the American side, the United States Army arranges his flights back home. He decides not to inform his wife, but to surprise her with his homecoming. Even though tired from the many long flights, he feels euphoric when a taxi drops him off at his house. He rings the doorbell, his heart beating in anticipation. When his wife comes to the door, he embraces her with the endless love he had held for her and then rushes inside in the hope of taking their child into his arms.

"I have to talk to you," his wife whispers, and explains her remarriage. He does not let her finish, but runs out the door, shaken to the core of his being. In a state of desperation he goes to the oceanside and hollers at the waves till he somehow manages to calm down...

He returns to the house, which is no longer his. This time, he begs his wife to listen to his truth. "I married you first," he utters with a trembling voice and continues to make his next most important point: "*We* have a child together!"

An unbearable silence follows, after which the wife replies, "But I am expecting..."

In the early years of my new marriage the theme of this movie kept haunting me. I was pondering my feelings of love for one husband while still feeling love for the other. In the movie, a P.O.W. wife finds herself married to two men in real life. In my dream life I experience a similar dilemma, which to the dreamer is as real as life. To find understanding about this subconscious psychological drama of my own life story, I began looking for spiritual answers.

After reflection on this topic over many years, I came to think that there had to be a deeper meaning to Harmen's passing, but that the full knowledge and the full explanation of his death would always remain an unresolved mystery. It slowly dawned on me that the least I could do as a survivor was to come to a place of acceptance of that which could not be changed. "God, greater than me, knows my whole story," and therefore, "I need to place my trust in him and know it is good." "Thy will be done on earth as it is in heaven," says the same. If a deeper purpose was served, this could only be understood from the multi-faceted point of higher Consciousness.

I was finally able to let go of conflicting thoughts regarding Harmen and Jon, as I knew this new insight benefited all our souls. I began to see that instead of sadness, I needed to look back to the years with Harmen with gratitude. With Jon I lived my continuing Earth existence, while Harmen played his role from afar like a loving spirit surrounding us and also for his own soul's purposes, which mysteries only he *now knows*. At last I was able to integrate my two men within me without hurting anyone. Each had their place in my heart and I could be loyal to both. I knew I had plumbed the depth of death in a way that enriched life, bringing forth more love. As I held on to this new perspective, dreams about Harmen returning never plagued me again.

Love does not stop at death, but continues to grow from the depth of death into a greater expansion of understanding life and thereby removing all fear of death as it grows. Death is only the dying of the physical body, which encases the soul like a garment. After death the soul or spirit frees itself to continue its journey ever closer to the light of God. Death is a doorway to more light for the spirit and the survivors. I had experienced that the departed can appear to us and that we can call upon them if truly needed.

Once, in a state of great despair regarding one of my children, I prayed for divine intercession. At the same time, I screamed inside my mind for the deceased father of my child,

"Please, I need your help for our child!" The following night, Harmen appeared in my dream:

> Intensely happy to see him, I rush "as if carried on wings of love" towards him. I am about to put my arms around him, when, painfully, I bump up against a large glass wall that I had also encountered in other dreams. I know that this glass-like wall forms a separation line between the earth plane and the spirit world. In anguish, I press against the glass, not knowing what to do next... Then... I feel Harmen's hand reaching for my hand through the glass. His hand takes my hand in his and caresses it with a love not of this world. "Please take care of our child," I whisper in English, while waking up.

As I awoke, I realized that Harmen was still holding my hand. I recognized the sweet vibration of the touch of a real hand of flesh and bones, one I had known so well.

Through revelations, I learned that the spirit-souls in the hereafter are able to see and help us. There is an ethereal cord of love-energy connecting souls. That thread of love is the highway upon which souls travel between the various worlds. Through death, I learned to expand in love. Love is what God is, the unbound everlasting unconditional love, which lives in man's higher Consciousness.

Seeing or experiencing that love often occurs to me like a sudden flash of lightning. This revelation of light is available to all of us and can happen to anyone in a flash even when it is least expected. Through seeking it we all can be certain to find that immeasurable immense power of infinite luminous Light.

Chapter Twenty-five
Reiki

It was Memorial Day, 1982. Femke was spending the day with her friend in the country. I got a phone call from the emergency room at Sacred Heart Hospital late that afternoon. The mother of Femke's friend came on the line to talk to me. "I am sorry to tell you, but Femke fell off her pony and broke her arm. It looks serious and it is best for you to come to the hospital at once."

I rushed to the hospital to pick Femke up and bring her home. When I entered the emergency room an orthopedic doctor was with her. He explained, "Your daughter has a complicated fracture of her elbow and to make sure the arm will continue to grow normally I put her arm in traction. She must stay in the hospital till the fracture heals." I looked at my eight-year-old daughter with her arm hanging in traction, and memories of Harmen in traction with a broken femur in Curaçao flooded back to me. I immediately made plans to stay with Femke in the hospital for the coming nights and days to comfort her as much as was possible.

When Femke adjusted to her hospital stay, Jon and I came to visit during the daytime. Jon read her favorite stories and brought cassette tapes with music. Femke's room filled up with letters, balloons and presents from friends at school and church. "But how long," I thought, "is this orthopedic surgeon going to let her hang like that?"

After two weeks Jon and I found Femke crying in agony with severe muscle spasms. We became concerned and I asked for a doctor. The regular bone specialist was not available. A pediatrician happened to be walking through the hallway and was called in to have a look. After his examination he took me aside and said, "Your daughter needs special care. I know a woman who does visualization work that has proven to be helpful in the healing process. Would you be interested?" Of course I was.

79

Doctor Magnus gave me the phone number of a woman named Luellen. I phoned and made an appointment to meet her at the hospital the next day. I found that Luellen did not do visualizations. She explained, "The kind of work I do is a practice called Reiki, a healing method that directs universal life energy through my hands into an afflicted area of the body." She added, "The application of the Reiki energy accelerates the healing time." It sounded wonderful and I gave Luellen the go-ahead to start her work at once.

The air-conditioned set temperature in Femke's hospital room felt rather cold when Luellen began her the Reiki treatment, but within minutes I felt the temperature rising and I broke out in sweat. Something was clearly happening in the room, and it fascinated me and gave me hope. Femke liked the session with Luellen and we asked her to come back for additional healing sessions. The new X-rays showed that her elbow bones were finally knitting together. After a painful seventeen-day hospital stay, Femke was discharged, looking radiant. I was impressed with Luellen's hands-on healing work and had no doubt Reiki had stimulated the bone growth. I asked her if I could learn this Reiki method. "Of course you can," she said, and referred me to her Reiki master, Marta Getty, who lived nearby.

I signed up for the next Reiki-I workshop. I learned how Dr. Usui, a former principal of a Christian seminary in Kyoto, Japan, mystically conceived the Reiki healing method. It all started when his students challenged him by asking why the Christian church did not perform healings like Jesus did. Dr. Usui took the challenge seriously, resigned from his position and began a search for clues to spiritual healing. He studied first in the United States and later on in a Japanese monastery, where he had to learn enough Sanskrit to translate the texts of ancient Sutras. He discovered healing symbols in these texts, but felt frustrated because he had no idea how to make practical use of them. Following the advice of the head of the monastery to meditate on the inner meaning of the symbols, he set out for a three-week silent retreat and fast on Mount Kuriyama. He went into states of deep silence and surrender, but the weeks went by and nothing happened... By the twenty-first day, about to give up and ready to leave the holy mountain, he noticed a sudden flicker of intense light rapidly moving in his direction. Frightened, he tried to avoid being hit by this light, but it struck him with force right in the center of his forehead, from where millions of bubbles of colored lights emerged. Then a great white light appeared before him displaying in golden letters on a large screen the keys to unlock the symbols of the Sanskrit text he had studied. This was his initiation into the higher levels of the healing arts granted by the universal Light.

As he returned to normal consciousness, he descended the mountain in a state of indescribable euphoria. Rushing down a steep slope, he badly stubbed his toe and spontaneously put his hand on the cut. A strong pulsating energy rushed through his hands, bringing instantaneous healing. This event marked the beginning of the reintroduction of a healing method known long ago by the sages of ancient India. Dr. Usui gave the energy the name Reiki, a Japanese word for universal life force energy. The most important part of learning Reiki is the initiation, a mystical opening-up to the universal life force.

When my turn came to go in for my initiation by Marta Getty, I did not expect anything. I had never been able to feel energy, but during the initiation I immediately became aware of higher energies around me. It was as if I was lifted to a higher plane where I heard myself singing, "Nearer my God to Thee, nearer to Thee." I was rapt in an expanded awareness. Afterwards I went for a quiet walk and then realized that I simply loved everyone.

I began my Reiki practice by working with the universal life energy on my own body as taught in the first Reiki level. Harmen's death had aged me beyond that of my contemporaries, and the Reiki energy reversed that process of deep grief and I felt youthfulness returning to my body and spirit. I signed up for the next workshop, Reiki-II, with initiations intended to open one's healing potential to heal others. Both initiations filled me with a renewed zest for life. I started participating in group-healing sessions, where I met spiritual people who practiced meditation. Some healers invited me to their Sunday morning meditation-*satsang* (meeting).

With all the new impressions I gathered, new ideals awakened in me. I imagined a whole new Earth where people would respect each other's differences of race, culture, religion, country, political convictions, social class and sexual orientation. This would be a world order in which people took care, not only of the human species, but also the animal, plant and mineral kingdoms. With this new model, balance and harmony would be restored on Earth. I had always been idealistic, and the sense that these visions would be attainable stirred the essence of my being. I felt the light growing stronger inside me.

Chapter Twenty-six
Huna Initiation

I met Nadia at my alternative healing-group meeting. Some said Nadia was too powerful. That she had powers and an enormous understanding of science not yet revealed to mankind seemed obvious to me after talking to her. Nadia was just not an ordinary person. Nadia was a Huna master and had the knowledge of the ancient shamanic healers that originated some 35,000 years ago in Hawaii. The basis of this healing is the understanding that everything is interconnected; anything is possible and separation is a useful illusion. I heard that Nadia was giving classes in Huna healing and I was most eager to learn more about mystical healing. As I longed to expand my knowledge of using spiritual power to find the answers of why we are here, I signed up for the next Huna seminar.

Prior to the seminar, Nadia asked me to select a special secret word that she, during the initiation, would connect with the Huna power of healing. It would, in my healing practices, act as a trigger to call upon the Huna power. I was guided to three words in the Book of Revelation and felt the tremendous power and a connection to the revealed light that always subtly nudged me on the path to inner knowledge.

The workshop started with an introductory lecture about the techniques of Huna mystic shamanic healing. Subsequently, Nadia invited each student, one by one, to come to a separate room to receive initiation into the higher realms of the Huna powers of healing. My turn came, and as I entered the semi-darkened room, I saw Nadia standing, cloaked in ceremonial dress, with an ornamental dagger in her hand. She made me lie down on my stomach. I was asked to think of my magic secret word. I revealed the three words from the Book of Revelation to her. Nadia was surprised and said, "These are very powerful." As the sacred words flooded my consciousness I remained stretched out on my stomach. It was quiet in the room and I felt Nadia stirring the energy fields in the lower part of my back with her dagger without touching my physical body. Working with Reiki had made me super sensitive to these invisible subtle energies. Changes in the energy field were occurring near the very bottom of my spine as if a physical object were touching my body.

When the initiation was finished I was sent back to the main meeting room where the other students were waiting their turns. A student who had already been initiated told me how wonderful it had been and how the initiation had brought about a spiritual experience. I immediately wondered what I had been missing. At the appropriate time I went back to Nadia and told her that the initiation had perhaps not worked for me. I asked her, "What are you actually doing during this initiation?" Nadia explained that the ornate ceremonial dagger she was holding in her hand would open the bottom of my spine in the ethereal fields and awaken the slumbering *Kundalini* energy. I had no idea what this meant as I had never heard the word *Kundalini* before. I lay down on my stomach to receive my second initiation.

This time, I immediately became aware of an enormously powerful surge of energy flowing from the bottom of my spine to the top of my head. It was moving slowly and felt cold like a huge river of molten ice. I was in another awareness when I gradually stood up and told Lydia what I experienced this time. I left the room to join the others. An older man amongst the students came up to me and said, "Do you want an experience of the light?" He then began to explain that I should imagine a star in my left eye and then imagine a star in my right eye. "Bring these stars together in the middle of your eyebrows," the old man said. As I followed his instructions I saw the middle of my forehead open and a beautiful brilliant white light appearing. I began to shake immensely because the light was too intense to behold and yet it was the same light already known to me.

The great light that took presence between my eyebrows first appeared in the week after Harmen died when I focused on the photo of the psychic Peter Hurkos. In my mind's eye, later known to me as the third eye, I had looked at Peter's face and said to him straight from my heart and soul, in contrast to my parents' disapproving remarks: "You are not a bad man. You are a good man, a very good man!"

In my life today, I acknowledge seeing this light almost every day, and when this happens I am for a split second pulled beyond the veil that separates this world and the next. Besides seeing it in my third eye, it also appears outside in midair or penetrating the density of ceilings or walls made of wood or stone. I feel a great deal of gratitude and respect for the immensity of its appearance. The light tells me, like other experiences I have had, that there are gateways between our physical world and other realms of spirit. The experience of the light reveals the reality of God and brings me closer to a full merging into divine essence, or source of all knowing, which I already experienced when I was twelve. To come closer to this light and to understand it is why we are here.

At the time I was initiated by Nadia I did not know that only a truly enlightened guru should do this type of cosmic energy release. I had not the slightest idea that the awakening of the cosmic power could be harmful to me. I trusted Nadia and had only positive feelings about the seminar when I went home. I soon forgot about *Kundalini* and only remembered the experience with the light.

Chapter Twenty-seven

A Beacon of Light

My meditation friends often quoted spiritual knowledge from the teachings of Astara, a secret mystical school, resembling the old mystery schools that existed during the times of ancient Egypt and Greece. Mystical knowledge always had held an attraction for me and I was happy to enroll as a student of Astara. The school was based near Los Angeles and I received my monthly study material, the "Astara Lessons," by mail. After reading the first material I felt so at home with the teachings that I could not put them down. I became absorbed in the teachings and practices of *pranayama*, the ancient yoga method of breathing, and *lama yoga*. Both methods can lead to states of enlightenment or union with God. I left my real estate occupation to study full time at an accelerated rate. At the same time I continued practicing Reiki. The studies of the revelation of the mysteries of life and the work of applying universal healing techniques complemented each other.

I attained the seventh level of Astara within a few years. The acquired knowledge changed my worldview from the material to the spiritual. It made me understand that the underlying substratum of all things is of a higher vibration, unseen yet truly real.

The mystical teachings and the revealed knowledge moved me onward to the unraveling of the hidden mysteries of life and death.

In this, dreams also held a fascination for me. It all began with my mother, who dreamed about the liberation of Nijmegen before D-Day in the exact way it happened later on when the Allies landed by parachute in front of our house. I had married Jon because of a dream that pointed to choosing the most humane person of the two men that proposed to me. Curious to gain more knowledge on the topic of dreams, I signed up for a class in dream interpretation offered by our community college. Gary Reiss, a process-oriented psychologist, taught the class. In this class I discovered how to find deeper meaning in my dreams through understanding ancient symbols and by using Gestalt theory, where all things in a dream are seen as part of the Self.

One evening while driving to Gary's class, I turned on the car radio and heard Schubert's *Ave Maria* broadcast and fell into a complete state of supreme ecstasy. By the time I entered my classroom I knew myself only as a beacon of light. I hardly remember what happened in the class that night. All I do remember was that when at some point we had to select a partner for some dream interpretation exercise, I knew I could just sit and wait for someone to choose me, because I was not the normal me, I was Light.

When I came home that night I said to my husband, "I am in ecstasy." Jon did not hear me. He was busy packing his suitcase for his trip to New York City the following day. His *Robert Louis Stevenson Songs for Voice and Piano* were going to be performed in Carnegie Hall in New York and his mind was focused on attending that event. He didn't appear to notice that I was in such exaltation. I remained in ecstasy for hours. It is a state of beauty beyond any mental understanding. I thought, "This is perhaps how saints must have felt all the time."

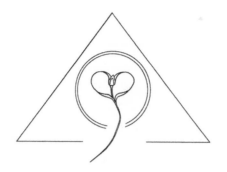

PART IV

Dwesha and Raga

Chapter Twenty-eight

Breakdown

In the summer of 1985 Jon and I went to see the movie *Back to the Future*. Halfway through, my attention shifted and I could no longer follow the storyline of the movie. My brain functioned differently as if something had broken inside my head. Suddenly I was mostly aware of the screen rather than the story projected on it. I looked at Jon, who was intently absorbed in the story. Alone and out of sync, I turned around and stared at the other people in the theater all wrapped up in what was happening on the screen.

A big change had come, causing extreme alarm inside me. The levels of distress were so overpowering that I could hardly wait for the movie to finish but, at the same time, I did not want to interrupt my husband's pleasure in watching it. After the movie ended, I was in a state of panic. When we walked out of the theater I said, "Jon, I have got to talk with you. I do not know what is happening to me; I do not feel normal anymore." I embraced him and said, "Please, please, stand by me! Help me! I think that I am having some kind of nervous breakdown."

Little did I know at that time that some nerves near the crown *chakra* (*Brahma-randha*) had broken inside my head, a first sign of the beginning stage of spiritual awakening. In India these nerves are called *dwesha* and *raga*. The breakage signaled the first scaling down of the ego by which I had lived most my life. I am talking about the ego as that sense of self which the thinker believes is the Consciousness. The ego is the part that, in the beginning of time, separated itself from the totality of Light, also known as God. The pathway back to God lies in the reduction of ego so that in a diminished state of ego, the light of God can fill up the emptied channels. Through meditation and other spiritual practices, preferably guided by a genuine spiritual master-teacher, the stage can be set to help the ego understand that its place and importance are wrapped in a greater dimensional realm of all-knowing.

It took years to come to have the full understanding as to what had actually happened during the movie. But in this not-knowing time, I became quite frightened. I knew that Jon could not help me, but it was important to have him by my side. I desperately needed someone to listen to the terror I was facing. I did not know then that the first shattering of the ego is a spiritual blessing. My life as I had known it seemed gone forever and pointed to the beginning of a different phase in my life. After my break at the movies, nightly frightful vibrations inside my spine would interrupt my sleep. The sensations felt like lightning attacking the core of my spinal column. I experienced a sense of inner heat and became increasingly thirsty. No matter how many glasses of water I drank they did not quench my thirst, nor did they lessen what I began to call my electrical attacks. The attacks were followed by severe muscle spasms in parts of my spine making me feel sick and nauseated. I consulted several doctors, but no one had the slightest clue about this type of condition.

Left without medical help, I began to look more deeply into what could have caused this strange new energy to occur inside my spine. I was still a daily practitioner of *lama yoga* and *pranayama* and had some inkling that the symptoms might be related to these practices. I decided to contact my Astara School. On the line with the secretary, I asked to speak with Robert or Earlyne Chaney, my teachers. Neither was in. "But I must speak to either of them without delay," I said in a begging tone. "It is extremely urgent." I felt completely out of touch with the world I had known. It was as if I was hanging on the edge of a cliff from which I could slide any minute into a deep dark unknown abyss.

"What is the matter?" the secretary wanted to know. I explained.

The secretary replied, "You are experiencing *Kundalini*," and then added, "Your nervous system may not be strong enough to deal with it."

I was shocked. "If this was true, what could I do? Who could help me?" I had believed with all my heart that all the spiritual practices I had been engaged in were completely safe. "Had I done something irreversibly wrong?" I recalled how Nadia had initiated me twice into *Kundalini* and how completely trusting I had been. I absolutely knew nothing about any negative impact of such initiations.

Much later in my process I became aware of the enormous dangers of *Kundalini* initiations, sometimes called *shaktipat,* by an unqualified practitioner. Only in those later years could I under-stand that *Kundalini* is a God-cosmic force whose awakening can only be granted by God or activated by an enlightened Guru.

"Was my situation to be permanent and was I lost forever?" was the thought that kept flashing through my mind. Nadia was no longer in town and my only recourse was Astara, whose eso-teric teachings and practices meant to awaken the *Kundalini* force.

While suffering continuing tormenting anxieties, I had no other choice than to phone Astara, once more. This time Mr. Robert Chaney was in and I got the chance to talk with him. He kindly listened to my long description of perturbing sensations that so intensely affected my body and mind. In response he remarked, "You are in the *Kundalini* awakening and your system has to cool down. You can do this by visualizing a cold waterfall rushing down your back when the *Kundalini* heat and the elec-trical-like sensations are present." Mr. Chaney paused and then emphatically assured me, "That will take care of it."

The next days, I tried to follow suit, but the prescribed

imaging did not produce the needed relief of my symptoms. Nothing else I tried changed the situation. I was terrified and felt myself sliding down into a period of great uncertainty. I lived in altered states of consciousness, separate from where the mainstream of humanity was living. I was not able to come back to what I called a normal state of being. A strange sense of isolation came over me. I could not read books, see movies or watch television. After Harmen's death in 1973, I had also experienced similar states of mind. But whereas deep grief understandably brings on feelings of disconnection, this new state was different. Its intensity and strangeness completely overwhelmed my being. I also realized how stories portrayed in books, movies or television, as well as the stories of peoples' lives, were illusions on the screen of the grand divine. I felt I was no longer a part of the world of matter. As I later understood it, "I was no longer connected to the perishable impermanent world. A shift to the eternal and non-perishable had occurred." Without that knowledge, at that time, my situation became extremely disconcerting. I began to lose weight. People I knew looked at me and said, "You look so beautiful, so slender!"

"If they only knew," I thought, "how odd I really feel." Little did I care how I looked; I only cared about how I felt.

The newest Astara lesson came in the mail. I opened the booklet and the first words that caught my eyes were: "From this level onward your road is straight to the heart of God." I completely fell apart because I thought that such a road was not attainable for me now. Every time I reread the words "straight to the heart of God," I wept uncontrollably.

Many healers tried to help by the laying-on of hands hoping for symptom release. I also went to my group healing sessions as I had done before, this time not to give but to receive healing. Grace, a compassionate elderly woman, was the only healer who temporarily could alleviate my symptoms. At the Cottage Grove healing center she would go into a trance-state and pound on my back while speaking in unknown tongues. The more she pounded the more I would scream and these screams eased my altered states but unfortunately the effect was always of short duration. Again and again I would slip back into altered states of consciousness and continue to feel sick with nausea. By now my isolation from others was complete. Jon helped me as best as he knew how. He took care of the children whenever this was called for. I was almost certain that I would soon lose my life.

One day I remembered the ecstasy I had once experienced while listening to Schubert's *Ave Maria* on the car radio. I asked Jon if he would play the melody on the piano. The moment I heard the music, scream upon scream involuntarily burst forth from my throat. By the time Jon finished playing the piece I felt healed but within hours, as with Grace's poundings, I fell back into my altered states far away from the self (ego) I knew.

Whenever my states became totally unbearable, I set out for Grace's house for a beating treatment or asked Jon to play *Ave Maria* on the piano. My regular Reiki friends did not understand my situation and could not offer any help.

Chapter Twenty-nine

An Ancient Prayer Revealed

Disillusioned with Reiki, which so far had not produced any relief, I turned to my alternative healer friend, Martin. Martin was part of the group of healers I had practiced with once a week since I became a Reiki practitioner. He was a dentist by profession and was devoted to a new body energy healing technique taught by a Californian internist specializing in lung and heart diseases, Dr. W. Brugh Joy. Desperate and open to try anything to find relief from my altered states I asked for a private healing session with Martin.

At his house Martin asked me to lie down on a massage table and began to apply Dr. Joy's method in combination with cranial sacral therapy. He channeled energy to my sacrum and heart *chakra*, the region of the spiritual heart, located on the right of the middle of the chest. I felt myself shifting into an alpha state of meditative consciousness. After a short while tears welled up in my eyes but I was not crying. Then more tears began flowing down my cheeks like small rivers. Words came to me in a language I did not know. I intuitively sensed that they held a message for me. The words were: *Eleison Panakrene.* I had not the slightest idea what they meant.

Some weeks later I told a close friend about the mysterious words, wondering whether I would ever find a translation. My friend said, "Wait a moment, my next-door neighbor is a theologian who knows many modern as well as ancient languages. I will ask him about the words you heard." To my surprise, the neighbor told my friend that the words are a prayer to God in ancient Greek. He said the translation is: "Have mercy, Source of All."

I wondered if I had been in ancient Greece in a past life, and whether this prayer had been meaningful then and if invoked, could help me now with my *Kundalini* problems.

To receive the ancient prayer and translation so quickly made it clear that a different plane of consciousness existed from where help was offered to ease my torment. I realized that I was no longer entirely alone while going through the *Kundalini* experience. I began to pray this Greek prayer often in the hope that God would indeed "have mercy on me."

Chapter Thirty

A Vision

My husband did most of the cooking. I appreciated his help and forced myself to eat even though I had no appetite. I was still losing weight and I was certainly concerned about it. My alternate states of consciousness kept me separated from the world in which I once found my security and balance. I was so frightened by the strangeness of my situation that I sometimes wondered whether I would actually lose my mind.

One evening Jon made a nice fresh salad. I sat at the kitchen counter eating a bowlful of appetizing greens. I was weak physically and felt like a wilted plant. After eating half of the greens, I suddenly felt a rush of pure life energy revitalizing my body. I said to my husband, "This salad makes me feel so good that I am going to lie down on our bed and enjoy this wonderful feeling I have, as though life is returning to my body." I went upstairs to lie down on top of the covers. I was very relaxed. As I looked up I noticed an ethereal substance rising up from my body like a small cloud and subsequently floating upward toward the ceiling. I saw this substance exiting through the skylight on the east side of our bedroom. I like to call it a form of condensed energy, almost invisible. I had never seen it before. As soon as this substance separated from my physical body, I felt as if my whole body began to beam with light. I heard my husband coming up the stairs. He said, "I am tired and I have a slight headache. Can I lie next to you?"

"Of course," I said and then continued, "Jon, something strange is happening to me. I feel as if I am one big smile that is beaming from one ear to the other. In fact my whole body is smiling."

The moment I spoke those words, another incredible powerful but unknown surge of energy began to move through my body. I described it to Jon as it was happening. Enormous electromagnetic fields were taking hold of my body and were strongly felt in the region of my heart. At the same time my hands began to radiate with super-charged energy. The sensation grew stronger and stronger till I was totally overtaken by this huge power. I was forced to breathe in a most unusual manner or else I could not withstand the extreme energy and would succumb to it. The force itself guided me in this, and for some unknown time I continued breathing in this extraordinary way because I knew that if I didn't, I would certainly die. I looked towards the ceiling and became aware that Harmen was standing there in midair. I could see him in color and at the same time, I could also see the vaulted cedar ceiling straight through his image. Harmen looked at me and spoke... Again, as in that dream I had in 1975, he spoke to me through the third eye in instant thought transfer while standing in a garden of flowers. He said, "These flowers are for you, for all you have done. I give you a garden of flowers for all you have done." He kept repeating the message. I thought that I was perhaps having a heart attack and that my late husband had come to take me to the other side. I heard his message over and over again and had the impression that I had to decide whether I wanted to live or die. I thought deeply about where I wanted to go for some time and slowly came to the conclusion that there was a reason for me to go on living in this world. As soon as I made that decision the vision faded and my breathing returned to normal.

The next day my life force was still strong. Life felt normal. Jon and I wanted to celebrate our joy by inviting our neighbor Lesley for breakfast. I could hardly wait to tell her what took place the prior evening, but unexpectedly, before I could relate the story, I felt the life force ebbing away from me... I had to excuse myself and lie down on the sofa. Lesley never heard what happened to me that prior night.

Chapter Thirty-one
To the Coast

Jon decided I needed rest and took me to the coast for one week. We hoped the fresh ocean air would be healing for me. The children were invited to stay at a friend's house for the seven days.

The coast was beautiful but my altered states did not improve. I became quite desperate. During meditation one morning, I received an ethereal message that there was a book for me in the bookstore in Newport. The message seemed harmless and Jon and I decided we should go to Newport, a town not far from our motel. Close to the tourist downtown-center of Newport we found a lovely bookshop with a delightful tea restaurant. I walked to the book section and looked around for a book of which, oddly, I did not even know the title. I spent half an hour looking and was about to give up when I suddenly noticed a red book at the bottom of the bookcase that had halfway fallen off the shelf. I wanted to put it back in place, but as I picked it up and read the title, *Science of Breath*, it dawned on me that this was the book I needed. The author was an Indian teacher, Swami Rama, who headed The Himalayan Institute. I quickly flipped through the pages and recognized that this book could be of great help to me. Jon bought it and I immediately started reading on our way back to our ocean-view motel. Since my *Kundalini* activation I had not been able to read any book and surprisingly I read *Science of Breath* with ease. I found helpful information about the intricate interrelationship between mind, body and breath. After I finished the book, I knew it was telling me to pay attention to my way of breathing.

The Himalayan Institute offered classes in yoga and meditation with emphasis on proper breathing techniques to promote health and well-being, as well as classes in homeopathy. I found a postcard in the *Science of Breath* book about an upcoming seminar in Stress Management conducted by medical doctors at the institute in Honesdale, Pennsylvania. I phoned the institute. I got one of the doctors on the line and his first question was, "Are you vegetarian?"

This question hit right in the heart of my being. All my life I had wanted to be vegetarian. After WWII when meat came on the market again I refused to eat it. I thought, "Animals are like us. They have eyes, ribs, flesh, blood and bones. If you eat them, why not eat humans?" As a malnourished war child I had become physically weak. When I was eight, our family doctor diagnosed me with severe anemia. He directed my mother to force me to eat meat, preferably cooked liver, or else, the doctor advised my mother, "your daughter will surely die!" Slowly I succumbed to the notion, so contrary to my inner being, that I should eat meat to stay alive.

To hear the doctor of the Himalayan Institute tell me that I could be a vegetarian for a healthier way of life sounded like music to my ears. I felt my inner conviction "not to eat animals" finally validated. Still on the phone with the doctor, I described my altered states, the electrical-like attacks and heat sensation in my spine. The doctor's immediate response was "You are suffering from *Kundalini*." Instantly I felt waves of ecstatic joy running up my spine, as I thought, "I am no longer lost. This doctor, who is a scientist, actually knows about *Kundalini*."

After discussions with Jon, it seemed appropriate to us that I sign up for a two-week Stress Management seminar at the institute. I hoped to find relaxation and a new way of looking at what I should do with an awakened *Kundalini*. That same day I became a vegetarian, which made me feel more closely connected to my soul.

Chapter Thirty-two

The Beloved and
I Are One

Grace, the healer who had been working on me, said, "You will never make it to Pennsylvania. The flight will be too much for you and you will end up in some hospital." Grace was deeply concerned and her observation was correct. I was in a bad state physically, mentally and spiritually. All I had going for me was a strong determination to get well. No one could stop me and soon I was on my way to the East Coast. After a full day of traveling by car, plane and a three-hour taxi ride, I walked into the entrance hall of the Himalayan Institute, completely exhausted. A beautiful serene spiritual atmosphere welcomed me in its invisible arms and I felt wrapped in stillness, which was like a sweet balsam on my overworked spirit. Peace entered my mind and I instantly knew I was in the right place. The place was completely silent and hardly anyone was there, as most residents had left for India with Swami Rama. Mysteriously, the thought came to me that I too would be traveling to India in the near future but that it would not be with Swami Rama.

I was given a small room on the institute's ground floor. During my first night, I was unable to get to sleep. I had been advised I could call the doctors in my program twenty-four hours a day. I made an emergency phone call. Dr. W appeared and kindly taught me a new method to induce sleep by reciting the sacred mantra *So Hum* and coordinating the sound of the words with my breathing. While reciting this mantra, I was to inhale saying mentally, "So" and on the exhalation, "Hum." The clairaudient *rishis* in ancient India had heard the sounds of the inhalation and exhalation in Sanskrit, the language of the Gods. With this mantra, I was told to visualize the breath going in through the nostrils and out through the mouth. *So Hum* means:

"He is I and I am He, or The Beloved and I are one." The *So Hum* mantra became a great help to ease my mind. From that night onward I have used this mantra successfully, even to this day.

I was in the stress management program with two other women who came to find help for their health problems. We each received a lot of personal attention from the attending doctors. Part of the relaxation program was to be in silence and alone. We were served delicious vegetarian meals in our individual rooms, three times a day. The food was prepared and cooked by students of Swami Rama and empowered by the recitation of continuous mantras. I could tell there was a difference in the way this food tasted and how the body was absorbing it. I came to believe that cooking with mantras changed the food on a molecular level, thereby enhancing its life force.

The institute functioned like an Indian ashram. While silence was maintained, the permanent residents were assigned tasks not necessarily compatible with one's profession in life. I noticed my teacher-doctors mopping the floors of the long hallways of the institute. In the back of the main building was an organic garden where most vegetables were grown for use of the institute's kitchen.

The doctor, who knew about my awakened *Kundalini*, lent me a book called *The Chasm of Fire*, written by Irina Tweedie. Irina recounts how her Sufi teacher in India oversees her *Kundalini* awakening process, which ultimately leads to her liberation. Irina writes about periods of severe suffering on her path to realization. I felt close to her while reading her diary-style account. Her story was also my story. While I read on, I became a bit annoyed when Irina complains that her master outwardly seems to pay no attention to her, even though she knew that he fully supported her spiritually at all times. Unlike Irina, I did not have a *Kundalini* master-teacher standing by during my process. Even though the doctors at the Himalayan Institute recognized my symptoms, they could not offer any help I needed spiritually.

Besides yoga and homeopathy, the science of breath is one

of the institute's specialties. One day during the seminar, my turn came to have my breathing tested. Dr. M gave me the result and said, "If you continue the way you breathe now, you can soon expect a heart attack." To prevent that from happening, he taught me a new preferred way of breathing.

By the end of the fourteen-day program the corrected breathing, eating organic foods as well as practicing Hatha yoga had an amazingly positive effect on my health. I reflected inwardly on what I had learned during my daily walks through the beautiful hills, dales and forests of the many private acres surrounding the institute.

Back in Oregon, I introduced Jon to the Himalayan vegetarian style of cooking, the practice of Hatha yoga and the importance of taking forty-five-minute daily walks, which he wholeheartedly applauded. I practiced all that I had learned, and yet I missed the tranquil Pocono forests and the deeper silence of monastery living. My health kept improving, even though *Kundalini* still continued to have the ultimate control over my life. There was really no one to help me with the vicissitude of altered states. These states occurred less frequently, but when I slipped back into them, I also suffered panic attacks.

Whenever my situation became too hard to bear, I would listen again to Schubert's *Ave Maria* for release. And again, this release brought about involuntary screams that burst forth through me like bolts of lightning, hurting my throat and damaging my voice. But *Ave Maria* did not always work. Through trial and error, I found that tuning in to the divine Mother is actually the same as tuning in to the universal God in whatever name or form. When needed, I often remained in continuous prayer till I reached that higher Consciousness, which is a plane of such indescribable power that it instantly gave me substantial release. I definitely was beginning to see more light at the end of a tunnel of darkness.

Chapter Thirty-three

Fire Initiation in Montana

In the spring of 1986 I met a world-renowned psychic at Orly's house, the place where healers congregated once a week for group healing sessions. Orly had done healing work with Virginia F in the past and invited her to give us a talk about her extraordinary life.

Virginia began narrating her story by telling us that already at a very young age she could see the emanations of color in the magnetic energy fields surrounding the human body. She said, "I did not think I was unique in this. I thought that everyone else could see them too." At the age of five, while on an outing in the car with her father and other family members, she watched a car passing by. They were on the highway, and she noticed that the passing car did not have an aura like the other cars. She exclaimed to her father, "That car does not have any colors!" A few moments later, the passing car was wrecked in an accident in which all the passengers died. Her father understood from this incident that she had the same paranormal gifts he had. From that time onward, he taught her how to read and interpret what they both could perceive beyond the normal vision.

Later in Virginia's life, researchers in the field of para-psychology heard of her and began testing her abilities of the paranormal. Soon she became well known. Virginia hoped to help the scientists understand the phenomenal worlds she knew, which exist beyond the senses. She underwent extensive testing in Europe, the old Soviet Union and the United States.

Once during an investigative visit to France, Virginia and several researchers were driving through the countryside. As she looked at the scenery passing by, she noticed a beautiful aura that was so large that it expanded far beyond the horizon, filling the whole sky with ethereal soft living-like colors. In amazement she thought, "This aura must belong to God." Eager to meet

God, she asked that the car be stopped immediately. She flung the door open and ran out into the green-hilled countryside. The researchers, who did not understand what was happening, ran after her hollering, "Come back, come back!" But the aura drew Virginia so overwhelmingly that she ran towards the source from which it seemingly flowed. She rushed up a hill from which she would have a look into the next valley. From above, her eyes caught the back of a male figure that was radiating this most spectacular aura. Sure to meet God, Virginia ran down the hill and by the time she reached him, he turned around toward her and opened his arms to embrace her. He was a shepherd herding his sheep in the French countryside. Not able to speak each other's language was no a barrier in this eternal moment. Time stood still as these two great souls embraced.

In the meantime, the researchers, confused and frustrated as to what was taking place, caught up with Virginia. She turned around, and followed them back to the car with a heart filled with the miracle of this divine encounter creating ecstasy and exalted jubilation.

The research Virginia was participating in did not always include such sacred moments. She told us that she often had to endure excruciating tests to prove her paranormal perception. In one incident, she was lowered into an underground grave while her eyeballs were partially taken out of their sockets to test if she still could see in the beyond. This cruel trial stopped her from participating in research for good. Her gift also led her to assist doctors sometimes in reaching diagnoses that could not be made through regular medical screening. Soon she became a sought-after person for healing, psychic readings and spiritual development.

When I heard that Virginia was coming to Portland to give psychic readings and healings, I made an appointment with her. I hoped she could shed some light upon my ongoing *Kundalini* problems. It had been a few years since I had seen Virginia. As I entered the consultation room I saw her grayish eyes twinkling for a split second behind her granny glasses. Virginia was a small-sized woman, middle aged, with a broad face and blondish curly hair hanging down to her shoulders. She was sitting in a chair in a small room where a massage table was set up for healing treatments. I did not tell her about *Kundalini*, but said after re-introducing myself, "I have been sick and was guided to attend a workshop at the Himalayan Institute. I learned new ways of healthier living and my health has steadily improved."

Virginia looked at me with an unusual otherworldly gaze, never really looking at me, but tuning in to the invisible deeper me. She said after some moments of silence, "You are still not well, you may have improved, but your aura is blown to pieces! Come to my farm and healing center in Montana where I can help you."

I arrived at the Billings airport early May 1986. Virginia's manager, Sara, picked me up by car. It was still cold in Montana and I saw some patches of snow on our drive to the farm. The healing center was an extended farmhouse with various bedrooms painted in different colors. I was to choose the color of my bedroom for the week and ended up sleeping in the green room. Virginia's personal program for me consisted of gentle body massages under blue lights, and the use of a glass crystal room modeled after those built in ancient long-lost Atlantis, of which Virginia had esoteric knowledge. I was allowed to sit in the crystal room for limited periods each day. The crystals were extremely powerful and an extended exposure could cause damage. The crystals' transmitting capacity allowed the flow of higher Consciousness to enter and make my aura whole. Virginia counseled me about past lives and said, "In this life you are a seer and you will write books."

Many hours that week, I roamed the forest and hills around her property with Virginia's dogs, an adorable doberman and a joyful springer spaniel. Virginia did not live on the farm, and I stayed there with her manager Sara and another female visitor, a nurse. Every day after dinner, the three of us sat down for meditation in the living room. One night after meditation, Sara and the nurse went to the kitchen to clean up and talk and I stayed behind in the living room. I made myself comfortable on a sofa stacked with soft pillows, and listened to one of Virginia's healing-relaxation tapes. When the tape finished, I closed my eyes and meditated for a while. When I opened my eyes, I became aware of a figure standing at the foot of the sofa. Who it was I could not clearly see. I saw the outline of a person with long and somewhat curly hair, the body covered by a ceremonial mantle. My higher mind revealed the presence of a "master." In trance I stared at the mighty appearance. Suddenly a human hand of flesh and bones of the master struck me hard over my third eye. The moment this hand touched my forehead between the eyebrows, blue light flashed out of my third eye. I was quite surprised as well as a bit frightened and ran into the kitchen to see if anyone had noticed anything, but no one did.

When I came home, *The Voice*, a magazine of my mystical school, came in the mail. I opened the issue. The first article that caught my eye was about the fire initiation. Astarians like myself who were at the level of readiness to receive the fire initiation were invited to travel to the mystical school in California to receive the initiation. The description of the initiation was the same as I had already received in Montana. I immediately realized that the person who stood at the foot of my sofa was no other than my Astarian teacher Earlyne Chaney in ethereal form. I was overjoyed and considered receiving my fire initiation in Montana a wonderful blessing.

I realized again that even though I thought I was in the *Kundalini* process without a teacher, my teacher had been watching over me all along. I had gone through much turmoil to arrive at this new level of awareness. I had been tested. The blue light I received never left me but has remained anchored and alive in my third eye no matter where I am.

Chapter Thirty-four

Meeting Earlyne

I received an invitation from Astara for a *satsang* (meeting) with Earlyne Chaney in Seattle the upcoming summer. Ever since my fire initiation by the ethereal hand of Earlyne's spirit-form in Montana, I yearned to meet her in physical form.

I signed up to attend. It was midsummer 1986. Jon and I set out for Seattle with the children. We stayed with friends at their North Seattle home. David and Femke would be leaving for their second overseas vacation to see the family in The Netherlands. They boarded Martinair in Seattle to fly to Amsterdam, where my parents would pick them up.

After the children left, Ken, Jon's composer friend from the old days, offered to drive us to the Astara meeting place at a hotel near the airport. Jon, who was also an Astarian, preferred to visit with his friend Ken in the coffee shop of the hotel, while I attended the *satsang*.

I was full of high expectation, but after Earlyne's lecture and the singing of Astarian hymns, I was taken aback by feelings of disappointment. I had a strong desire to join Jon and Ken, but after reflecting on my strange uneasiness, I decided that I should force myself to stay for at least another half hour. I waited, witnessing my own inner conflicting thoughts and emotions.

Then Earlyne Chaney stood up and said, "The great masters of the ethereal planes are here and will transfer their blessings to you through my hands. A honey-like substance that has been miraculously seeping from a picture of the Virgin Mary will be applied to your forehead. Please come forward and bring your favorite items for a special blessing."

A long line of Astarians began to form. I waited at the end of it. I watched and was amazed to see how various people who stepped in front of Earlyne were falling over backward as if momentarily taken over by the powerful presence of higher

Consciousness. Volunteers stood ready to catch them before they hit the floor and healers came rushing forward to bring them back to this reality. I had the wedding rings of both husbands in my hand for a blessing. The line was slowly moving forward while the sounds of familiar church hymns filled the hall. Inside myself I screamed for a deeper revelation into God's mysteries. I felt restless, as if I still doubted the validity of the presence of higher Consciousness.

When my turn came to step forward, the hymns stopped and Schubert's *Ave Maria*, glorious *Ave Maria,* filled the meeting room. This was my soul song that had evoked ecstasy as well as relief from my *Kundalini* trances. When I stood before Earlyne, I felt inwardly lifted up by the divine. Suddenly, I was overcome by an overwhelming sense of great humility. I thought, "How ignorant I am to question the higher nature of this event!" Literally awestruck, I was ready to receive the blessing. Earlyne placed the sacred honey on my third eye and both wedding rings. I was speechless when I left to meet my husband and his friend Ken. "How was it?" they asked. I could not explain.

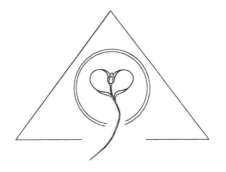

PART V

Drawn to the Eastern Light

Chapter Thirty-five

Touched by Divine Love

A year had gone by since my awakening in *Kundalini*. During my severest moments of altered states, I had learned to find relief by tuning in to the divine Mother energy presented in the sacred words and melody of Schubert's *Ave Maria*, the auditory form of the Virgin Mary. My vision of Harmen with his message of love and gratitude "for all I had done," as well as the clairaudient gift of an ancient Greek prayer, *Eleison Panakrene*, asking for the mercy of God, showed I received divine guidance during my turmoil. The teachings at the Himalayan Institute had opened my mind towards eastern thought and new ways of living: a vegetarian lifestyle, a deeper understanding and use of *prana* (life force) and the divine sounds through mantras like the *So Hum*, drawing my ego-self toward the light of God. I felt deeply blessed when, during my stay in Montana, I received the Astarian fire initiation by the hand of the bi-located ethereal form of Earlyne Chaney. When I stood, at a later time, before my master-teacher in Seattle, the touch of her physical hand brought the essence of the light of higher Consciousness when a materialized honey-like substance was applied to my third eye and the sacred sound-vibration of *Ave Maria* filled the meeting-hall. All these events moved me onward through a difficult year and gave new strength on the physical, emotional and spiritual levels of my being. I became aware that the road "straight to the heart of God" lay now wide open for me.

In the meantime I received *The Autobiography of a Yogi* by Paramahansa Yogananda, a gift from my friend Robin. I resisted reading it for some time, but when I finally did I immediately fell in love with Yogananda's narratives. He soon became another beacon of light revealing the depth and richness of the spirituality of India. He opened my mind to the concepts of reincarnation, enlightenment and *samadhi* (eternal rest) and the existence of yogavatar masters such as Sri Yukteswar and Lahiri Mahasaya. I soon embraced the eastern thought as a logical way to explain some of the unanswerable questions of life.

The Autobiography of a Yogi recounts how Sri Yukteswar came to send his disciple Yogananda as his emissary to the West in 1920. Yogananda lived in the United States for more than thirty years and introduced the ancient science of *kriya yoga* as a discipline for self-realization. I read the book many times over and became familiar with the various photos in the book. During this time, I was still a continuing student of Astara under the emanating lights of the Astarian masters of higher Consciousness. I still practiced my daily *lama yoga* and *pranayama*, an Astarian practice, but from now on also began to meditate on the image of Yogananda as he appears on the book cover of his famous autobiography.

One Saturday afternoon, Femke wanted me to meet the parents of a new school friend who had recently moved to Eugene. As I entered the house through the front door, the first thing that caught my eye was a small picture of Paramahansa Yogananda that hung over the fireplace mantel. I recognized it immediately as the last picture of Yogananda taken a few hours before the conscious leaving of his body (*maha-samadhi*) during his lecture at the Biltmore Hotel in Los Angeles, in 1952. The picture was called *The Last Smile*. The text under the photo from *The Autobiography of a Yogi* recounts the following:

The photographer here caught a loving smile that appears to be a farewell benediction for each one of the master's millions of friends, students and disciples. The eyes that already were gazing into Eternity are yet full of human warmth and understanding.

When my eyes met Yogananda's in *The Last Smile* that Saturday afternoon, I felt my soul merging with his and I became aware of streams of divine love flowing into my heart from the image in the picture. I was speechless. I entered a state of ecstatic joy, while the parents of Femke's friend were showing me around the house, which to my amazement turned out to be the Yogananda's Self-realization Fellowship Center in Eugene. In the upstairs, I was shown the center's meditation room. I again looked at Yogananda's face in the many photographs on the walls, and felt abundant radiant love streaming from his face towards mine, wave after wave, everywhere in the house. I sensed the whole house to be an ocean of his pure love. My heart filled to the brim with divine Light and by the time I left the house I was in a complete daze. All I could feel was love...

Chapter Thirty-six
Hearing About Sai Baba

Early fall 1986, my friend Bill Mirabella called and said, "You should watch a television program showing right now on the local station. They are featuring a man by the name of Sathya Sai Baba." Then Bill added: "Ella, I think he is the real thing." I had much respect for Bill, a retired government attorney and alternative healer, and listened to him with an open mind. After I hung up, I turned on the television. I watched Sai Baba filmed in his Indian ashram, with a summation of his teachings that sounded in essence similar to those of Astara. As I was committed to Astara, already advancing to the teaching level, I felt no desire to change course to study with Sai Baba.

But soon, I would not be able to withstand the draw to the eastern light, placed in me by the light emanations I received from Yogananda. With *dwesha* and *raga* (nerve clusters holding the ego in place) partially broken, my true Self (God in the eastern philosophy is often called the "Self" with a capital S) was beginning to break loose, nudging me to search for the deeper understanding of my own awakening process. This search had to lead to the eastern teachings where the pathway of *Kundalini* is more readily understood. Ann Ree Colton in her book *Kundalini West,* page 548, writes:

> In the West man turns to the Holy Ghost for miracles of manifestation. In the East man turns to *Kundalini,* seeking the essence.

Due to my unspeakable agony with *Kundalini* the year before, I had lost touch with my Reiki friends and practitioners. Reiki, the hands-on energy channeling practice, certainly another light-form healing modality, did not provide any insight into the *Kundalini* phenomenon for me when I needed it most. I had lost faith in Reiki, but when Marta, my Reiki master-teacher, unexpectedly called me in late September and asked, "Ella, can we do a Reiki-treatment exchange?" I nevertheless suddenly felt a strong impulse to accept the offer. We set up a meeting time.

During a talk in the healing room at Marta's house, I mentioned that her friend Joanna, a clairvoyant minister, had said to me, "Ella, a great living teacher in the east is calling you. To find this teacher you may want to become a master-healer." As I had decided not to become a Reiki master as yet, I wondered how I would find this eastern master.

Marta listened and said, "Maybe the master who is calling you is Sai Baba."

"Sai Baba? You must mean Babaji?" *The Autobiography of a Yogi* describes Babaji as the deathless *mahavatar* who lives amid the Himalayan snows. Yogananda's light that had touched my soul led me to feel drawn to this mysterious Babaji, the immortal teacher of teachers of the highest levels of consciousness. Marta, however, did not mean Babaji, but Sathya Sai Baba, who resides in Puttaparthi, in southern India, the same Sai Baba I had seen on the local TV show. Marta told me that she had visited Sai Baba's ashram even though she was not a devotee. She recounted amazing tales of esoteric dreams and spiritual happenings that took place during her stay in the ashram and showed me stacks of photos she had made. After we finished our Reiki exchange, I left with a photo of Sai Baba, a book entitled *Sathya Sai Baba: The Embodiment of Love* by the authors Peggy Mason and Ron Laing, a packet of Baba's holy ash and a small dried branch from the wishing tree in Puttaparthi. Marta explained that this branch came from the tree on which Baba, in his teen years, had spontaneously materialized a variety of different fruits desired by his schoolmates. It was seen as auspicious to have a piece of this tree.

Flabbergasted by Marta's stories, I came home with her stack of gifts and showed them to Jon, who was in the kitchen cooking dinner. I sat down with the book *The Embodiment of Love* on the other side of the kitchen counter and began reading to him. After just a few pages, we both became quite intrigued by the narration of Peggy and Ron's first trip to India. The following day, Jon had to deliver his music manuscript to the printer in Beaverton, a suburb of Portland, two hours north by car. On the road, as I sat in the passenger seat, I continued reading *The Embodiment of Love* to Jon. Our son David was sitting in the back of the car. Before going to Beaverton, we had to drop him off at his dorm at Reed College in Portland, where he was an undergraduate student. David was listening to his favorite music with his headphones on unaware that a transformation was taking place inside Jon and me.

When we came home late that night, Jon noticed that he had accidentally left some of his manuscript papers behind that also needed to go to the Beaverton printer. We headed back north the following day. On the highway, I resumed reading the Peggy Mason book. The deeper I got into the story the deeper I felt something stirring within my soul, especially when the authors described their interview with Sai Baba in which he declared himself to be the Cosmic Christ. I thought, "Was this perhaps the master from the east calling me, the one the reverend Joanna had pointed to, representing that eastern light which was magnetically drawing me to that source from where my questions of life would be answered? How would I know?" Bedazzled, I sensed I simply had to follow this call, as this was my destiny.

Jon had always been my spiritual companion. We were on the same level of spiritual understanding. He also was an unswerving humanitarian and certainly a student of the light. Even though he too was a student of Astara, he learned about the teaching through me when I read the lesson material to him. This often led to deep spiritual discussions. But above all things in life, Jon's main focus was composing classical music. His tuning in to the music of the higher spheres connected him to that same radiance of light emanated by the masters of Astara.

I continued reading. The words in *The Embodiment of Love* were so powerful and had such a spiritual as well as an emotional impact on us that it grabbed our hearts. Again I thought, "Was this Sai Baba the new savior, the promised messiah or the avatar, who as a beacon of light had come to straighten out the affairs of our world?" From my own religious upbringing, the belief that a Christ could return to Earth seemed plausible. In an extremely elated state, I read on for four more hours on the road to and from Portland. By the time we came home I had finished the book. An overwhelming sense of joy suddenly overcame both of us. Both Jon and I felt that meaning had come to our lives, as we had understood it thus far. We held a small ceremony in which we dedicated our lives to this eastern master Sai Baba, who, as we understood it, had come to save the world.

The dreadful year of the initial stages of my awakening through *Kundalini* suddenly seemed far behind. The process went into a new phase without the frightful experiences of the year before. Now I was called to embrace the eastern philosophies I had previously rejected in ignorance of their truth and power. A complete change had come over me, a change undoubtedly invoked by *Kundalini* awareness.

Chapter Thirty-seven

Lightning Strikes

One of Marta's gifts, the picture of Sai Baba, needed a frame and I wanted something special to elevate his image to the status of an icon. It was October 1986. My friend Linda, an astute analytical-minded stockbroker, was about to arrive for an early dinner. The dining room table was set. Jon appeared from his studio with an artistically rendered framed picture of Sai Baba in his hand. We decided to hang it on the wall of the living room. It was a small photo, yet its gold-leaf frame stood out against the rough sawn cedar wall. Immediately, my Dutch religious conditioning started to spook in my head. "What will Linda say? How do I explain this to her? Can I really hang Sai Baba, pictured in orange robe and wild Afro hairdo, on our wall? Will Linda ask who he is? What will I say to her? What will other friends say? Would I look like a fool believing in an Indian master and avatar?" I became anxious, with my thoughts running wild and my heart pounding noticeably. Deep down I heard the voices of my parents telling me that we were Protestants and should under no circumstance stoop to worship icons. "But, had I not through the Yogananda book already made a beginning to adopt the divine images of India as a genuine way to reach God?" Nevertheless, my emotions around Baba's iconic picture on the wall showed the power of parental and religious conditioning as still a part of me to be reckoned with. It took a lot of my inner strength to leave the picture on the wall. In a state of mental exhaustion, I went to the third floor and sat down under the large skylight of the upstairs bathroom. I tried to calm myself by meditating and letting go of those conflicting thoughts about the picture and to focus instead on the essence of Baba's teachings, the universal love.

As I looked through the garden window of the master bathroom, I noticed how beautiful deep blue the sky was that day. "Not a single cloud in sight," I murmured. Suddenly a tiny pitch-dark cloud appeared in the sky. It amazed me. "If this cloud were any bigger, it could be a thundercloud," I thought. Then my mind refocused on Sai Baba and "out of the blue," I spoke to him in a prayer-like fashion, "Sai Baba, even if lightning were to strike me, I still will love you." I had not the slightest idea why I spoke those words. After the prayer I stood up, right underneath the skylight. Before I could even blink an eye, lightning struck. The light was so powerful that I felt as if every cell of my body down to the atomic level had been exposed to its intensity. I looked in the large bathroom mirror and did not recognize myself. I felt my body splitting as if I had two bodies. I did not know whether I was dead or alive. All I knew was that I wanted to run and with that impulse started running down the stairs. It was as if one half of me was just screaming and the other half screaming: *"Om Sai Ram,"* the Sai Baba mantra devotees used. My husband, at work in his music-copying office on the ground floor, had heard an explosion and left his room. He saw me running down the stairs and was startled by my screams. "What is the matter?" he asked. "I have been hit, I have been hit by lightning!" I shouted. Together, we ran outside to see what had happened. Our son

David and his friend Don were standing on the lawn in front of the house with the lawn mower. Don said, "I heard an enormous sound blast, which made my hair stand on end!"

David said nothing. Next to our house stood a tall old fir tree with a trunk size so big that even two people could not fully embrace it. The tree towered to about one hundred twenty-five feet, its branches reaching towards the sky far beyond the three levels of the house. The tree stood a few feet away from the house. We discovered the tree had been struck by the lightning that had rushed downward from the top, causing deep rifts in the bark. Pieces of slashed bark were hanging from many branches and covered the ground.

Femke, our twelve-year-old, appeared, and told us her part of the story. She recounted how, after coming home from a bike ride on this sunny day, she had gotten off her bike and walked up the steep driveway towards the studio. All of a sudden, a huge ball of white light had appeared in the cloudless blue sky, "five times the size of the sun," Femke explained in bewilderment. The ball came tumbling down from the heavens with enormous speed. Frightened and with no time to lose, she had rushed into the studio to find shelter.

When our broker friend came for dinner that night, I had completely forgotten about Baba's picture on the wall. Instead we spoke about the lightning. The lightning had crashed most of our electronic equipment and numbed my ears, but I had no recollection of hearing the explosion.

Later, someone told me that I had been inside the vortex of the lightning strike and that this was the reason why I had not heard anything. It took three days for my ears to get back to normal. The experience of the lightning strike had struck the core of my being. I had certainly been exposed to the light, but whether this was the light of Sai Baba, I could not evaluate...

Chapter Thirty-eight

Pilgrimage

In November 1986 our house became a meditation center dedicated to Sai Baba. Thursday evening was called *bhajan* night and consisted of a program of singing devotional songs in Hindi, Sanskrit, English, Hebrew and Urdu to develop the ideals of seeing the oneness in the essence of all faiths. Jon played the harmonium and I became one of the *bhajan* leaders. We studied the teachings of Sai Baba, which were based on the sacred scriptures of India.

Every year, hundreds of thousands of Sai devotees were traveling from all parts of the world to see Sai Baba in his Puttaparthi or Whitefield ashram in India. I too felt drawn to go, but also had doubts. The trip was long and I could not quite figure out the total expense of travel, hotels and ashram stay. I was happily surprised when Femke, who participated in our Sai activities, got up one morning and said, "Mom, I had a Sai Baba dream. Baba appeared to me and said, 'Even though it is expensive to make the trip to India, I will make it worth your while.' Then, with a motion of his hand, he materialized a carriage full of diamonds for me."

Trusting that Femke's dream was a true sign from Sai Baba, I soon began to make preparations for our trip to India. Jon said he preferred staying home to write another symphony and take care of our dachshund, Stanley.

Inwardly, I asked Baba for guidance for our first pilgrimage. The only help I really wished for was to have a trustworthy and experienced person after our arrival at the Bombay International Airport who would be traveling onwards in the same direction. We needed help to find a safe taxi to the domestic airport, a person who had some understanding of the Indian ways.

It was in July 1987 when Femke and I boarded the first phase of our flight to India. We were full of excitement. Our first stop was Hong Kong, where we arrived jet-legged and worn-out. I had booked a hotel in advance and while waiting for our taxi, Femke fell asleep against the wall of the airport building. The Park Hotel in Kowloon was a modern glass and steel high-rise building. Our room felt peculiarly foreign: the air in our room had an overpowering muggy smell and the double Chinese bed made of dark wood had an uncomfortable hard mattress. Despite our fatigue, it took hours to get to sleep.

We woke up late the next morning and joined the other guests for a buffet breakfast. Gorging on fabulous-tasting unfamiliar Asian fruits, French croissants, and local juices and coffee gave a glimpse of the amenities of this touristy Chinese hotel. Still tired, but in a happy mood, we set out to tour Kowloon that day and do some shopping. In the afternoon back at the hotel, we tried for a short nap, but when that failed we decided to get to the airport early to continue on to India. At the airport hall, we had more than enough time to sit down and order a bottled drink in a small restaurant where we could observe other travelers assembling for our flight to Bombay.

As I glanced over the many passengers, I noticed an Indian woman in a dark red sari wearing diamond studs on each side of her nose. I became fascinated, as I had never seen such nose rings before. The longer I stared at her from a distance, the more I got the feeling that she might be the person I had prayed for. I said to Femke, "She might be the one who will be traveling the same way as we are!" Femke thought that it was odd I would say that, because more than three hundred passengers would be boarding our flight.

I was nevertheless drawn to walk towards the Indian woman and ask if she was going to Bangalore via Bombay. "Yes, yes, my destination is indeed Bangalore," the woman said as she introduced herself as Veena, a teacher for the hearing disabled in California. "My relatives told me my mother was ailing and without delay I decided I should leave for India and see her. I already missed one flight connection and I am now ready to board with you. None of my relatives know that I am coming. I can tell you I am very pleased to travel with you. It is much safer for the three of us." I believed with all my heart that this instant help came from Sai Baba.

After our arrival in Bombay and the collection of our luggage, the three of us walked through the large airport building towards the exit. I was aware that hundreds of small olive-colored Indian men were following our every move with their deep dark eyes, the white of their eyes shimmering by the neon tubes that lit up the hall. Their faces were expressing a sense of wonderment as if they were seeing some strange species that just landed from outer space. The men were dressed in colorful shirts and had white, blue, or checkerboard-design cloths pulled up around their shorts in Indian *dhoti* style resembling our miniskirts. I felt uncomfortable being stared at. I immediately realized that we had entered a completely different world. It was midnight, but India was still hot, humid and extremely noisy. Across from the airport exit, I saw a group of emaciated light-colored cows sleeping on a small patch of land that was covered with muck and garbage scattered amongst sparse grasses. We walked to the taxi stand in a pouring monsoon rain with our luggage stacked on a cart. With Veena in the lead we got to the government-certified taxi stand. On our behalf, our newfound friend negotiated in Hindi for the appropriate fare to the domestic airport. It was quite a scene to watch how she and the two of us were viewed as wealthy Americans, despite the obvious fact that Veena was Indian born.

The monsoon was still coming down in buckets, and by now I was soaked to the skin. Before sitting down in the taxi, I wrung out my new cotton skirt as much as possible. The taxi was a cream-colored Ambassador, a small Indian-made old-fashioned looking car. We had too much luggage, and the driver shook his head with the familiar Indian saying: "No problem, I will take care of it!" and tied our suitcases down inside the trunk. Some had to hang outside as the lid would not close. With wet clothes stuck to our bodies, the three of us waited in the taxi while our driver temporarily disappeared in the airport building. The dampness of our clothes steamed up the windows and we could not see out. Our taxi driver reappeared and took us on a fast ride on roads covered with soggy mud and dangerous potholes. For a moment, I panicked and thought, "Is this really an okay taxi?" As soon as that thought occurred, I noticed Shirdi Sai Baba's picture on the windshield to the left of the steering wheel. I relaxed. Shirdi Sai Baba was said to be the prior incarnation of Sathya Sai Baba. "To see Shirdi's picture is equal to seeing Sai Baba's picture," I reasoned. I sighed with relief, acknowledging that our trip was in divine hands.

At the domestic airport we tried to get some sleep in the uncomfortable seats of the departure hall. Veena showed us how to cover ourselves with large Indian shawls in a heroic attempt to keep the swarms of mosquitoes at bay. Six hours later, we crossed the airfield to our plane. Tired, and wet from the humidity and heat, we climbed the steps of our plane to Bangalore. After a relatively short flight, we touched the ground of our destination. Our prearranged taxi driver, Noor, was waiting at the airport terminal carrying a sign with our names on it. With gratitude we said goodbye to Veena, our friendly guide, who continued on home by separate taxi.

After loading our luggage, Noor took us to a brand-new hotel, the Ashraya. Noor was a light brown–colored man around forty, dressed in a white *punjabi*, his head covered with a white embroidered *topi* (hat of *nawaz*), signifying he had made the *Hajj* (pilgrimage) to Mecca. An Oregon devotee, an organizer of tours to India, had highly recommended Noor to us and I felt certain I could trust him.

When Femke and I entered our hotel room we were extremely thirsty. Warned about the drinking water in India, I did not trust the filtered water in the carafe on our table. Even though the bellboy assured me, "Madam, this is safe drinking water," while shaking his head, I nevertheless, as soon as he left, phoned the front desk and asked, "Please bring us bottled water right away!" I turned on the air conditioner while anxiously waiting for the safe water to arrive. Both Femke and I suffered from severe headaches, undoubtedly from dehydration. It took hours before the knock on the door came to deliver the water. This was India, a land where one can always expect the unexpected, as we learned later.

The next morning, our headaches were gone. In the hotel restaurant I struggled to figure out the breakfast menu written in Hindi. We ended up simply ordering cucumber sandwiches and Indian coffee, which I loved right away.

The Sai Baba ashram had a dress code, and we were required to buy some Indian clothes to conform to the ashram rules. Noor knew all about it, as he had been the driver for many devotees visiting the ashram. He picked us up to shop for *punjabis*, shawls and saris at a Hindu sari shop on Commercial Road. By ten in the morning we walked into the store during the performance of a morning ritual called *puja*. The storeowner moved burning incense sticks around his merchandise. The store filled with a sweet, delicate otherworldly scent while the storekeeper chanted Vedic mantras that were not known to me as yet. I was astonished as well as profoundly moved by this mysterious ritual so different from our ways of opening a store in the morning. In India I found that invoking God's blessing for a good day is common practice almost everywhere. Even though I did not know the mantras or prayers, I could sense a definite shift in the energy of the store. Worshiping God so openly was deeply gratifying to me. Stillness flowed into my heart... I immediately felt love for India and thought, "This is a land where God comes first."

The next morning at three, Femke and I, draped in our new silk saris, set off in Noor's taxi for the three-hour drive to Baba's ashram in Puttaparthi. It was pitch-dark when we left the Ashraya hotel. Dawn broke in vibrant colors just before we drove through the gates of Puttaparthi village leading to the ashram. Here, Noor handed each of us a small photo of Sai Baba. My daughter and I looked at each other with smiling faces. I sensed my intense hope for a spiritual adventure!

Chapter Thirty-nine

Ashram Life

Getting a room in Sai Baba's ashram was out of the question. The registration office directed us to the sheds, buildings as large as airplane hangars where residents set up camp on the large cement floor. I was impressed to see how devotees had built their individual sleeping places. The floor of the hangar-like building was covered with air mattresses and standing primitive cots covered with sheets and pillows surrounded by large mosquito nettings. Clotheslines were set up to hang saris and towels to mark each designated space – to give it some vague sense of privacy. Within these separate spaces, devotees put up small altars with pictures of Sai Baba, Jesus, or other holy images complete with incense burners and candles. I was touched by the sweetness and dedication of the devotional path (*bhakti*) to God, so different from my own upbringing. The spaces in the sheds were small but adequate. Femke and I made one large space out of the two assigned to us by placing our rented cots side by side.

Well prepared with American air mattresses and mosquito nettings, we were in no time part of shed living. One problem troubled us from the start: the sheds were filled with swarms of mosquitoes. Despite our superb mosquito nettings, Femke in particular was soon covered with bites. Remedies from the pharmacy did not get her huge swellings down. Femke felt miserable and our spiritual adventure looked less rosy. I proposed we return home if we did not get a proper room and for a second time I asked accommodation for help. To my utter surprise my request was suddenly granted. Not only did we get a room but a private one as well, just for the two of us. Its location was near the *mandir* (temple) and also conveniently near the ashram shops. With screens in the windows of our new room, the mosquito attacks and bites diminished considerably.

Step by step we learned the ways of ashram living. The most

important event in ashram life in 1987 and years hence was seeing Sai Baba walking amongst his crowds of devotees. His twice daily walk was a ritual called *darshan*. *Darshan* is a Sanskrit word that means seeing divinity and divinity seeing you.

Life in the ashram started at four in the morning for Femke and me. We washed with cold water, got dressed in a sari or *punjabi* and went out into the quiet pitch-dark Indian night carrying flashlights to light our way to the *mandir*. We joined devotees circling the temple in silent prayer. It surprised us how some devotees stopped for special prayers before the statues of Sri Krishna, the ancient Lord of the cowherds, and Sri Ganesha, the elephant God of wisdom and the remover of obstacles. The mantra-like sounds of feet shuffling on the sand circumambulating the half-lit temple impressed me as if they were silent prayers filling the cool morning air.

At five, devotees lined up behind the *mandir* hoping to obtain a seat on the marble floor inside to hear the singing of the Awakening Song, called *Suprabhatam*. Femke and I just followed suit. After the fifteen-minute *Suprabhatam* finished, devotees assembled at the Ganesha temple. From that point, lines of hundreds of singers formed to chant Sanskrit and Hindi songs led by a tall white-haired older Indian woman *bhajan* leader, and these throngs of devotees walked around the center part of the ashram, singing. How otherworldly and foreign this scene felt to us newcomers. Femke and I joined in, singing the *bhajans* we knew, which were the wake-up call for the still-sleeping devotees to get up and get ready for *darshan*.

Every day around seven, Baba appeared from his small room in the temple. Thousands of devotees, who had earlier assembled line by line, spiritually embraced the small figure of Sai Baba as their own God-Self strolling amongst them. While making his rounds, Sai Baba spoke with some of the devotees or took letters from them. The men sat on the left side of the *mandir* and the women on the right, facing the temple. During Baba's twice daily stroll, he selected a person or a country group to wait for him on the temple verandah. After *darshan*, these chosen devotees were invited for an interview with Sai Baba, who was better known as Swami in the ashram.

For the other devotees it was breakfast time, which consisted of pancakes with a spicy sauce, or *upma*, porridge with hot spices, and sweet coffee with cooked milk. Around nine, a group of superb Indian male musicians began their devotional singing inside the temple. Devotees could join for half an hour, inside or outside the temple. After *bhajans*, the ashram stores opened to sell vegetables, fruits and household goods. Around midday, people had the choice to eat their own prepared meals or eat lunch served in the ashram canteen. Siesta time followed at the hottest part of the day. At four in the afternoon, a second *darshan* happened, followed by *bhajans* one hour later.

Femke and I soon got the hang of Indian ashram routine. Occasionally, I broke the monotony of the repetitive daily rituals by taking Femke outside the ashram walls to shop in the many enticing village bazaars. In the small town of Puttaparthi, we had interesting encounters with colorful smooth-talking bazaar owners, who were all too eager to sell their wares to wealthy westerners.

Inside the ashram some of our breaks included indulging in eating vanilla ice cream or fruity ice sticks or lining up for ice-cold carbonated lemon or mango bottled drinks to cool off in the extreme heat of the day. Another cherished excitement of the day was to listen to devotees who came back from their interview with Sai Baba. These so-called "lucky ones" had tall tales to tell and a few showed materialized gifts they had seen miraculously flowing out of Swami's hands.

During *darshan* line-up, it was the custom to read one of the hundreds of Baba books for sale in the ashram bookstore. The contents of these books were amazingly mind-blowing and pointed the reader conveniently to Sai Baba's divinity. The books certainly kept me inspired and I thought like many others that we were literally sitting on holy grounds. Many of the resident-devotees were telling us with true devotion how Swami had turned their lives around.

"Was it too good to be true to believe that Sathya Sai Baba was the Godhead descended on Earth in times of moral decline as the Indian scriptures had prophesied?" In those days I held for almost certain it might be true, even though, on occasion, doubts slipped in.

One such occasion happened in that first year in India, when I was sitting on my ashram pillow across from the *mandir*. After interviews, Swami was known to sometimes walk around the sandy grounds before afternoon *bhajans* began and eager devotees would wait outside hoping to get another glimpse of their Swami, and I was one of them.

It was raining. A cement roof sheltered us from getting soaked. Suddenly a shock wave hit the seated devotees when a bald young woman, her head covered with a kerchief, ran towards Sai Baba, who had just appeared from the temple. The woman shouted at the top of her lungs, but we could not hear what she said. Obviously she wanted to see and speak with Swami. In no time, volunteers (*seva-dals*) who kept law and order in the ashram appeared on the scene and grabbed her. The woman struggled to get free. The *seva-dals* subdued her and carried her away from the temple grounds. People started talking and I heard that the woman was Italian and that she had cancer. She obviously had lost her hair during chemotherapy and no doubt ran to Baba for healing. I was seriously troubled by witnessing this scene and even more so when Sai Baba came walking toward us. The rain had saturated the sands and to avoid getting his robe stained by wet sand, Swami pulled his flaming orange robe way up above his knees, a most peculiar sight. He spoke and murmured as if to himself, "A crazy woman, a crazy woman, what can I do?"

I was shocked to say the least and pondered why he would make such remarks, if he was indeed the avatar (highest descending Consciousness on Earth). But the serene spiritual atmosphere of the ashram and the continuous stream of devotional tales of Baba miracles made me doubt my own critical analysis again and again.

After five weeks, we heard that Swami was leaving for his Whitefield ashram near Bangalore. Most devotees followed him there, but Femke and I decided to explore the tiny town of Puttaparthi and take time to rest up before our long travels back home in the week ahead.

First, we set out to visit the "wishing tree" shrine on the outskirts of town, considered a miracle tree where Baba, as I wrote before, had manifested a variety of different fruits for his schoolmates during his teens. The tree still grew on top of a small hill at the end of Chitravati Road, overlooking the Chitravati River. As we climbed the steps to the shrine, village beggars beleaguered us for rupees and it was hard to shake them off. But once at the shrine, I was deeply touched not only to find poster-size pictures of Sai Baba and the God Shiva, but also a large one of Lord Jesus Christ portraying his compassionate heart. All images were garlanded with fresh sweet-smelling jasmine flowers. In contrast to many of the Western religions, which so often exclude the holy names and forms of other religions, I realized for the first time that India includes Jesus and recognizes him as a spiritual master. This inclusion of the different forms of God elated me. "This is the 'true catholicism,' which means inclusive and universal," I thought. "God is all names and forms and Hindu India understands that."

Our last sightseeing stop was a walk through the garden of the last resting place of Baba's parents. Femke and I walked on our bare feet over the soft sandy grounds behind the *samadhi* (eternal rest) temple-grave, the soles of our feet burning from the scorching heat of the sand. Behind a wrought iron gate we found a small pond filled with pink lotus flowers. In the middle of the pond stood a statue of a blue Krishna, dressed in his yellow *dhoti*, with the golden *murali* (flute) at his lips. I was struck by an intense silence when I stared into the eyes of the statue. The large dark mysterious Krishna eyes came to life, like living eyes, through which streams of divine love flowed towards me. The energy of heavenly love came through the denseness of the plaster statue, just like the light that had appeared to me so often through ceilings and through walls. The experience made me feel that the India trip had been divinely blessed. Ecstatic, I was ready to go home.

Chapter Forty

Ponderings on the Path

Since that first pilgrimage, I felt mysteriously drawn to India as if it were my own home. This is what I made clear to the devotees at home who were eager to learn about the trip. I described India as the land where God's presence can be seen and felt in the forms of many deities that come alive through the rituals of burning incense, fresh flower offerings and the reciting of mantras. I explained that I still had a lot to learn and understand about India and Sai Baba. I did not tell the story of the bald-headed Italian woman, who had sought healing for her cancer. Nor did I relate the dream I had about Sai Baba that he was a fake and false teacher. I kept these things to myself to ponder.

In the year 1987, I was a new devotee bubbling with enthusiasm who, beside some doubts, still believed that Sai Baba was the teacher of teachers and the redeemer of all mankind. His teachings that emphasized serving one's family and community as part of a new divine order seemed logical. It impressed me that the Sai organization never solicited pecuniary donations and that the Indian ashrams operated on nominal fees for room and board. The Sai ideals, as I understood them then, were to bring forth goodwill towards one's fellow man. These ideals fitted with who I was then, and who I am still today.

To see large groups of people flock to India from every part of the globe to focus on Sai Baba, who in their minds represented positive change in the world, was awe-inspiring. During my first visit, I too sat in *darshan* with my neck stretched to the limit to get a glimpse of the five-foot-tall man in his flaming orange robe and wild hairdo. I experienced how the atmosphere electrified as he walked slowly through lines of devotees, who yearned to be called for an interview. It was not unusual for Swami to walk by me without paying any attention to me. As a dutiful devotee I nevertheless followed him with my eyes when, one day, he moved on to the left from where I was sitting. I noticed an Indian woman-devotee who eagerly held out a stack of letters to him. He bent over two lines of devotees to take her letters and then proceeded to create the holy ash, which was seemingly flowing from his fingers into her hands. I stared at this woman as she received the *vibuthi*, and in that instant became part of her. She and I seemed to share a great moment of joy that overflowed our hearts. My jubilation was so strong that I was placed once more beyond time, in a state of transcendence, deep and silent. Swami moved away from the woman, turned around, and looked deeply into my eyes. Even though he was at a distance, I was immediately aware that he knew what I experienced. In this, I recognized the presence of divine love that flows from God to man and from man to God and through which all souls are connected.

At home our Sai Center was doing well. Many serious spiritual seekers attended weekly *bhajan* singing and study group. I enrolled in a class the *Religions of India* at the University of Oregon. I wanted to have a better understanding of the history of Hinduism and the meaning and chronology of the ancient Indian sacred texts. One day, I took the well-known wrought iron statue of the dancing Shiva to class. My professor pointed out the symbolic meaning of the various parts of this statue. After class, an Indian woman came up to me and asked, "Where did you buy that statue?"

"In southern India," I replied.

"Which town?"

When I answered, "Puttaparthi," her face lit up. "You must be a Baba devotee," she said, as she pulled out a Sai Baba pendant from under her sweater. "Do you know if there is a Baba Center in town?"

"At our house," I said.

"It is my birthday today. I prayed to Swami to find a Sai Baba Center for me. This must be my birthday present!" That was how I became acquainted with Sunu and later on her sister, Jaya, both students at the University in my town. From then on, the two sisters from Singapore attended our *bhajans* singing.

I wondered, "Had Sunu's fervent prayer been answered by Sai Baba, her guru in India, or had her plea reached her own inner elevated consciousness, which higher power connected the dots for her?" In those days I would have answered that it was without doubt Sai Baba himself, but today I believe that all prayers are answered from the universal mind of God residing deeply within each of us and consequently also in Sai Baba.

Chapter Forty-one

Parents

In the early spring of 1989, I received a phone call from my sister with an urgent message: "Meggy [a term of endearment for Mother] suffered a heart attack. She is in the intensive care unit of the hospital. Please come at once if you wish to still see her alive."

I immediately took action and within twenty-four hours, I arrived at Schiphol, the Amsterdam airport. Herman, my brother, picked me up and drove me to my parents' house in The Hague. I was to stay with my father so that we would travel together to visit my mother in the hospital. Amazingly, my mother recuperated rapidly and was soon able to come home again. I decided to stay on for a while to be near her.

My parents knew of my interest in Sai Baba. In 1986, I had sent them the book, *The Avatar,* written by the Australian theosophist Howard Murphet. I had hopes that the book would give my parents some inkling why I had joined the Sai Baba movement. My parents, both bibliophiles, spent a lot of their time reading the best of world literature. The rooms in the house were lined with bookcases filled to capacity. Knowing my mother's appetite for reading and her earlier interest in the theosophists, it struck me that regarding the avatar, she remarked: "I simply got stuck in the fifth chapter, unable to continue any further." She gave no further explanation.

The prior year when I was in India, I had bought a photo of Sai Baba. While I was meditating on his image, an intense diamond-like star of light had sparked from his third eye. It was the light that always guided and connected me with the higher vibrations of consciousness. I understood that my own higher Self had touched that picture and as it was special, I took it to The Netherlands.

At my parents' house, I placed Baba's picture on a shelf in the bookcase in the guestroom where I slept. That same day my father asked me to go shopping with him at a supermarket outside our immediate neighborhood. We took a bus. At a stop near a hospital, I saw a huge crowd of people holding up large signs as they came flocking towards our bus. I heard that they were hospital employees "on strike" to protest unfair labor contracts for which they sought public awareness. Some of the strikers entered our bus and handed out flowering orchids in small vases with an attached pamphlet voicing their demands. To my surprise I was one of the bus riders who received a pink orchid. I happily thought, "This is the perfect flower to put next to Baba's picture in my room." To adorn a guru's picture with a flower is the

Indian way of showing devotion for one's guru. When we came home, I placed the orchid by Baba's photo.

A few hours later, I heard my father hollering as he came storming out of the guest room. He had seen the Sai Baba's picture adorned with my flower offering and was extremely upset. "Do you not know we are Christians?" he screamed, pointing to the Bible in the front room. I had never seen my parents read the Bible, except on Christmas Eve. They never talked about the Bible, never quoted it, never referred to it. What my father was shouting came as a total surprise. I was shocked, and said, "I am going for a walk," and left the house. I walked around the block in my old neighborhood, while trying to figure out what to do next. I felt extremely hurt. In my way of seeing the world, I held deep love for Sai Baba and my life was centered on my convictions. In 1986, Jon and I had dedicated our lives to him in the belief that he had come as God on Earth or as the second coming foretold in the *Book of Revelation*. I felt extremely alone as I reflected on my father's fury.

"What was I to do?" I turned around and went back to my parents' house. I rang the doorbell with my heart pounding wildly. My mother, who was always the peacemaker, opened the door and said that she had been trying to discuss the incident with my father.

When I entered the living room, my father threw a Dutch translation of a Sai Baba book on the dining room table entitled *Leringen van Sai Baba (Teachings of Sai Baba)*. My father said, "I bought this in a bookstore some time ago." On the cover was a picture of Sai Baba's face in shiny silver colors. My chest still felt heavy and tears were welling up in my eyes, but the moment I glanced at Baba's face on that book smiles broke through my tears like sunlight breaking through after a storm. To see Baba's face connected me with my own God-Self and in that connection, I could feel joy again.

My father gave *Leringen van Sai Baba* to me, and when in a quieter moment I browsed through the book, I noticed that my father had actually taken time to study some of the teachings. I found his notes lying in between some of the pages with his remarks. Apparently he regarded the contents as self-serving promotional material to draw people into the Sai movement. Trying to be sensitive to my father's feelings, I removed the photo and orchid from the guest room and put the silver-image-covered book under my bed pillow. That night, before sleeping, I took the book out from under my pillow and looked at it again. Inside, I spoke to the image and said, "This morning you came to me, I know!" At that instant, intense white light appeared from the picture in such abundance and intensity that my whole body shook as if experiencing an earthquake. To me the message was: "Yes, I am with you, always."

My sudden awareness of the appearance of this light came from the higher Consciousness, which lives in all beings. With full concentration on God, this light can be seen coming from all that is alive, as all is alive with the great spirit-energy of light. This light is in and beyond any form and that light came to me again and again, and not only through Sai Baba.

On a later occasion, my father told me how worried he had been about my association with Sai Baba. He remarked, "I saw a group of Hari Krishnas in downtown The Hague chanting words that included Sai and Baba," from which my father concluded that I must be in a similar cult and that this cult might take away all my money. He worried that I too would shave my head and sing in public. He had a genuine concern and did not want to see his daughter brainwashed and impoverished by any religious group. I was happy my father told me how he felt. "But was he coming from fear or from love?" was the question. Years later, long after my father had passed away, I reflected on my father's remarks. I realized that at that time in 1989, it was exactly right for me to embrace eastern thought and connect with its high vibrations in India.

I believe that humans are constantly guided towards the light by the invisible forces of higher Consciousness. It is always best to stay mentally open and aware, not to imagine, but to literally see God's guiding hand in one's life.

When I visited my parents, it seemed obvious to me that the light and Sai Baba were one and the same. This light clearly showed I was on the right track. My father's opinion at that time did not fit my life's plan. I still had much to learn in that ancient land India, whose hidden spiritual treasures would come to define a major part of my life.

Chapter Forty-two

Puttaparthi 1989

During my first pilgrimage to India in 1987, devotees in the ashram told me I would be back the next year. I refused to believe it, but I did go back to India the next year and now I was making plans for a third trip. This time, Jon wanted to join Femke and me even though he disliked traveling and large crowds. We invited our son David, but he was not in the least interested to see what he called "that man in India."

It was pitch dark when we arrived in Madras, India. Around midnight, our taxi drove into the courtyard of the Connemara Hotel, where our reservations had been reconfirmed a week before. I had purposely booked a room in a five-star hotel to give Jon the taste of Indian upper-class luxury living before going to the ashram, where living conditions were austere. As I walked into the hotel lobby, the smell of fungi and clamminess hung in the air like a neglected steam bath. The high humidity showed pockmarks of deterioration on the indoor walls, creating an atmosphere of a certain lost glory of former colonial days. And yet, I also recognized the presence of a mysterious otherworldly beauty revealed in the old dark woodcarvings of Indian deities displayed on every wall.

The receptionist who checked our reservation said with a sad look in her eyes, "Some mistake must have been made, Madam. We have no room reservation for you!" adding, while looking at the three of us in dismay, "I am so sorry!"

"But then what are we to do?" I asked, while sweat poured down my face and swarms of black mosquitoes began their attacks.

The receptionist, draped in an eye-catching tight-fitted green silk sari, looked at us in a strange pondering mood. Apparently she was waiting for us to solve the dilemma. But we just stood there speechless and tired. Finally, after some minutes, the receptionist broke the silence and said, "We will give you our best suite for the same price." This good news brought a big smile on my face, as I remembered for a split second my days with Harmen in first-class Caribbean hotels. The receptionist rang for the bellboys, who stacked our heavy suitcases with seeming ease on top of their heads. We went with the boys in the elevator, which brought us up to a musty-smelling hallway leading to our luxury suite.

The suite included a living room, a separate study with a single bed, and a master bedroom plus bath. A vase filled with red roses mixed with jasmine stood on the living room table. I rushed to set the air conditioner on cold. Exhausted after three days' travel, we went to bed covering our heads with sheets to avoid the bites of hungry mosquitoes. In no time we were off to sleep.

The next morning after breakfast Jon and I took a taxi to the railroad station to buy tickets for the express train to Bangalore. Femke stayed behind, as she wanted to sleep in that day. The area around the station was packed with buses, cars, taxis, auto-rickshaws (a motorized three-wheeled rickshaw), bikes and pedestrians. The sounds of horns, bells and shouting vendors were causing severe auditory pollution. In addition, the smells of decaying garbage, cow dung, urine and diesel exhaust overwhelmed our senses. About fifty taxi drivers eager to attract the attention of us bewildered-looking foreigners began competing for our business. We shook our heads at them, which really means "yes" in India. Some taxi drivers followed us as we were trying to find our way through hordes of different vendors offering their wares and coolies looking to us in the hope that we had something to carry. We had to walk cautiously around people asleep on the grounds, while beggars accosted us for rupees. The area was swarming with young manservants busy doing their masters' chores of the day. I believe we were the only ones who did not know how it all worked. Even though I had been to India twice, I still felt much like a newcomer, as the complexities of the layers of Indian life are too subtle to be easily understood. Inside the railroad station, we noticed multiple long lines of Indian younger men patiently waiting their turn at the various ticketing offices. It was extremely hard to determine where we needed to go and the lines did not seem to move.

"We must take some action," I thought; after all such is our western way. Hot and disoriented and yet determined to get information, I knocked on some far-off office window. An older fleshy woman, gray hair knotted in a bun and wearing a brown-green colored sari, opened the door. "Come in," she said. "What is your problem?"

To my relief we had miraculously landed at the "Office for Foreign Tourists." "Finally, the right place," I sighed with relief. The now perspiring older woman clerk sat down at her computer. In no time our names appeared on a printed sheet of paper that was to be attached on the outside of our train compartment the next morning to confirm our reserved seats.

The next day I was in high spirits while enjoying our ride on the express train with its smoke-puffing steam engine pulling us through arid lands and mountainous terrain. Looking through the train window, lush palm tree forests, sugarcane, rice and banana tree fields, small villages and many rivers slowly opened up to our view. We saw villagers working the fields or lining up at water holes. At every stop, vendors came on board to sell bananas, oranges and Indian delicacies. As the hours progressed,

I slowly got back in touch with that mysterious otherworldly feeling of India, my transcendental land, where all things spiritual are possible.

Seven hours later at the Bangalore train station, we found our new taxi driver Suleman patiently waiting and ready to take us on the familiar three-hour bumpy road-ride to the Puttaparthi ashram. Exhausted to our limits we came to Puttaparthi, where Suleman dropped us off at the accommodation office of the ashram, to secure a room. This year we were most fortunate to get a room assignment in one of the attractive-looking round houses. Our unit luckily had a clean vinyl-tiled floor. Jon, Femke and I put our self-inflating air mattresses down, attached the mosquito netting to the hooks in the ceiling and draped the netting in a tent-like fashion around our make-believe beds. I set the alarm for six to be sure to make it for early morning *darshan*. Soon the three of us were sound asleep.

Interviews with Sai Baba never came easy and seemed to be only for those lucky ones who, in our minds, apparently had good karma. I had been sitting for many *darshans* in the two years I had come to India. Every day, I had watched devotees' faces glowing with light after they had an interview with Swami. I wanted to know and experience what it was really like to come face to face with him. I told Jon, "I have discovered that groups have a much better chance for an interview." I had never belonged to any group, and when Jon heard that devotees from various countries were thinking of forming an international group, he asked, "Can my family and I join?" They invited us to a meeting where I was introduced to devotees from India, the Soviet Union, Germany, New Zealand and America to discuss group ideas. I spoke with zeal and enthusiasm about what I would like to see a group do for *sadhana* (spiritual group practice). Everyone voiced opinions, but because I had spoken quite boldly, I feared being ostracized. To my astonishment, however, they offered to make me the group leader. Elated, I took our new group to the tailor shop to have scarves made for each member to symbolize our group-status and unity.

Our group member Alex, a Muscovite artist, was the first Russian to come to Baba's ashram, which made him extremely popular. At this time, the United States was in the Cold War with the Soviet Union, an arms race in nuclear weapons in which each country pointed their nuclear rockets at the major cities of the other. The Iron Curtain prevented not only Russians from coming to the west but also the rest of the world from seeing the Russians as people like us. One can imagine how impressed I was when Alex during a group meeting spoke about his mystical experiences in the Soviet Union. He was clearly deeply religious, which I had believed nonexistent in such a controlled political state, where Karl Marx had termed religion "the opiate of the masses." Jon, my composer-artist husband, soon befriended Alex and another member, Wilhelm, a German composer. Later on, back home, we lost contact with Alex, but Wilhelm's friendship would last the rest of these men's lives.

Before each *darshan*, our group met on the sands in the shade of the big banyan tree to sing *bhajans* to invoke unity and peace, visit with each other, pray and meditate.

Chapter Forty-three

Interview

I did not expect an interview, and found it emotionally increasingly trying to sit for *darshan* and see other devotees called in. I was happy for them, but wondered when and if our chance would ever come, especially since we were going home soon.

On the last day before our departure I was sitting on the temple grounds praying with all my heart to have an interview.

After a while, I let go of all expectation to be called in. I was still in deep meditation when I heard a lady of our group shouting, "Look, Alex, look... Alex is called for an interview." By the ashram rule "if one member of a group is called, the whole group is called," I knew that all of us were invited to have an interview. I picked up my ashram pillow, as did Femke and the other women, and ran to the verandah of the temple. The psychological impact of being called brought tears to my eyes. When our group sat down, I noticed that everyone was going through similar emotional states. I sobbed, while tens of thousands of eyes of devotees, who remained seated in the *darshan* lines, were staring at us, "the lucky ones" of that day. I suddenly thought, "Stop crying and pull yourself together!" Immediately, I began my *So Hum* meditation, which brought me up to a higher state of being.

Swami returned from giving *darshan*, and cordially invited the international group and some Indian devotees to come into the interview room. We filed in and sat down on a marble floor, Indian yogi-style. The room had no furniture except a throne-like chair with dark wooden carvings and a deep-red velvet seat with a high back, displaying the AUM symbol in silver Sanskrit letters at the top. A large kitchen-type clock hung on the wall. Swami was the last one to come in. He switched on the lights. With a wave of his hand he materialized *vibuthi,* the holy ash. It miraculously seemed to flow from his hand as he handed it to all the ladies seated on the right side of the room.

Swami sat down, looked at us and asked, "Where is God?" No one spoke. As group leader, I felt that I needed to show courage and break the silence. I said, "Swami, God is within and without." His reply came quickly, while he looked at me, "No, no, no, God is never without." Then he gave us teachings on the omnipresence of God, how we live in God and God lives in us. "It is like a fish swimming in water. If God is the water, that water is in the fish, above, underneath and in the back and the front of the fish. We are like fish swimming in God, but God is also inside us." He looked at the group again and asked, "Is God in this handkerchief?" Someone answered: "Yes," but Swami immediately replied, "Then God must be very small!" Everyone laughed. Then he asked the question, "What is Joy?" No one dared to give any more answers. Swami proceeded, "J stands for Jesus, O stands for others and Y stands for you. Jesus first, then others, then you."

Then Swami motioned two Indian boys, about thirteen years of age, to come with him to the inner interview room. Our group and some other devotees remained seated on the floor of the larger interview room. A black curtain separated the inner room from the outer room. The curtain was not completely shut. From the angle where I sat, I could see the two boys standing in front of Sai Baba, who presided from another throne-like chair. "How odd this is," I thought, as no one was ever allowed to stand straight up in front of Sai Baba. People always knelt before him to make themselves smaller than Swami's five-foot figure. Such was the ashram protocol. I kept my eyes fixed on Sai Baba and the Indian boys, who kept standing before him. The situation puzzled me so much that I kept staring. Suddenly, to my bewilderment, I noticed that Sai Baba unzipped the pants of the young man on the left, from my perspective. I felt dismayed. Baba's gesture looked as if he was making a sexual approach towards the young man. I glared at Sai Baba in disbelief and in that moment my eyes and Sai Baba's eyes met. Acutely aware that I could see what was happening with the boys, Sai Baba jumped out of his chair and rushed towards the curtain while looking at me intently. With his eyes fully fixed on mine, he pulled the curtain closed. Shocked, and at the same time trying to be a good devotee, I did not know what to make of it. After all, Swami was said to be all knowing. "Could he have known my thoughts, or was he simply protecting himself from what he suspected my eyes had seen?"

When it was the turn for our international group to go into the innermost sanctum sanctorum, we all rushed forward to find the closest spot to Sai Baba's chair. I felt some delight that I ended up sitting at Swami's feet. "This is the time to speak with God himself" is what we all believed. When my turn came I asked a question for my son David, who had absolutely no appreciation for the Sai Baba phenomenon. Swami, despite David's feelings, showed interest in my son. He talked at length about David's schooling and life. I had a strong feeling that Baba was trying to draw David to him. He further made some remarks to Jon, who was sitting in the back of the room, and recognized him as the father. He also made remarks to Femke, which were impossible to comprehend. When the interview was over, Swami walked me to the door and again emphasized in his typical Indian accent, "Tell your son that Swami will give him a long and happy life." Strangely, when David said goodbye to us at the Portland airport, this was exactly what he had asked for. When our group walked out of the interview room into the temple compound, I cast my eyes downwards as I sensed tens of thousands of eyes watching us, perhaps in the belief that by doing so our good fortune would rub off on them. I was in seventh heaven and so was Femke beside me, shown by the triumphant big smile on her face. Our whole group was glowing and our feet were barely touching the ground.

The day after the interview, our last day in India, an interesting event took place. It was *darshan* time and Femke and I sat in the first row waiting for Baba's appearance. I reflected on Alex, the artist from Moscow, and the cold war conflict that still might erupt in a full-blown nuclear war. I fell into deep contemplation and asked God with all my heart that I, in some modest way, be used to break the barriers between our two nations. I requested, "Swami, walk straight towards me and allow me to touch your feet as a sign that my prayer to help the Russians has been answered." The touching of Baba's feet, called taking *pade namaskar*, was considered a special blessing. Amongst the throngs of devotees few were given this opportunity. I was still repeating my prayer when I saw Swami leave his room in the temple. When he came around the corner, he walked straight towards me and allowed me to touch his feet.

Swami had given special attention to me twice, defocusing my mind from what my eyes had seen in the inner interview room. My ego or limited self enjoyed his attention. I felt special, not only for myself, but for my whole family, as Baba had addressed all of us, each in different ways. Drawn into these joyful psychological heights, I was already forgetting the incident with the Indian boys, even though the mind really never forgets. After *darshan* was over, Jon, Femke and I left the ashram in a blissful mood to make our long journey back home to the United States.

Looking back so many years later, I find it still strange that I did not report what I saw to anyone, not even my husband Jon.

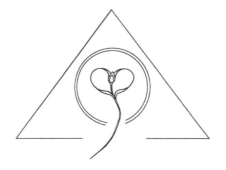

PART VI

Practicing the Teachings

Chapter Forty-four

Russians

Shortly after our return from India, Femke went back to high school. She was in her second year of studying Russian. Her Russian teacher, Mrs. Loblinskaya, informed the class that the city of Eugene had started a Sister City program with Irkutsk in Siberia, U.S.S.R. The program sought to promote cultural exchanges and commerce between the two cities, as well as a high school student exchange. Mrs. Loblinskaya chaired the student exchange program. As parents of the Russian language students, we were asked who could volunteer to host one Russian high school student for three weeks. "This is exactly what I am meant to do," I thought, and enthusiastically offered our house. Mrs. Loblinskaya formed a committee of students and parents to prepare a program of outings and other activities. The plan was to get our whole community drawn into welcoming the first Russian students from behind the Iron Curtain to come to the United States. I asked several large stores in Eugene to donate food for our parties and American souvenirs to give to the students. All were more than happy to oblige. "Russian students coming to Eugene" was an exciting event and most people were eager to show the Russians that Americans are good-hearted generous people and not the enemy.

One afternoon, when we had a parent-student meeting, Femke was unable to come, and I went by myself. Other parents and students did not show up either and I was alone with the Russian teacher. There was no reason for me to stay, as we needed to have all people on board to make decisions. Mrs. Loblinskaya walked me down her driveway to where I had parked my car. Unexpectedly, she stared at me, put her arm around my shoulder and said, "You are glowing." When I came home, I looked in the mirror. I was indeed glowing with radiant light that seemed to pour from my very essence, quite impossible to fully describe. As I had asked Sai Baba, in prayer, in India that I might in some small way help ease the tension between Russia and the U.S.A., I wondered, "Had Sai Baba something to do with this light emanating from my body?" All I knew was that this light illuminated me. That the Russian teacher had been able to detect this phenomenon with her physical eyes made it even more credible.

With enthusiastic anticipation we waited for the Russians at our local airport. A heavy fog rolled in and the airport officials announced that no plane could land at Mahlon Sweet Field, the Eugene airport. The Russians, who had already landed in Portland, were bused to Eugene despite the heavy fog on the interstate. After a wait of many hours, the bus arrived. It was an enormously thrilling event to see the first Russians from behind the Iron Curtain descend from their special shuttle bus. We welcomed them with armfuls of rose bouquets of all colors donated by a local floral wholesaler. From the airport, we carpooled them to the home of one of the participating parents for an official welcome. As I looked into the faces of these so foreign young Russian students, I felt such joy that I spontaneously made an impromptu welcome speech. I still sensed that glowing light within me, and from that place of light I found the right words. Afterwards, I could not remember what I had said. The words were flowing through me from somewhere else, but not from my personal self.

Our student's name was Yulia. We took her home and showed her around the house and had her settle into our American ways.

We slowly became acquainted. Yulia was very quiet and never spoke about her home in Siberia. She did her homework with utmost discipline. Every morning promptly at seven, I found her silently standing in the dark at our front door on the ground floor, ready to be taken to school, with her schoolbooks neatly organized in her backpack. Yulia had an identical twin sister, Olga, who stayed with another family. The girls were inseparable and could hardly bear to be apart. We often invited Olga to the house to be with her sister. Femke taught the twins Monopoly, the capitalistic game of the West. After some games, the girls got the hang of it and started buying houses and hotels, while we cheered them on. I had a strong feeling that even the tiniest effort on our part to be kind, helpful and to promote fun and laughter would help in the ultimate meltdown of the Iron Curtain.

It was November 9, 1989. I heard Jon urgently calling, "Please come to the TV room, the Berlin Wall is tumbling down!" We rushed with Yulia to watch the historic moment as it took place. I found the event awe-inspiring, but soon realized that this was different for Yulia, whose parents were Communist elites. Yulia showed no emotion and said absolutely nothing...

On the day before their departure, the twins shopped extensively for American products to bring home. When Yulia and Olga had their last supper with us, we all enjoyed the Russian beet salad they taught us to make. The girls gorged themselves on typical American ice cream, topped with red cherries and heaping mounds of whipped cream, their farewell dessert. All these foods were incredibly scarce in the Soviet Union. The girls, who were very artistic, presented us with some beautiful drawings they made for us. They had the same birthday as Jon and like him showed remarkable talent for composing classical music. Jon had fun taping their voices singing haunting Russian folk songs. On that last night, I felt barriers between our two countries melting away. The girls finally ventured to speak about their hopes and dreams for their future in Siberia. We had come to love the twins and we were truly sad to see them leave. There was no longer any doubt in my mind that the light of humanity was present in the hearts of the Soviet people and my hope was that this light would soon find its way to the hearts and minds of the officials of the Politburo.

Chapter Forty-five

Graduation Time

In the summer of 1991 David received his bachelor's degree and Femke graduated from International High School. Both children had done well with their studies. David left for San Francisco to experience what earning a living was all about, and Femke was scheduled to start the College of Nursing in San Francisco the next autumn. Since her fall from a horse at the age of eight, followed by a fourteen-day hospital stay, Femke had been dreaming of becoming a nurse. "Why not become a doctor?" people often asked, because she was such an outstanding student. Femke always replied in the same manner: "Nurses save lives!"

During David's years in college I always had the chance to see him, as it took only two hours to drive to Portland. Paying visits to Femke in California was a different matter, as it would take ten hours including some stops to drive to San Francisco. Not only would I see Femke less, but also I would miss my after-school walks and talks and our spiritual summer vacations to India.

Kahlil Gibran in *The Prophet* writes:

> Your children are not your children,
> They are the sons and daughters of Life's longing for itself.
> They come through you, but not from you,
> And though they are with you yet they belong not to you.

My children, from now on, had to attend their own "school

of life" and learn their own lessons. I could stand on the sideline for support only when required. Detachment in the spiritual sense was about stepping back to let their life's stories unfold.

When I realized that my graduation time as a day-to-day parent was soon coming up, I enrolled in financial classes to get licensed for a post in the financial field. How thrilled I was to be offered a position at a financial institution. Jon, the artist, composer, designer and poet had an innate capacity to live in each moment, giving him an easier time graduating from day-to-day parenthood. For him the departure of the children signaled a new beginning of increased creative activity. Jon, whom I had married by following the guidance of a spiritual dream, had been a remarkable stepfather. With the children gone, new avenues were opening for Jon and me to support each other's unique pathway in life.

Besides starting my career in the financial field, I also intensified my studies in Indian philosophy with a special interest in the *Bhagavad-Gita* (Song of God). The texts in the Holy Scriptures always pointed to the inner knowledge or that "full awareness" I had known when I was twelve. I believed in the importance of understanding these ancient scriptures that pointed to an alignment with higher Consciousness, from where a more perfect world would come into existence.

I tried to apply my spiritual understandings in my work at the financial company. Unfortunately I found that the old thinking of taking advantage of people rather than serving others still strongly prevailed in my company's philosophy. Fortunately, I also met other employees who thought as I did, but together we were not strong enough to effect change. Ultimately, I left the company, which was not ready to incorporate creative ideas that would bring a win-win situation to both buyers and sellers of financial products.

Chapter Forty-six

When Silence Speaks

After WWII, my parents' post-traumatic stress disorder constantly surfaced in talks about the ordeal of living under German shellfire. The death by the executioner's bullet of my 29-year-old uncle caused deep emotional scars as did the stories of my mother's brother, Uncle Jo, and my cousin Bob about their incarceration in a Japanese concentration camp in Indonesia. My parents' constant wartime review touched my being deeply. I grew up with a different awareness than children born in peacetime. As a child, I meditated to make peace with war, even though I did not know the word that describes that silent practice. In Chapter Thirteen, "Revelation of Truth," I already wrote that when I was twelve, my mind and body disappeared during meditation and I entered a state of full knowledge of "all that there is to know." I realized who I was, namely knowledge itself without boundaries. Even though the sacred revealed knowledge changed me, I nevertheless seemingly grew up like any other person. I kept the secret of what I knew hidden till I disclosed my spiritual side to Harmen a few days before he died. A week after the funeral, my third eye opened revealing the diamond light, which is the central consciousness and force of the Divine according to The Mother, an enlightened saint in the Sri Aurobindo Ashram in Pondicherry, India. From that moment on, this light of higher Consciousness quietly guided and nudged me in the direction I was to take in this life. When Femke suffered a fall and broke her elbow I learned about alternative healing and got in touch with meditation groups.

I was forty-two when I officially learned to sit for meditation. The objective of meditation is to still the mind and enter the deep space of silence where one's soul essence resides. My practices were initially irregular, but I still meditated during the day while not sitting in the official cross-legged lotus-yogi position. While doing the dishes or mopping the floor I could be in either a state of letting go of excess thinking, or in a state of inquiry and self-reflection. According to many spiritual teachings, seventy-five percent of meditation is witnessing the self, in other words seeing-observing one's own thought processes. Being the I-witness, without judgment, leads to experiencing higher Consciousness or God. God, the ultimate I-witness of all things, is also the ever watchful "I" within each person.

During the teen years of David and Femke, I often felt uncertain whether I should protect or guide my children or allow them their own experience without my interference. One morning, when I felt extremely weary and unsure in my mother role, I descended to my silent room to sit for meditation hoping to regain some clarity of mind. Suddenly, I received a distinct message spoken to me in a clear audible voice: "Have *faith* in the beauty of your own being." The message amazed me and I repeated what I heard like a mantra. I realized I had received a universal message applicable for all mankind. It dawned on me that my own true being is God, perfect and beautiful created in His image.

During this time of renewing my meditation practice, I picked up the insert of a Sunday newspaper called *Parade.* My eyes glanced over the pages stopping at some photographs of monkeys. I remember a tiny baby monkey and a monkey with a metal strap around its head. Reading the story, I found that scientists intentionally had separated the tiny baby monkey from its mother to test psychological reactions for their research purposes. I saw the agony in the face of the mother monkey and her baby. Appalled and sick to my stomach, I screamed and cried inside, and asked the question, "What can be done to stop these tests? What must I do about this?" Utterly distressed, I rushed to my meditation room, shut the door and sat in complete silence, and then asked God, "What can be done to stop these horrific and cruel laboratory experiments on animals?"

I did not expect to receive any answers soon, but a clear voice spoke from deep within, saying: "When you change, they change!" The message touched me profoundly and I kept repeating the words, "When you [Ella] change, they [the scientists] change!" You and they are both part of God and live in that same field of higher Consciousness, in the east known as our true Reality. The message was clear. "Do not judge the cruelties you see outside, but instead look deeply within to see if there is anything that has taken you away from God." The attitude of blaming others can lead to not questioning what we ourselves do, or omit to do. We can make it a spiritual task to find our own shadow parts knowing we are not different from others in whom we clearly see foibles. With inner change, outer change comes. Every individual who is willing to look deeply within helps our world towards more peace and harmony.

When I was a member of a small meditation group in the early eighties, our group leader said, "Ask God in meditation this week for a special gift." I pondered upon that, as I was not particularly in the habit of asking God for favors. That whole week, I actually never sat for meditation. I did not want to ask God anything, and yet one day when I walked down the stairs, I heard from deep within, "You are carried in love, no harm can come to you." I was extremely surprised. "A gift without asking!" I thought. From then on I also used this divine message as a meaningful mantra. "I and all people are carried in God's love." It is the truth. God's love is the glue that holds this whole universe together. We need to trust that what we perceive as harm and suffering is but God's gift to move us closer to his heart, where peace is always present.

I like to reiterate that silence speaks not necessarily only during sitting meditation. It can take place whenever or wherever the mind transcends into stillness. I like to illustrate this with my following story.

In March 1993, I attended a Sai *satsang* (spiritual gathering) in Portland with my friends Ruth and Mira. On the way back home, I was in deep contemplation about my relationship with God when we drove by an Oriental gate and building complex that looked like an Asian temple. Ruth, who was driving the car, suddenly said, "Mira and Ella, what is this thing we are just passing by? Maybe we should see what this is."

My immediate reply was, "Yes, let us turn around and see." We turned and arrived at an entrance gate with an inscription indicating that we had come to a Buddhist temple. Ruth slowly drove her car inside the temple compound. I saw a garden and in the distance a towering statue of the Buddha. In the front of the garden was a statue of a large reclining Buddha lying under a roof. We got a glimpse of a man, who looked like a Buddhist priest, entering the house on our right. Mira suggested that we walk around, but a bit uncertain, decided we had better go to the house to ask for permission. When Mira came back, she said, "We have permission to see the gardens."

I got out of the car and walked alone toward the reclining Buddha. While I observed the statue, I recognized that it represented the Buddha's *maha-samadhi*. That thought somehow touched the inner me. I moved closer towards the statue and folded my hands, touching my forehead and bringing them back to the region of my heart. By doing this I began to feel a deep reverence for the Buddha shown in his state of union with God. The statue was some fifty feet in length, clothed in the orange robe of renunciation. A serene smile of stillness hovered around the face, and small black ornamental curls were draped around the Buddha's head as if that part of his body was a temple most high. My reverie moved me into a trance state in which I felt the essence of God in the Buddha statue. Tears welled up from my soul as I continued walking along the path to the next statue, also approximately fifty feet tall and likewise dressed in an orange robe. As I looked intently at this Buddha's beatified face while greeting him with my deepest reverence and devotion, I remained in a transcendental state of awareness. I walked back to the reclining Buddha in the *samadhi* temple and stood there without thoughts, when I heard, "*I AM* the Living God." The words came from the transcendental statue, the formless beyond the form. I realized that God had spoken... I felt as if I was standing on holy ground. Then I experienced ethereal waves of divine infiniteness floating toward me repeating, "I AM that I AM, I AM that I AM... I AM..." When we drove away from the temple area, while tears were flowing inside my inner Self, the words, "I am that I am" kept resounding deeply within me, and I found myself in ecstatic joy and beauty from far beyond any description.

The blessings I received through the Buddha were special teachings. As I stood before the statues, I felt immense love for the Buddha as that higher level of myself, that beauty within me. In this awareness, the higher Self responded in sounds I could understand. I suddenly understood the Buddha to be the source of all beings and all life. In union with the Buddha essence, the revelation came that there is no difference between the Buddha and other forms people worship. All forms of God are but images or icons representing the holiness and wholeness of God through which holy words flow in different tongues. Through the appearance of diversity emanates the unifying principle of God as the Creator of all things. In that sense, all that is worshiped in his name and his form is ONE.

Chapter Forty-seven

Destiny for David

It was summertime 1993. David declared that he would like to visit his parents' home country, of which he still held a passport. For many years in a row, I had taken Femke to India. Now it was time to spend a summer abroad with my son. I made plans to travel to The Netherlands to reunite with my close relatives and friends. David, who wanted to continue on to graduate school, made plans to check out a variety of Dutch universities as possibilities for advanced studies.

My parents were delighted that we were coming. I still remember them waiting for us, standing quiet and dignified on the train station platform at Amsterdam's Schiphol airport. My parents had not seen David for eight years; it was moving to reintroduce my son, their grandson, to them. In my parents' silence and inner poise, as they stood there, lay an ocean of human recognition that meeting their grandson was part of life's continuing future, but also pointed to a painful rift on a subconscious level between the cultures of America and The Netherlands. This inner knowing that sought no expression in words brought with it the sense of the wisdom of old Dutch souls who take everything in observation at a deeper level. This was the richness of the culture and the depth I knew, and wished now for David to know.

I wanted David to become immersed in his old ancestral background. I was aware that it would feel strangely foreign to him to be in my birth country. The way of thinking and thought patterns and consequent conversing are derived from completely different roots, which would be untranslatable in modern American language. The Dutch historical roots go all the way back to the Middle Ages, the days of Charlemagne and the Roman Empire. In The Netherlands, in contrast to the United States, this connection to the past can be seen and felt almost everywhere. From the seventeenth-century houses to the still-standing ancient city walls, castles and cathedrals from medieval times and before, history has carved its well-defined marks everywhere. The sturdy historic Dutch brick buildings and the medieval cobblestoned streets give a feeling of longevity and ageless solidity.

Walking on the sidewalks in Amsterdam connected me with floods of memories of old rhymes, songs and poetry learned by every Dutch child from kindergarten through high school. It was as if the sidewalk whispered the old rhymes to me, and it filled me with awe for the Dutch spirit, which still remained so much a part of me.

From Dutch political history to Dutch art, music and philosophy, I showed David its unique richness in bits and pieces. We visited the many great museums where wonderful and interesting exhibitions of art and culture, not only of The Netherlands, but also from every part of the world, can be admired. In the outdoor cafés, we found it enjoyable to sit on one of the many large terraces filled with rattan chairs and tables for a *gezellig bakje koffie*, a cozy cup of coffee, or a large glass of excellent Dutch beer. Here one can hear the Dutch discussing politics, philosophy, religion and culture for hours on end. One may find that the Dutch are seldom afraid to voice strong opinions and to strongly disagree with each other.

I tried to tell David as much as I could to give him an understanding of my upbringing and past. I was able to point out the Dutch ways of things, which more often than not, made us roar with laughter because of the charm and fun of the different ways of looking at the same things from completely different angles of thinking.

When I reintroduced my son to his relatives on his father's side of the family, we stayed for a few days at his aunt and uncle's house. On the morning of David's twenty-fourth birthday, he came running down the stairs shouting, "Mom, I had a Sai Baba dream and I want to tell you all about it!" This was most unusual, because as I said before, David was never a Sai devotee and often scoffed about the Indian guru. After David told me his dream I became so intrigued that I wrote it down as if it were my own dream.

> The scene of the dream is our house in Eugene. David and I are sitting at the dining room table. We are talking about what David should be doing with his life... Our conversation continues to a more general dialogue as to what anyone should do be doing with his or her life.

David had not only come to my home country to visit relatives and friends, but also to find a new way and direction in his life. Thus far, it had not been clear to him whether he should stay in The Netherlands for further academic studies or continue graduate work back in the United States.

> In the dream, going back and forth about the questions of life, I am saying to David, "I do not even know what is right for me either. I am confused like you." I seemingly question my own spiritual beliefs, while gazing off into the kitchen area. Then, David and I hear a swooshing sound at the sliding doors leading to the outside deck. The sound turns into a red-orange blob, which to our surprise materializes into the form of Sai Baba in flesh and blood. Sai Baba walks over to me and puts his hand on my left shoulder, making me understand that I already found my direction and purpose in life through his teachings, based on the ancient scriptures of India. Sai Baba and I in the dream say some words to that effect to David, who then asks Sai Baba, "But what about me? Don't I have a purpose or destiny?" Sai Baba communicates to David that his destiny is: "Switz-her-land," which David interprets to mean Switzerland, the country known for its large banking industry. David answers, "That cannot be realized now, because my father died, and that is why my life is forever changed." Sai Baba shrugs his shoulders, suggesting symbolically perhaps that David has to find his own destiny...

David and I tried to figure out what the dream meant. To both of us, Switzerland represented the banking world. Had his father been alive, he might have steered his son in the direction of the banking profession, but we no longer had any connection to that world. David and I did not tell anyone about this interesting dream, but I kept pondering its meaning.

We planned to see David's Oma (Grandma), who had always stayed in close contact with us through letters and loving attention at birthdays and Christmases. My mother-in-law had recently suffered a serious stroke, and I was not sure what to expect during our visit in her assisted-living home. Oma's flat (apartment) was on the second floor of a solid brick building surrounded by beautiful park-like gardens. The flat was small, but large windows visually enlarged her space, which included a balcony where the intensity of the northern European light illuminated planters filled with purple, white and yellow pansies (viola), her favorites. When David and I, accompanied by his aunt and uncle, entered her room, her thin and frail appearance startled me. Oma was eating her lunch and I noticed how difficult it was to swallow every bite of the food set before her. "The stroke must have affected her throat muscles," I speculated anxiously. "No wonder she has lost so much weight."

In 1973 after his father died, David and I had to switch from the Dutch language to English to better adjust to our new life in the United States. David had forgotten most of the Dutch he knew when he was three. I felt sad that on this special occasion he could not converse in Dutch with his dear Oma. After our initial greetings, my mother-in-law looked intently at David and said, "He looks exactly like his father, like two drops of water." I became still for a moment feeling the pain once more of my husband's untimely passing. I understood the depth of sadness of Harmen's mother. I recognized that she saw her lost son now in my grown-up child and my heart went out to her. I gazed at my mother-in-law and felt suddenly overcome by deep sorrow. I ran out of the room into the hallway and wept bitterly, intuitively knowing that Oma's time on Earth was nearing its end.

While continuing our exploration of The Netherlands, David and I also checked out graduate schools. We learned that the University of Amsterdam had a master's program for overseas students taught in English. The application time was closed, but the department head was willing to make an exception because of David's excellent academic background. The decision to enroll needed to be made at once. Unfortunately all available university housing had been taken and David was to secure his own rental in Amsterdam. We asked for a one-hour decision time and sat down in the university restaurant to consider the options.

I told David, "I will help with the tuition funds, but the final decision whether you want to enroll in the master's program is yours alone!" We sat in the cafeteria in utter silence, while I nostalgically sipped a delicious Dutch cassis, a carbonated black currant drink unavailable in the United States.

After a while, David finally broke the silence and said, "Mom, without university housing, knowing the scarcity of rentals in Amsterdam, it might well be impossible to find a place." David concluded, "Mom...I think my destiny is likely to be in the United States, after all."

Back in the United States, David went to work at a new job in Portland, Oregon. I had left my financial job earlier and applied for a new position at a mortgage company. Three months later Oma passed away, as I had suspected she might. Out of love I sang my favorite spiritual songs to her for a week, hoping her spirit would hear and know how much she had meant to me.

A year later, I went back to India to stay in Sai Baba's ashram. David in Portland was pondering again whether to go to graduate school at the University of Amsterdam or at San Francisco State University. He applied to both schools. I had not forgotten about David's Sai Baba dream the year before when I was having coffee with my psychic friend Annette in India. I recounted the dream to her and said, "I am frustrated that Baba did not indicate any direction for his life," and added, "to both of us the word Switzerland had absolutely no meaning."

Annette shook her head and replied, "*Switzerland*, just wait a minute, I am getting something... It means 'switch-the-land.' In other words, it means that he is to settle in Holland, and switch from the U.S.A." When Annette uttered those words, I felt cold chills running up my spine.

As I had always heard that the inner Sai Baba speaks to devotees directly and not necessarily through other people, I wanted to meditate on what Annette had perceived psychically.

I went to my room in Kadugodi, near the ashram, and sat down under my mosquito netting and asked my own higher Self for a direct answer. To my utter astonishment, I heard, "*Switzerland* means Switz (h) er Land," in other words, David is to stop and start flowing (meaning of switch) in a different direction in his life, which would take him to his mother's land, The Netherlands. The moment I perceived the inner explanation, incredible brilliant diamond-blue and white lights appeared in my third eye. My whole body shook with the intense force of this divine power. I also received another strong message: "Do not interfere with David's decision-making process."

I called my husband in Oregon to ask how things were going at home. Jon said, "David has signed up with the University of Amsterdam. He will leave the first of September." I could not say goodbye, because my return home was to be on September the thirteenth! David decided on his direction in life in the United States while I was in India having the divine revelation that this was meant to be. I fully accepted the separation from a son I loved so dearly as part of David's own divine plan. "Had Sai Baba directed my son in this mysterious way, even though David did not want to have anything to do with that man in India? Or, was the man in his dream simply a manifestation of his mother's higher Self?" In any case, I stood in awe recognizing that true divine guidance had come to David as a belated birthday present.

Chapter Forty-eight

Reflections

I believe that in general most religions of the world try to expand the awareness of love and compassion for all living beings. In the Hebrew Bible we find in Leviticus 19:18:

> You shall not take vengeance or bear any grudge against the
> sons of your own people, but you shall love your neighbor as
> yourself.

In the first place this means that amongst the people of your land one should not have conflict, but only love. In a more expansive way of looking at the same text, "the sons of your own people" encompasses all sons (which includes daughters) of the human race. First we must find peace at home, then in our neighborhood, our town, our state, and our nation to ultimately embrace the whole world of humanity as our brothers and sisters of the one Earth we share. The phrase "You need to love your neighbor as yourself" means that we must extend love to the other next to us, who ultimately is our Self, inasmuch as he or she is part of that same higher Consciousness.

In the teachings of Jesus of Nazareth in the New Testament of the Holy Bible, we find in Matthew 5:44:

> Love your enemies and pray for those who persecute you, so
> that you may be sons of your Father who is in heaven;

These teachings go even further and ask us not to hate ever, no matter what is done to us. "You may be sons of your Father who is in heaven" really says "When you have the unlimited universal view of all things, like God, you know the other to be part of the same Consciousness." Jesus on the cross asked forgiveness for those who crucified him. This is also a demonstration of the unconditional love of God. Jesus knew that his persecutors were ignorant of what they were doing. They simply did not know that he was a teacher of higher Consciousness, a harbinger of a wider interpretation of the Torah.

The death and resurrection story of Jesus meant a new beginning: a new and deeper way of love, which, when implemented, would be the man or woman in God's own perfect image. The vertical part of the cross stands for the "I," the Father, or the eternal Light that comes across our life story, symbolized in the horizontal part of the cross. This "I" or "I AM" is permanent and our own true awareness, or our witness or seer within.

In the Bhagavad-Gita Gita (Chapter 18 of the Mahabarata), or the Song of God, I learned about the path of devotion *(bhakti)* to God, which is said to lead to the knowledge *(jnana)* of God, making mankind into the enlightened beings they are meant to be. Such an accomplished human being could only act righteously *(dharmic)*, harming no one. With such realized souls a new world of peace and love for all living beings will come to pass. In the same Gita, translated by Eknath Easwaran, in Chapter 12:18, "The Way of Love," is written:

> The devotee who looks upon friend and foe with equal regard, who is not buoyed up by praise nor cast down by blame, alike in heat and cold, pleasure and pain, free from selfish attachments, the same in honor and dishonor, quiet, ever full, in harmony everywhere, firm in faith – such a one is dear to me.

All people have hearts longing for the fulfillment of love. People look for love in relationships – a spouse, children, nephews, nieces and/or friends – but ultimately they will find that all these relations are of a temporary nature and that the relationship with God is the only permanent one. God is not easy to find because he is invisible to the eye and yet Mark 12:30, in the Holy Bible, emphasizes:

> ...and you shall love the Lord your God with all your heart, and with all your soul, and with all your mind, and with all your strength.

This commandment is a pathway, like the *bhakti* path, to find God.

The sacred texts of Hindus, Jews, Buddhists, Christians, and Muslims, and the revealed knowledge of the mystics all point to the fact that all humans are God's children created in his image, no matter what race they are or where they were born or by whose ideals and religions they were raised. God's message was and is always about love, which humanity, so far, has never fully implemented into daily life to the extent it was meant to be. The oneness of the human race can be understood through the scriptures and is, as yet, still mostly ignored, due to economical and political and subsequent social boundaries set by greed, which is always selfish. This type of selfishness I like to define as ego.

The power in our world today greatly reflects the accelerating power of the ego, which lives in man's individualized self. It is self-centered and separated from the universal God-Self. It cherishes its own opinions in disregard of others. This separate self-centered part of man is happy when it achieves its objectives of obtaining power over the other. This ego exists on the personal level, on the group level and on the level of governments. On a personal level such ego would say, when relating to others, "What is in it for me?" On the group level such ego might say, for instance, "Our church practices the right interpretation of the Bible. God is with us. We offer you God, come to our church!" On the governmental level, the ego often expresses itself by saying, "What or where is our national interest in this?"

If, symbolically speaking, God is the ocean, the individualized selves are the waves. These waves are part of God, part of the full body of water. Carried by the water, they are also the water. Today the waves have forgotten they are the water and fight the fight of survival of the fittest. I believe the illusion of this concept is dawning, out of which a new world is to be born.

I was raised in The Netherlands in the Protestant faith, which is iconoclastic. This meant one should not have any image in mind when thinking or reflecting on God. That God is the Light I learned at a very young age from my Sunday school teacher and I never wavered from that concept. Pictures or statues of the Virgin Mary, a crucified Jesus, or the saints were not part of my Dutch Protestant tradition and upbringing. I had always believed in God, but a God without form.

When I was a young librarian, I used to walk past the French Church in The Hague on the way to my work at the law library. On the façade of the church building stood engraved in large bold lettering: *"Je suis le Chemin, la Vérité et la Vie"* meaning, "I am the Way, the Truth and Life Itself."

Every day I looked at those words and repeated them to myself and pondered their meaning. Jesus, who spoke these words, did not imply he was "the only way" to God, as so often interpreted. When Jesus speaks, he is speaking from his God-Consciousness as a messenger of the Absolute, to reveal truth and the essential meaning of life. "I am the way, the truth and the life" meant that God is saying, "I, God, the father, the creator of all, am the way of revealing to humankind my true reality (truth) and life itself. That which is alive in you, *I am*. The ways by which you can find me are multiple as I am the total multiplicity, the all in which humanity plays its part." God created, and is still creating by his command, mankind. For humans to find who we are, we must return to our creator God, back to his divine plan for each of us, which will lead to the revelation of all sacred mysteries.

The way to God is never the exact same road for all people. There are as many ways as there are viewpoints, religions, beliefs and imaginings. Religions have either abstained from imaging or seeing God in form or have purposefully given him or her form. Many religious or spiritual leaders who spoke from their God Consciousness have appeared over the ages and led people back to the way of their creator. In Judaism these teachers were called prophets, in Christianity mystics and saints, and in Islam, the leader-revealer of Allah is the prophet Mohammed. In Hinduism we find the path to God through the studies of the *Vedas*, *Sutras* and *Upanishads* and their prescribed practices, as well as the auspicious sitting in the presence of an enlightened master. Similarly in Buddhist studies, the enlightened ones, the *bodhisattvas*, lay down spiritual practices to assist the seeker on the road to find nirvana or one's own Buddha nature.

In a sense, it does not really matter which religion is practiced as long as its basic principles lead to respecting human life as a gift from God, which should be lived by honoring the highest principles of one's innermost sense of morality. All religions have God in whatever name as their base.

In 1986, my dedication to Sai Baba had led to a new journey, the study of the ancient sacred teachings of India. From those texts arose the knowledge that all forms in our world are God's forms. The Hindu concepts of God became helpful in re-educating and expanding my awareness to understand that if God exists everywhere, he also exists in the statue, the stone or the painting a devotee uses for worship. I had to admit that no matter what form people worship, it is the desire to know and love God that counts. For some, worshiping a form of God may be a beginning spiritual tool and when deepening occurs, that form may gradually fade, as more of the formless light stands revealed, the Light that transcends all things known.

Chapter Forty-nine

Hypnotic Spell

I believe that all major events in life happen on a schedule or soul imprint of the divine. We come into this world with a kind of internal blueprint of experiences that need to happen, because of the lesson we came to learn from them. We are seldom aware of this on a conscious level. Sometimes though, by looking backward, we can clearly see how our soul plan is unfolding by intuiting the reason behind our experiences.

I had accepted a new position at a mortgage company, but when the president heard that I had plans for six weeks in India the next summer, he forced me to make a choice between the two, as the company wanted me on the job that summer. I chose Sai Baba and walked away from an interesting job for good.

Then Ellen, a former colleague, called and said, "Ella, some of my friends and I are going to attend a hypnotic therapy session for weight loss and it would be fun if you could join us." I always wondered why Ellen called, because she knew I was not particularly overweight. I was fond of Ellen, a spiritual friend from my financial company days. I had not seen her for a while, and first wanted to oblige, but remembering my Astara teachings, I said to her, "I want to point out that according to the mystical teachings, hypnotism should be avoided for a spiritual aspirant." I felt an enormous reluctance to participate in a weight-loss hypnotism session.

At the time of Ellen's call, I was in excellent health. I always ate healthy and exercised, but suddenly the idea of losing some extra pounds, the easy way, began to have an attraction for me. Contrary to my better judgment, I began to reason that a weight loss session could not affect my vibrant health but only add to it. Finally, in total disregard of my own spiritual warning, I decided to join Ellen and her friends.

The session was scheduled in the early evening at the Ramada Inn, on the eighth of March 1994. As I entered the hotel conference room, I was shocked to find myself amongst seriously obese participants. I had an acute sense of being in the wrong place, but stayed on despite those feelings. The hypnotist, who claimed to be a devout Christian man from California, announced, "I will use a new method of hypnotism never used before. It is a method combining hypnotism with neuro-linguistic programming." He proudly added, "My program is the only way around to obtain results of losing weight permanently. I guarantee that this method will work."

The session began. The hypnotist guided us first into states of complete relaxation. He subsequently planted a thought in our subconscious that overeating would cause the worst thing ever to happen to us. He said, "Image your worst possible fear."

At that instant the symptoms of *Kundalini* flashed before my mind's eye. I had been free from *Kundalini* suffering for almost eight years and my states of altered consciousness seemed to belong to the past. I was perhaps not quite under the hypnotist's spell when I thought, "How incredibly unfair to connect the minds of desperate people to negative thought patterns!" Even as I fell deeper and deeper into a hypnotic state, I remained in control of my mind. I fumed, "How dare he...how dare this man make us believe that the terror of our worst fears will restrain us from the affliction of over-eating."

The hypnotist slowly brought us into yet deeper states of the unconscious and stated, "Those of you who meditate will go quicker into deeper levels of the hypnotic trance."

The announcement frightened me, as this applied to me... I felt an enormous impulse to leave the room. But with the notion that my sudden departure would upset the hypnotist and the participants, and embarrass my friends, I stayed on, even though reluctantly. In my inner awareness, I called on my higher Self to stand by me, while the hypnotist led the participants through the different doorways of the subconscious. The hypnotist described in gross detail the cancer that would grow and spread in us if we were to overeat. By now my inner being was screaming, "Never, never will this happen to me."

When the session finally ended, I stood up wondering why I was there amidst overeaters. I quickly left. "It is best to forget what happened here and go home," I said to myself. But by the time I came home, I had lost my appetite completely. A mysterious aversion to food had taken hold of me. I was no longer in control of my own body, but seriously caught under the spell of the hypnotic neuro-linguistic programming. My own will had been usurped. I became acutely aware how food is really a major part of the joy of daily living. My life suddenly became gray without meaning. I had been programmed that eating would trigger negative emotions in me and no matter how hard I tried, I was unable to shake off the induced questionable instructions.

I began to lose weight. I felt I was living in a strange dream.

This went on for weeks. One time, when I was on the road with Jon, I wanted to test myself and see if I could enjoy ice cream. We stopped at my favorite Dairy Queen ice cream place. I ordered the smallest soft–ice cream cone and began to eat it with apprehension. To my surprise I still loved eating it! I hopefully assumed that the hypnotic spell was beginning to fade. The following night, I had a nightmare. I dreamed I had cancer with only five more days to live. I was shown that I had a hole in my solar plexus, the area located above the navel, where the energy fields of the human willpower reside. The dream scared me. "Had a permanent change taken place inside of me without my approval? Had I freely given away my own will power?"

I called the hypno-therapist in California to find out. After I discussed my state of being, he said, "Nothing can be done for you. The input was irreversible." I was devastated, but decided that I did not need to accept his concept of irreversibility. After all, the therapist was not God and I believed I could always call on the higher power of the divine. But, being acutely aware that I had knowingly overstepped a spiritual boundary, I began to have panic attacks.

Caught in a daunting spiritual and mental dilemma, I turned to my best friend Beverley for advice. I admired Bev's clarity of thinking and the practical ways by which she approached life. I phoned and recounted my hypnotic horror story. Beverley was a good listener and understood immediately I was in some sort of serious trouble. She advised, "Ella, I cannot help you directly. Through my connections with the School of Music I know of a hypnotist who assists students to overcome stage fright during their university performances. This hypnotist has an excellent reputation. Consult with her. If someone is able to understand what is going on with you, I think that person is Donna."

I immediately phoned Donna and was lucky that I could see her the next morning. Donna was a calm-mannered person who sat me down across from her and asked that I tell her my story. After I finished she fell quiet for some time and then said, "Ella, that hypnotist acted in a highly unethical manner, but he is correct to say that the hypnotic input cannot be reversed. However you can select your own most clear statement regarding eating or overeating to create a new input into the subconscious mind, while I bring you again in a trance state." I sat for a while in meditation... Then prayerful positive words regarding food flooded my consciousness, connecting me to my soul essence. I felt a sensation of energy release happening deep inside me. Within days the panic attacks vanished and soon I could eat again.

Later in the year I saw my friend Ellen, who told me that her middle-aged and overweight friend, Richard, who was programmed under hypnosis with us, had died from cancer two months after our weight-loss session. How fortunate I felt to have escaped such an outcome.

Chapter Fifty

Shirdi Sai Baba

Fully recovered from the hypnotic session, I was able to organize a group-pilgrimage to India, which included six devotees from our center. We all loved being in India again, but soon after our arrival, conflict broke out between the group members, who were faced with disease, excessive heat, problems with housing and a rigorous ashram schedule. But, when our group was called for an interview twice during our five-week stay, the spirit of unity and joy rekindled.

A wondrous event took place in one of the interviews. I was sitting on the floor of Baba's lotus flower house in his Whitefield ashram, minutes after I had my turn to speak with him. I was sitting in a relaxed fashion leaning backwards, and completely tuned out what was going on between other devotees and Sai

Baba. I fell into some kind of trance-like state... I looked upward toward the ceiling, and became aware that streams of liquid gold appeared in mid-air, one large band after another covering the whole room. These bands of pure living scintillating gold moved over the devotees' heads in a fanlike, circular slow motion. Mesmerized, I watched, filled with awe-struck wonder, as I had never seen anything like it before. I knew that in the moment when all my reasoning stopped, the invisible divine became visible to me. I never told anyone about this event, but the wonderment remains with me to this day.

When I left with my friend Annette for Bombay, I was still in high spirits about what I had witnessed. We were invited to stay with the Agarwals at their Yuhu Beach home in Bombay. I had met the Agarwals in Eugene, when they visited their daughter Alka, a graduate student at the university. We had become close friends. I felt greatly honored when our wonderful Bombay hosts kindly offered to take us on a pilgrimage to Shirdi Sai Baba's tomb in Shirdi.

Shirdi Sai Baba, a well-recognized Indian saint, became known during the later nineteenth and early twentieth century when he took residence in Shirdi, a small insignificant village northeast of Bombay. He was sixteen years old when he first appeared sitting under the neem tree in Shirdi in a *samadhi*-like state, absorbed in the eternal vibrations of the Absolute. No one knew where he came from and he was obviously no ordinary lad. Soon people flocked to him for help with health and family problems, which he offered freely. Sai Baba of Shirdi wore the clothing of a Muslim, but had markings on his forehead like a Hindu. He would sleep one night in a temple and the next in a mosque. Though a *Siddha* (he who has attained Shivahood or enlightenment in Shaivism), he always acted like a *sadhaka* (spiritual student). He was humble and completely selfless. Shirdi Sai performed miracles and helped the poor. In his biography *Shri Sai Satcharita or The Wonderful Life and Teachings of Shri Sai Baba*, adapted from the original Marathi book by Hemadpant, by Nagesh Vasudev Gunaji, B.A., LL.B., Shirdi Sai Baba says the following to his devotees:

> Be wherever you like, do whatever you choose, remember this well that all what you do is known by Me. I am the inner Ruler of all and seated in their hearts. I envelope all the creatures, the movable and immovable world. I am the Controller – the wirepuller of the show of this Universe.

According to the Puttaparthi Sai Baba, Shirdi Sai, before his death in 1918, had indicated that he would reincarnate eight years later. Sai Baba's birth date was said to be November 23, 1926. Thirteen-year-old Sathya Narayana Radju, later named Sathya Sai Baba, declared he was that Sai Baba of Shirdi, come again. I learned that despite Baba's declaration, most Shirdi Sai Baba devotees and the official Shirdi Sai organization do not adhere to the myth that the Puttaparthi Sai was the reincarnation of their Saint of Shirdi. I understand that it is even forbidden for their members to visit Puttaparthi.

Our trip to Shirdi took place during the monsoon period. The heavy rains had been pouring down for some time and most roads to Shirdi were in a deplorable state. The chauffeur of the Agarwal family kept us safe by avoiding treacherous holes and challenging traffic situations. To reach our goal we drove nine hours under heavy dark-gray skies often producing pouring rain while we passed through luscious green landscapes of rolling hills.

Upon arrival in the small village of Shirdi, the four of us were most eager to visit the Shirdi temple called *Shirdi Sai Baba Samadhi-Mandir*, before checking into our hotel. The temple stood in a narrow street. We had to leave our shoes with a special shoe attendant, cross the street barefooted and trudge through sticky mud toward the temple. Inside the Shirdi temple, an atmosphere of complete otherworldliness immediately took hold of my being. An immense stillness entered my heart, as I was being touched by the old saint's invisible divine emanations. The presence of these higher vibrations quieted my spirit.

Afterward, alone in my hotel room, I took a bath to scrub my crusty muddy feet, rested and meditated. On one of the walls I noticed a Shirdi Sai Baba photograph. I focused on this picture with love and devotion and made an inner connection with the image. For a moment I was elevated to the higher realm of consciousness, which was so intensely powerful that it made my body shake and tremble. Then a flash of golden light sparked from the picture. It was as if God was saying, "I am here also!" Later on, I realized that it was my own intense devotion calling for that higher Light, which as the underlying principle of all there is, responded.

The next morning we attended Shirdi Sai Baba's *darshan*, which is the seeing of his marble image on top of the tomb that holds his physical remains and the receiving of the blessing of the cosmic energy that continuously emanates from it. A throng of Shirdi devotees and visitors shared a tiny space to touch the shrine, while barefooted Vedic priests performed a *puja* of Vedic rituals on top of the cream-colored marble tomb. The priests ceremonially washed the statue of Shirdi Sai several times and then dressed it. Squeezed by the crowds that were pushing me forward, I was still able to throw a bouquet of roses on top of the *samadhi* tomb as my gesture of reverence and love for the saint. The whole scene made such a profound impression on me that I wondered whether I could have been a Shirdi Sai devotee in a prior life.

Chapter Fifty-one

Book of Bhrighu

Back in Bombay, my friend Salek surprised me when he said, "You have an appointment with Mr. Pandya, who will do a reading for you from the *Book of Bhrighu*." To have a reading from the *Book of Bhrighu* had been my long-time wish since I read Phyllis Krystal's book *The Ultimate Experience*. In that book, Phyllis describes the story of a *pandit* who had a collection of ancient palm leaves, maybe thousands of years old, on which the destinies of the people who would be coming to consult them were written. The *pandit* Mrs. Krystal met had died, but his son continued the work of his father.

When I walked through the door, Mr. Pandya was sitting behind a large desk doing some writing in what looked like a large checkbook. He asked me to spell seven hundred in English and seemingly did not pay any further attention to me. The house was an old-fashioned concrete building and the room I had entered was sparsely furnished. The walls were whitewashed and bare. While the *pandit* continued his personal work, I called on the Divine. I wanted the reading to serve only a spiritual purpose, and I asked God, "Please be present during the reading. May I only hear what you want me to know. May it be your reading."

In general, the palm leaves that are read correspond to the length of one's shadow measured in the sunlight. With monsoon clouds hanging low over Bombay, there was no direct sunlight to measure my shadow. Instead, the *pandit* took some measurement with a compass of the palm of my hands and then proceeded flipping through a stack of palm leaves from which he pulled several leaves presumably pertaining to my life. He read that I had been a woman Shirdi Sai Baba devotee in a prior life. In that life, I had moved from India to America. Now I lived in America and was drawn to reconnect with the Shirdi Sai and Puttaparthi Sai emanations of light. I would like to add that Mr. Pandya had no prior knowledge that I just visited the Sai Baba shrine in Shirdi.

Earlier in the Sathya Sai Baba ashram I had hoped to receive a mantra for meditation. Mantras are often given by one's guru or intuitively imprinted during meditation. I had received my mantra on the inner level, but one word seemed to be missing. The *pandit* said, "You should recite a mantra three times a day," and gave me the exact mantra I had received earlier, but with the addition of the missing word. This perplexed me, since I realized that he could not have known on a conscious level that I had asked for a mantra, or that I was looking for a missing word as part of that mantra. The *pandit* furthermore revealed from the palm leaves, "You will be writing books like the author Phyllis Krystal." He continued to tell me how my life would continue from year to year, what experiences would come and where and at what age I would die. The reading was in-depth, personal and intense. The information drew me deeply within my soul-self. Suddenly I was filled with the exhilaration of ecstasy. I felt myself glowing, touched by the essence of divine light. When I looked at the *pandit,* I noted that he too was glowing with light. His face shone radiantly, as I felt mine did. Mr. Pandya spontaneously took my hands in his and for a moment we shared the depth of oneness in God. The beauty of the meeting stayed with me for several days.

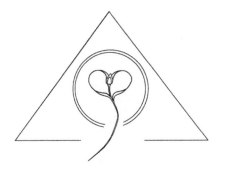

PART VII

Pathway of *Kundalini*

Chapter Fifty-two

Kundalini Returns

Before I continue my story, I want to give my reader a better understanding about the meaning of *Kundalini*, which I discovered much later than when the first signs of *Kundalini* awakening appeared, as described in Part IV, Chapter Twenty-eight, "Breakdown." I want the reader to know that *Kundalini* is a direct sacred pathway to God-realization, but for most not an easy one. As *Kundalini* knowledge did not come to me all at once, I want to illustrate throughout the next stories in my book what happened to me in response to dealing with this God-force.

Kundalini is the cosmic evolutionary energy we all possess. In India, the power of *Kundalini*, also called the serpent power, has been known throughout the ages. India has always been a country where exceptional men and women willingly renounced the objective world to find union with God. In ancient times, accomplished souls who had found liberation from the bondage of the mind's limitations, or ego awareness, were called *rishis*. Many *rishis* had knowledge of the Absolute or God through clairaudience, the hearing beyond the normal range of sounds, and clairvoyance, the seeing beyond the three-dimensional world. Clairvoyantly, they noted along the spine of the human body seven major vortexes of energy that look like wheels and move in spinning motion clockwise or counterclockwise in a variety of colors. They called the wheel-like vortexes, *chakras*. The first *chakra*, called the root or the *muladhara chakra,* is located at the bottom of the spine. In all human beings, the cosmic *Kundalini* energy lies dormant, rolled up like a snake in this first *chakra*. *Kundalini* awakening happens when the *granti*-lock, an ethereal protective lock of nerves that keeps the energy in the root *chakra* from escaping, breaks. *Kundalini* then is activated and travels through the central spinal canal, the *sushumna*, to the sixth and seventh *chakra*, where illumination or God-realization will take place at the time designated by *Shakti*, the divine Mother. The sixth *chakra* is also called the seat of God, the eye of God, *ajna* or *trikuti*.

The *Kundalini* activation is sometimes performed by unqualified people, as was likely the case with me when Nadia broke the *granti*-lock during the two initiation ceremonies of Huna mystical shamanic-healing. The safest way to receive *Kundalini* initiation is from an enlightened guru, who has the god-power and is thereby qualified to raise this cosmic force. After long practices of various yogas, as I did with Astara *(lama yoga), Kundalini* may rise spontaneously when the two ethereal channels called the *ida* and *pingala* (the polarities of left and right, female and male or the moon and the sun) are in balance, which puts such considerable pressure on the *granti*-lock that it breaks, thereby bringing the *Kundalini* energy force upwards. Detailed information about how this may be accomplished can be found in an excellent book on this subject entitled *Kundalini and the Third Eye* by my mystic-teacher Earlyne Chaney and William L. Messick.

I have been on the path of *Kundalini* since my breakdown in the summer of 1985. My life has never been the same, as the breakdown involved the breaking of the nerves near the crown *chakra* where the human conditioning is held in place. These nerves, the *dwesha* and *raga*, are of an ethereal nature, and form part of the astral subtle body. They are not physical. The human conditioning could be likened to a house well constructed to function in the world around it. When *Kundalini* happens, that house of conditioning, that human ego, gets smashed as the foundation that holds the ego is stripped away. As a first reaction, enormous anxieties and fear follow because the house of ego has lost its solid footing. The shifting of the structure brings about altered states of mind and physical changes never experienced before. The breakage causes a diminished state of ego, and opens new channels to receive more of the light of God. In my experience this sudden opening was enormously scary and it set me apart from my fellow humans. As a reader may, at one time or another, experience the same shift, I want to share my own ups and downs in this process while going through the awakening stages.

Besides receiving the enormous blessings of more light, I, in all modesty, admit that the process of spiritual knowledge is still evolving and unfolding in me. Besides the blissfulness of seeing light and knowing God, there can be states of terror when *Shakti-Kundalini* rises and brings up the mind's conditioning to be burned by her fiery firepower. *Kundalini*'s severity of suffering depends on one's individual karma. This book has an Appendix called *Checklist of Symptoms of Kundalini*, which lists *Kundalini* symptoms alphabetically as a guideline for those interested in, and those already on the *Kundalini* path.

In early 1994, after Donna helped restore my appetite after the weight-loss hypnotic programming, I suddenly felt intense *Kundalini* symptoms stirring my physical being like the ones I suffered after my breakdown in 1985. It came as a complete surprise, because during the last eight years these symptoms had not hindered me. In the past I had found release by listening to the sacred sounds of Schubert's *Ave Maria* or by connecting with divine power through meditation. When I focused on God, screams would rip through my throat involuntarily, making my body shake uncontrollably. I became frightened, as before, by an immense fear of going insane. I phoned my former alternative healer friends hoping for relief. My special friend, Grace, who in the past could release the intensity of *Kundalini* by pounding on my back while speaking in tongues, had recently died. Another friend from my alternative healing days suggested, "Ella, get in touch with Mr. X on the East Coast. I know him as the most powerful healer in our country. People from all over the world consult with him." I followed Orly's advice. Mr. X, on the phone, led me through imaginary light meditations, which helped to ease the symptoms temporarily. Unfortunately, soon I was unable to live through the day without his help. I had become attached to this man, like one clinging to a straw.

In the midst of re-experiencing these intense cosmic energies, I asked myself, "How did it happen again?" While reflecting, I remembered how my deep-seated fear of altered states had flashed before my inner eye when the Californian hypno-therapist asked the participants to imagine their worst fear. During my hypnotic state I had called on God to stand by me and I believe it was the already freed divine *shakti* energy that responded, causing a full upward surge of *Kundalini*, not to hinder me, but to bring me to my ultimate home in God. To live my life with *Kundalini* was never a choice for me because once the cosmic energy is activated it will never return to its slumbering position at the bottom of the spine. My fear of *Kundalini* was tied to the experience of altered states, which I call a falling out of the normal dimension.

Today I believe that, no matter what happens to me, the only certainty I have is that *Kundalini* will ultimately bring me to the final state on the spiritual path, namely self-realization. I have no doubt that before I came into this world it was written in my soul's blueprint that I came to experience the forces of *Kundalini* not as a curse but as an ultimate blessing.

Once again, reawakened *Kundalini* symptoms manifested themselves as before: the feeling of ants crawling up my spine towards the crown *chakra*, the tingling electrical-like sensations, the pins and needles, and shaking vibrations coming up from the root *chakra* and moving towards the crown *chakra* inside the *sushumna* (ethereal channel inside the spine). These sensations caused severe pressure on the top of my head. Sometimes I noticed a wave bringing heat up through all the cells of my body, one wave followed quickly by another, working in the brain as if a burning process was going on. I felt dizzy and nauseated, but could not vomit. I felt stabbing pains in my big toes and spasms in my legs, back and head. Sometimes the intensity of *Kundalini* would take place at night resulting in sleeplessness. When it changed to day-time, I felt sick, confused and disoriented. Inside my head I sensed a constant circular motion as if I was hanging on a string that was attached to the crown *chakra* at the top of my head. I felt various sensations of other magnetic fields moving through my physical being, bringing alteration to the physical, emotional and spiritual realms of my being. The altered states once again produced an indescribable feeling of separateness from the rest of the world and yet I could function intellectually in the outer world. I played the game of life, while inside I was constantly falling apart.

One night the *Kundalini* swept slowly and softly through my physical heart. My heart rocked back and forth and I thought I had a heart attack, but after the rocking was over, the *Kundalini* moved upward to my head again. As I became once more a wit-ness to my symptoms, I wrote in my diary one morning, "I witnessed a different *Kundalini* rising. It opened my throat *chakra* and penetrated it with loud piercing sounds and blue light." Times of increased involuntary body movements, called *kriyas*, followed, which made my body shake without prior notice. I did not know at that time that these sensations are all quite normal in the *Kundalini* process.

In my desperation, I wanted to take the invitation of the healer on the East Coast to stay with him and his wife for a few weeks and have energy work done on a daily basis. When I asked the healer, "How much will you charge per day?" and he answered, "three hundred dollars," it shocked me. Despite my dire need for healing, I still functioned mentally well enough to know that this was an unacceptable fee for me. I permanently severed my connection with Mr. X.

I began to experience panic attacks, making it hard to live

through the day. Without any help in sight, I prayed for a sign to shed light on the situation. *Kundalini* had distorted my dream-life and most the time I could make neither head nor tails out of it. One morning, to my astonishment, I woke up and remembered that Velma, a well-known Sai Baba devotee, had appeared in my dream. Desperate for any kind of help, I called her at the spur of the moment. Velma referred me to a yoga teacher in California, who told me over the phone, "Ella, I just know the right person for you, namely a medical doctor who has personally experienced the power of *Kundalini*."

Chapter Fifty-three

Help Offered

The doctor was Dennis Gersten, a psychiatrist in San Diego. Extremely anxious to get in touch with him, I called his office as soon as it opened the next morning. When the doctor's secretary asked, "How can I help you?" I said, "Please tell Dr. Gersten that I must speak with him as soon as possible; tell him I am in an emergency!" The inner experience and the effect on the physical level by the cosmic force were so intense that I felt certain that my life was in imminent danger.

The secretary replied, "The doctor will call you back as soon as he can." I waited anxiously near the phone all through the day and yet tried, with all my might, to practice patience. Finally, around seven in the evening, the psychiatrist called. We had an hour-long conversation. In the end he said, "You are probably thinking that you are going insane, but I can assure you that you are not insane. I deal with insane people every day, so I know!" I felt relieved. Dr. Gersten then recounted his own *Kundalini* experiences to me. To speak for the first time with another human being who actually understood what I was going through felt very reassuring and it uplifted my spirit immediately. Dr. Gersten urged me to buy an important book on the subject written by Dr. Lee Sannella, a Californian psychiatrist, called *The Kundalini Experience*.

Two days after my phone conversation, I finished reading the recommended book. What joy it was to find my own *Kundalini* symptoms amongst the many case histories recounted in *The Kundalini Experience*. Dr. Sannella's book proved that my experiences were real and that I was not losing my mind. To read that I was not alone in the *Kundalini* experience was a tremendous comfort. I recommend this book to everyone who has *Kundalini* symptoms as a first start to understand this phenomenon rarely known in the West.

I also want to give you other techniques to help with *Kundalini* symptoms that I learned from Dr. Gersten. During my talk with him, he instructed me to use breathing techniques and visualizations to deal with the excess *Kundalini* energy in my body. These techniques can also be found in his later published book, *Are You Getting Enlightened or Losing Your Mind?* Dr. Gersten also gave a warning: "Take *Kundalini* seriously, do not fight it, and learn to surrender to it." His breathing techniques were designed to lower the *Kundalini* energy in the body by inhaling to the count of four, holding the breath to the count of four, then exhaling to the count of eight, and to repeat as needed three to four times a day. He also told me to visualize the cosmic energy escaping out of the top of my head, like the steam leaving a pressure cooker. With the implementation of these techniques and my new understanding of the *shakti* energy, my anxieties leveled off.

Besides using Dr. Gersten's methods, I also began to develop techniques of my own, which I can highly recommend. The most important help I can give to a *Kundalini* sufferer is to first of all surrender to the power of the cosmic energy, which will reduce many of the unwanted symptoms. One can surrender to the force by speaking affirmations aloud or on the inner level by stating,

"I am not in control of *Kundalini*, God is. I welcome *Kundalini*. I am open and unafraid, knowing all is in divine hands and for my ultimate benefit." For success it is best to repeat this type of affirmation often in your own words like a mantra and believe in it. This method has worked for me and I know it will work for you, because as you surrender, this tremendous energy is unhampered and free to rise up through the body without injuring it. Obstructing the force by fear leads to pain and unbearable suffering, which could produce insanity.

One can also imagine the spine as the divine flute, the *murali* of Lord Krishna, and its holes the *chakras* through which the divine breath needs to flow fully and uninterrupted. In other words, "Surrender by emptying out that which is the ego-self, which is your resistance, and allow the divine *Shakti-Kundalini* to do her work. That *Shakti* is the only one who really knows and understands and even grants this process. Be unafraid to die from it. Say always, 'Yes' to it. Observe it and love it. Know this power to be your ultimate best friend." After following this method of help, when surrender is truly happening, your *sushumna* (inner spinal canal) becomes hollow like the flute. Then God can blow his divine breath through, granting the total experience of divine love, which is oneness with him, forever inseparable.

Chapter Fifty-four

Guided to the Third Eye Book

By using my own mantras of surrender and some breathing and visualization techniques, I slowly began to see how to adjust and move with the cosmic energy. In a few months I was able once more to travel to India. It was late summer 1994. After a few weeks' stay in Sai Baba's Whitefield ashram, my friend Annette and I strolled to Sai Towers Restaurant for some strong coffee. We sat down at a table covered with a dark red cotton tablecloth full of greasy stains, not uncommon in India. Sai Towers Restaurant was a hub where devotees from all parts of the world gathered for spiritual discussions, good coffee or a simple Indian meal. While we were slowly sipping our coffee, two young men walked into the restaurant and asked if they could join us. We were happy to share our table and while Annette began a lively conversation with one man-devotee, I chatted with the other. The men had just come from a private interview with Sai Baba and were in high spirits.

The person I talked with was in his late twenties and came from California. He was dressed in a white *punjabi*, as worn by most men in the ashram. He told me that he had suffered from severe problems caused by a sudden awakened *Kundalini* earlier that year. As my reactivation of *Kundalini* symptoms had also happened during that time, I felt an immediate kinship with the young man. We went into a deep discussion about the various unusual experiences we had, which are sometimes impossible to explain to those not in the awakening process. After one hour of talks, the young man stood up and said, "Come with me; I know something that will really help you." He took me to Sai Towers Bookshop, just one store away from the restaurant. He led me to a thick book with a bright yellow cover on one of the shelves and said, "This is one of the best books in India on the subject of *Kundalini*." The book was written by Dr. B.S. Goel, entitled, *Third Eye and Kundalini, an Experiential Account of Journey from Dust to Divinity*. I had no idea at that time that this book would forever change my life.

Without any hesitation, I not only bought the *Third Eye* book but also *Psycho-analysis and Meditation* by the same author. With the two books tightly tucked under my arm, I walked back to my small rented space in the women's dormitory at the ashram. I settled down on my air mattress on the cement floor, draped the mosquito netting around me, and began to read. When my other four roommates appeared and seriously interrupted my reading, I knew I needed other sleeping arrangements. I yearned to have more quiet time to study Dr. Goel's book from cover to cover. When I heard that one of our group members was leaving for the United States, I quickly decided to take over her privately rented room in a simple but charming house occupied by an Indian family of four. The house was surrounded by a lovely garden and located on a country road in the small town of Kadugodi, close to the ashram. I intended to spend lots of time there immersing myself in the various aspects of the *Kundalini* phenomena, as expounded by Dr. Goel in his writing.

Third Eye and Kundalini is a narrative of the spiritual revelation of knowledge in the life of Dr. B.S. Goel, in somewhat of a diary format. He writes:

> Due to faulty practice of yogic postures and *pranayama* my
> *Kundalini* once got uncontrollably activated in 1964 and
> I went into a state of unbearable depression after passing
> through an initial state of ecstacy.

Dr. Goel calls this type of awakening an abortive awakening, because the *Kundalini* arousal did not have the grace of God. Much of the *Third Eye* book is about his suffering from depression and how he sought help through psychoanalysis. The book also narrates that in one of Dr. Goel's most desperate hours, a Swami appeared in his room asking if he could wait there because he had to visit someone in the building who was not home yet. While waiting, the Swami learns about Dr. Goel's interest in yoga and about his depression. Without hesitation, the Swami taught him his technique of meditation and gave him hope for the cure of his depression. Dr. Goel realized that this meditation technique was God-sent. Along with the psychoanalysis, it helped him to alleviate some of his suffering. But once he understood the superiority of the divinely guided *Kundalini* process, he gave up psychoanalysis as a healing tool for the psyche.

Dr. Goel's *Third Eye* book lists the *Kundalini* symptoms that often resemble mental and physical diseases, as well as psychological ailments. Some are included in the *Kundalini* symptoms list in my Appendix. Dr. Goel writes that he suffered from schizoid trends, insomnia, extreme restlessness and delirium. He adds that on the physical and psychological levels one may experience occasional loss of hunger, loss of confidence, fear of death, fear of insanity and increased sexual feelings, which all can emerge quickly.

Readers who experience one of the symptoms described so far should know that most people suffer from time to time from some of the mentioned symptoms, but this does not indicate that their *Kundalini* has awakened. The most important indication of genuine *Kundalini* arousal is that bad and good states emerge alternately in the process. I too have observed the same. For me, the tuning in to divine energy and the surrendering to the *Kundalini* process produced healing like the deep meditation did for Dr. Goel.

Since my *Kundalini* awakening, I became aware of strong energy movements that last about half a day in which the removal of my psychological bindings takes place. This often affects my mental realm and can cause physical pain. The rest of the day milder *Kundalini* energy release usually follows in my spine and head, often accompanied by joyous blissful feelings. I want readers to know that if their symptoms follow this pattern, they need not panic because release is close at hand.

I am certain that there are patients in mental institutions misdiagnosed as having a mental illness but who, in fact, are going through *Kundalini* awakening. Dr. Gersten mentioned in my phone conversation with him that he tries to find such patients, as he believes himself to be one of the few psychiatrists able to recognize the difference.

I learned much from reading Dr. Goel's *Third Eye* book,

especially that the *Kundalini* is literally the Goddess Mother, the *Shakti,* who with her powerful cosmic energy rebuilds the whole nervous system in the body. The *Kundalini* process forces the individual to unlearn all that was learned, and this unlearning releases the spirit from accumulated karmic bindings. *Shakti* will ultimately free the spirit, called *jiva,* to go back to Shiva, the unbound birthless and deathless consciousness. When *Shakti* and Shiva unite, self-realization takes place. At that point all body identification leaves and the greater Self, which is God, emerges.

I include a quick checklist of essential characteristics of a risen *Kundalini* (for further information, see my Appendix):

Waves of powerful energy moving up the backbone, like the movements of a snake.

Shaking of the spinal column and/or the head in perceptible motion.

Extreme pressure near the crown *chakra,* located on the top of the head.

No voluntary control of deep weeping, laughter or extreme screaming.

A tongue coated with thick white saliva.

Nausea.

Fear of insanity, as the alternate states of consciousness cannot, as yet, be understood.

Chapter Fifty-five
An Invitation to India

During my absence in India Jon had begun to remodel the kitchen, but soon realized that he bit off more than he could chew. On our way home from the local airport he told me about the project. When I entered the living room, I had to jump over stacks of dishes, pots and pans, jars, and cans of staple foods spread out over the entire floor. It was quite a mess and mice had gotten into the dog food, leaving droppings as noticeable evidence.

I was also greeted by a large oil painting of Sai Baba, prominently placed on our dining room wall. Every time I had come back from India, Jon had welcomed me with a newly created piece of art, but this Baba oil was the most beautiful and life-like piece he had ever done. Jon deeply believed in Sai Baba as the modern-day avatar. He detested travel, but always kept urging me to go to India to see Baba for the two of us.

A young man who had been part of our center's spiritual group in India asked if he could stay with us during the next school year to finish his studies at the university. With our own children gone, Jon and I were of course thrilled to have Chris live with us. Chris immediately offered help with the finishing of our kitchen project and we had a lot of fun working together. Chris was a wonderful young man dedicated to the spiritual way of life. Every day, in the early morning hours, I heard him play the tabla (set of Indian drums) and sing *bhajans* with his melodious voice in the meditation center on the ground floor. His living with us made me feel I was still in an Indian ashram.

Since the return of serious *Kundalini* symptoms in early 1994, I noticed that every time I visited India, my *Kundalini* symptoms faded, but as soon as came home, I again was faced with that tremendous *shakti* power. While I was practicing surrender to the force, a video entitled *An Interview with Dr. B.S. Goel* came to my attention. It was the same Dr. Goel who had written *Third*

Eye and Kundalini, which had become one of my best reference books on *Kundalini.* I ordered the video, viewed it, and learned that meditation camps were held on a regular basis in Dr. Goel's ashram. I immediately felt drawn to attend the camp and wrote a letter to his ashram in Haryana to obtain more information, but unfortunately no answer came.

Time went by, and in early 1996, I again felt a strong pull to see Dr. Goel, the expert supreme on *Kundalini,* who was undoubtedly able to answer all my unresolved questions regarding my personal struggles with the unleashed cosmic force. I studied the map to his ashram included on the last page of the *Third Eye* book. The ashram is located in Bhigaan, Haryana, north of Delhi. As I had never been to Delhi before, I felt wary of going without any knowledge of the local situation and without having heard from the ashram administration that meditation camps were still offered. In India I also needed the name of a trustworthy taxi-driver to pick me up at the airport and bring me to the ashram. I went into deep meditation and spoke to my innermost Self: "If you want me to go, please send me an invitation to India!" I immediately regretted what I had asked for. After all, "Who was I to ask for a personal invitation from God?" It felt absolutely presumptuous and I quickly tried to forget the whole matter.

Nevertheless, a week later, my friend Alka called from Bombay and said, "Ella, you have an invitation to India. My brother Sanjive is getting married and the wedding is going to be a grand event." She informed me that the two to three weeks' wedding ceremonies would commence in Bombay for the groom's family and friends. Consequently, the groom, his family and guests would board the train for Delhi (a train ride with one overnight), where a chartered air-conditioned bus would bring the wedding party to the bride's city, Chandigarh, at the foothills of the Himalayas. I looked at the map of India, and was flabbergasted to see that Dr. Goel's ashram was somewhere between Delhi and Chandigarh. Still I had doubts and meditated for months on whether I was called to go. Suddenly the brilliant diamond-light appeared illumining my question. I took it as a sure sign and immediately started getting ready for the Indian wedding, a possible stay at the ashram of Dr. Goel, and a trip to southern India to pay my respects to Sai Baba.

I left in early May 1996. Alka welcomed me at Bombay International Airport. The family's chauffeur drove us to her private flat where I would sleep the next nights. I loved India. I was always drawn by the spiritual vibration of the country, which I could even feel in cosmopolitan Bombay (Mumbai) despite the extreme heat, humidity, smells, noisy chaotic traffic and poverty. Bombay, located on the Arabian Ocean, with a population of well over eleven million, spreads out over poverty-stricken shantytowns, opulent districts for the lucky few and areas of many multi-leveled apartments for the many. The palm trees, bougainvillea, and other tropical trees and plants I had come to love when I lived in the tropics always provided that touch of home. As a vegetarian I enjoyed looking at the cows, however meager, as they stood peacefully amidst busy traffic looking for a hard-to-come-by meal. The cows, holy and respected, seemed to have that awareness that no harm would come to them.

Every morning Alka's family car appeared at my flat to take me to the main family house on the Arabian Ocean where wedding preparations had been in progress for weeks. Family and friends were coming and going. I watched a *pandit* performing hour-long Vedic wedding *pujas* on Sanjive, the groom. I did not fully understand the rituals, but had no doubt that the deeper meaning was for purification to ready the groom for the upcoming wedding ceremonies in northern India. The kindness and hospitality I received during the ceremonial events warmed my heart. My hosts invited me for a special celebration that was for women alone. The ladies were invited into one of the bedrooms, where soon musicians appeared. The women, both young and old, in their best delightful brightly colored saris, took turns dancing to tantalizing melodies of Indian music. After the dance, two beautiful-looking young women artists appeared to tattoo our hands with ancient temple designs in brown henna. I requested an A-U-M sign in the center of my hands as a reminder why I actually had come to India that year. This part of the hand is connected to the heart *chakra*, the spiritual center in the middle of the chest near the physical heart. The artist who applied the henna said, "This henna will stay on your hands for several weeks."

The wedding party boarded the train to Delhi, and after a one-night struggle to sleep on a hard bunk bed we arrived in Delhi late midmorning the next day. The squelching temperatures of well over one hundred degrees caught me by surprise. I felt my heart weakening and was quite relieved when we boarded the special chartered air-conditioned bus to take us north. A few hours later I was curious as to where Dr. Goel's ashram might be located while passing through that particular area. I was wondering how I would ever find his ashram after the wedding, but then decided to best leave everything in divine hands. The wedding party stopped for lunch at a resort at a lake near Kurukshetra, the ancient region where the Mahabharata war took place around 3100 B.C. It was a spiritual delight for me to be in this well-known area where Lord Krishna granted Arjuna the vision of his divine cosmic Self, dazzling Arjuna with the blinding splendor of a thousand suns. What he saw was the true Light of God often seen by saints and sages. The diamond-light I see is a powerful spark of that same greater Light drawing me heavenwards. From the ancient battlegrounds we continued our bus ride to Chandigarh. At the steps of the Shivalik View Hotel, the bride, Reena, her parents and entourage welcomed us by lavishly throwing handfuls of rose petals over us as a blessing.

The wedding rituals, ceremonies, and events during the next two days were like the tales from *One Thousand and One Nights* I read in elementary school. The formal wedding ceremonies began on the last day. A small tent was set up for the bride, groom and their immediate family. Inside the wedding tent, a *pandit* sat next to the couple chanting Vedic prayers. From my guest bench outside the tent, I watched Reena and Sanjive walking around the fire that was lit in the center. Reena wore an exquisite bejeweled sari woven with pure gold-thread embroidery. At times it seemed hard for her to move under the sheer weight of her wedding gown. The wedding ceremonies lasted well into the early morning hours. I left the bride's house by taxi at four in the morning to catch some sleep in my suite at the Shivalik View Hotel. Quite worn out, I fell asleep in an instant. At eight in the morning I heard Alka, who had not slept all night, shouting, "Ella, Ella, hurry, hurry, get up, you have to leave right now!" I jumped out of bed, packed my suitcase, and rushed down to the breakfast area. Mr. Agarwal, the father of the groom, had kindly arranged to have his own family take me to Dr. Goel's ashram and we were ready to take off.

Chapter Fifty-six

Dr. Goel

The taxi became quite overloaded once I got in. I had a large suitcase plus some hand luggage. All the suitcases were stacked up in the trunk and on the front seat next to the driver. Four people were squashed together on the small back seat, like sardines in a can. I felt guilty, because this tightness was caused by my quest to visit Dr. Goel's ashram. I had to let go of my embarrassment of sitting halfway in Alka's uncle's lap. I thought, "Indians are much easier about squeezing together and feeling each other's bodies than us Westerners." On the highway, while my friends' aunt and niece were sleeping, I softly sang mantras and *bhajans* to Ashok, the uncle, who was surprised to hear how much I was in tune with their Vedic culture. Soon he too began reciting the mantras he remembered.

Close to Murthal we took a right turn towards Bhigaan. The narrow sandy country road was full of deep potholes, and we got seriously stuck in one of them. With some careful maneuvering, our driver slowly but successfully pulled the taxi up and out to continue again along the main road of the village. Besides the bumpy dirt roads, Bhigaan consisted of rows of clay huts and small cement houses. I noticed dogs, chickens and goats running loose all over the place. Many houses had a water buffalo tied to a tree or iron post on a short chain. We passed little ponds where buffaloes were standing up to their shoulders in the water with their owners, who were washing their faces to cool the cattle down from a scorching 105 degrees Fahrenheit. The scene brought smiles to my face.

Finally we arrived at the ashram gate. The taxi driver got out and found the front gate to the ashram locked. Observing the locked gate, I thought, "Sai Baba does not want me here." I said to the taxi driver and Ashok, "The ashram is closed, let's go on to Delhi to take the train!" But the taxi driver did not take heed of what I was saying. He climbed over the iron-gate and unlocked it. Then Ashok said to me, "Come, Ella, let us go in!"

The two of us walked into the ashram grounds. Not a soul was around and total silence reigned. I thought, "One cannot even hear a pin drop," and remarked, "No one is here. This is an empty ashram. Let's go back." I was ignored and Ashok continued to walk toward some buildings. I followed reluctantly. All of a sudden I recognized a large Sai Baba photo on a wall. I was momentarily overwhelmed with joy seeing Baba's familiar face in this middle-of-nowhere place. "Maybe this is the administration building," I uttered as I noticed a door next to the picture. Ashok took charge by pounding on the door. A small person opened the door, but remained standing behind a screen door. I could not see who it was, but heard his voice. Ashok began a conversation in Hindi. I did not know what was being said. The man behind the screen door suddenly said in English, "I am Dr. Goel," and then to Ashok, "She can stay." The door closed. In that moment my heart overflowed with tears. I was ecstatic. "Finally, no more obstacles," my heart sang. This was the final blessing, the divine permission to stay with the *Kundalini* master.

I went back to the taxi to collect my luggage. Alka's aunt and niece looked at me in dismay, because they did not believe I wanted to stay in this forlorn far-away ashram. "But I am very happy," I said, and with tears of joy flowing from my eyes, I said my goodbyes. Ashok helped carry my luggage to the house that displayed the Baba's picture and left. A burly Indian boy appeared. He said, "My name is Puneet; I am here to bring you to your room." On the way to the room Puneet declared, "In the ashram we call Dr. Goel, *Guruji*. You can come and talk to him in the classroom next to Guruji's house at four o'clock." He put my luggage in a small room in a concrete whitewashed building and left. Finally alone, I set up my bedding on the wooden cot, hung my mosquito netting from the ceiling hook and rested for half an hour. Then it was time to meet Guruji.

I found the classroom, sat down on the rough carpet laid over the hard cement floor and waited. I was the only one in the room. The ashram was completely silent. I realized how deep and different the vibrations were in this ashram than what I experienced during the wedding ceremonies in Bombay and Chandrigarh. I looked at my hands still covered with the wedding henna tattoos, the A-U-M sign still visible inside the palms. I closed my eyes for a moment, sat without any expectations, and opened my mind to whatever the next moment might bring.

At four on the dot Shri Guruji appeared. He was a small silvery-white wavy-haired man wearing old-fashioned dark-framed spectacles and dressed in an orange Indian *kurta*-pyjama. Guruji sat down on his special guru chair in front of the classroom. On the wall behind his chair hung pictures of the goddess Kali, Lord Shiva, Shirdi Sai Baba and Sathya Sai Baba. "Come," Guruji said, while looking at me, "Sit here." He pointed at his feet. He spoke English with the sweet accent of northern India, the Punjabi language. I stood up, walked over to him, and sat down in the lotus position at his feet. Shri Guruji put his thumb on my third eye and his hand on my head, and said, "Think of Sai Baba, Jesus, or God and repeat *Om Namah Shivaya*." After a few moments my head started to move involuntarily. Guruji continued holding his hand on my head for a while and then stopped. He took a small amount of sacred ash that had some cardamom seeds embedded in it out of a crystal bowl next to his chair. He dropped the ash into the middle of my hand, where the tattooed Sankrit word for God met his divine guru touch. He said, "Eat this and inwardly recite the mantra *Om Namah Shivaya*."

In my ignorance, I did not know what was happening to me. I did not know until later that I had just received my official initiation into the path of *Kundalini*. I was not aware of the profound sacredness of that moment. When Guruji held his thumb on my third eye and his hand on my head, he drew up the *shakti*, the cosmic energy from the base of the spine to the top of the head, the place where Lord Shiva resides.

Two middle-aged men dressed in white *punjabis* entered and sat down in the lotus position on the right side of the room. I found out through their questions that one was a journalist from Sweden and that the other had come from Bosnia. Classroom time, I gathered, was the hour for students to ask Guruji spiritual questions and by answering them, he taught. I felt as if I was back in the ancient days of the *Upanishads,* sitting at the feet of an enlightened guru and listening to the teachings from infinite unbound Consciousness. It brought me into a state of immense spiritual joy.

The night following my initiation I fell sick. I vomited for several hours and had great difficulty doing the clean-up. My body weakened and became weaker yet after I managed to get back into bed. In the early morning hours a knock at my door startled and woke me. A voice said, "Good morning – tea!" It was the ashram's wake-up call with an offering of hot sweet Indian chai-tea with rich buffalo milk poured into a stainless steel cup. Without opening the door, I spoke to the young man who had knocked on my door through a screened window. "I am too sick and too weak to have tea, please, let me rest!"

One hour later Rachna, the office manager, came to check on me. "You should not have come, Madam, May is too hot," she said, looking concerned. She then told me that there was neither a doctor in the ashram nor any pharmacy nearby, but promised that she would bring a local remedy for nausea. She left. A few minutes later Rachna reappeared and spooned a bitter-tasting remedy into my mouth. After tugging my mosquito netting back under the mattress, and snuggling down under the bed sheet, I said to her, "Please, be sure to tell Shri Guruji, that no matter how sick I may feel, I will come to the four o'clock class even if I have to crawl."

Chapter Fifty-seven

Classroom in Paradise

Physically weak, but much improved from the nighttime, I appeared in the classroom promptly at four in the afternoon. I asked Shri Guruji in class, "What happened to me?" Guruji replied, "The initiation sometimes causes people to fall ill." He looked at me with penetrating eyes and a most beautiful smile. I left the classroom and went back to bed to meditate, rest and sleep.

When I woke up the next day I felt strong as a horse. Then I knew Shri Guruji was the One, that supreme Consciousness itself. To be with my guru was like a beautiful dream in which he gave answers to all my spiritual questions, on a daily basis. Every day I longed with all my heart for the teaching-hour with my sweet enlightened guru. As I sat at his feet, he looked deeply into my eyes to see if there were any questions. Whatever came to mind, I would ask him. The moment I said, "Guruji" – and posed my question, *Kundalini* spontaneously rose up my spine, bringing my whole being into a state of pure bliss. While writing these words I experience it again very deeply.

I ask my reader to take a moment to connect with the essence of my guru, so that you too may understand what lies beyond the description of the words of this world.

At some point my questions did not seem to matter anymore; just to sit with Shri Guruji was sufficient.

The author Irina Tweedie, in her book *The Chasm of Fire*, writes that disciples of her Sufi teacher often went into states called *samadhi*. To me *samadhi* meant being in the uninterrupted state of bliss and full knowledge of the Self. I knew there was no higher state to attain in spirituality and I yearned for the opportunity to experience it. One afternoon, while looking at the three of us, Shri Guruji asked, "Any questions?" "Guruji," I said, "I would like to know and experience the state of *samadhi*." He looked at me for a while and then said, "To be granted such a state is determined by one's karma." I became quiet, for I did not know whether I spiritually deserved to attain such a state. It humbled me to realize that I asked a bold and daring spiritual question. I thought it best to forget the question and to surrender instead to whatever God had in store for me.

I was so happy to stay in Shri Guruji's ashram that, in a sense, I really did not need anything. The ashram reminded me of a place I had known before, ages ago. The heat so devastating to most people was totally acceptable to me. Few students come in the month of May due to extreme high temperatures in that part of India, but this gave me the great advantage of being practically alone with Shri Guruji. The ashram exuded such peaceful beauty, with its gardens of multiple blooming colorful flowers and young trees lining the roads that Guruji himself had helped build. I often felt that I was either in a mysterious dream, in paradise, or in a higher heaven where divine teachings on truth were taught. Guruji himself radiated total compassion, and sitting with him brought such continued deep joy to my being that all other desires vanished completely. Guruji was all that I needed spiritually. I did not want to leave. I asked him if I could stay. Shri Guruji said, "You have my permission."

I called Air India to change my ticket Delhi-Bangalore to a later date, which meant I would cut my time with Sai Baba. Despite my extreme longing to stay on, I did remember the pledge I had made to Baba some ten years ago. As a person of extreme loyalty and dedication, part of me felt drawn to adhere to the pledge. Another part drew me to stay on in Guruji's ashram. I felt torn and confused. To resolve the dilemma, I decided that if I could get my ticket changed, God meant for me to stay. But when the airline official said, "We cannot change your ticket date," I did not feel peaceful about it.

After lunch in the ashram canteen, I left to rest from the squelching heat in the coolness of my room. Every afternoon I had set my alarm for three-thirty to give myself sufficient time to get ready for "class with Guruji" at four and I believed I had done so that afternoon. It was Friday and I had only two nights left in the ashram. That afternoon I was not woken up by my alarm clock. My eyes opened with a sensation of an enormous powerful flow of energy slowly coming up my spine from the root *chakra* (*muladhara chakra*) like an earthquake and volcanic eruption all at once. This eruption of unimaginable cosmic power overtook me completely. With it I felt the complete power and fulfillment of love slowly ascending my spine, almost like a broad river of lava. It was love, only pure love. I was speechless, thoughtless, bodiless and only aware of love. I felt completely alone and yet completely fulfilled. I was merging in love; the love was merging me. When I came out of this wondrous state of *Kundalini* I had solely one thought, and that thought kept repeating itself, "only God, only God, only God" – it was a most sacred moment, and I felt an enormous sense of humility that is unexplainable.

I looked at the clock. It was three-thirty in the afternoon. The alarm had not been set. Slowly I became aware of Shri Guruji's books on the shelf in my room. I picked one up, vaguely remembering that I had inserted a list of questions for the afternoon class. I glanced at the questions, and suddenly realized there was no longer a need to ask Guruji anything. Out of the questions flowed the immediate answers as if questions and answers were one. All knowledge was available to me at once while I remained in this state of revealed God knowledge. I do not know how I arrived at the classroom that afternoon. I was completely unaware of my body. I remember being at my guru's feet feeling complete. There was nothing more to add. I realized that both Guruji and I exuded that same light of truth. No words were spoken between us. All was known in the supreme silence of that moment. I did not know what day it was. Time had stood still as I had entered another awareness and vibration that does not relate to time.

The next morning, I participated in ashram *seva* (service) in the canteen. I was mopping the floor and felt fortunate to have yet another whole day before my departure. The journalist from Sweden who had been staying with Guruji for some time managed the ashram canteen. He said, "You should know that many people will be coming to the ashram this morning," and added, "and on Sundays, know that Guruji's class is scheduled at eleven in the morning."

Shocked, I thought, "Oh, my God, if this is Sunday, I am supposed to leave for Delhi airport in the early afternoon!" I quit my canteen mopping at once, rushed to my room and started packing. I found it hard to believe that I could have lost a whole day. I did not understand where all of Saturday had gone and wondered, "Could I have been in *samadhi*?" and "Do we have remembrance of being in a state of *samadhi*?" I venture to think that such a state of supreme Consciousness cannot leave an image on a three-dimensional conditioned mind, and the answer most likely is "no" to remembering *samadhi*. Only a self-realized person, most likely, would know the real answer to such a mystery.

I packed my suitcase in a hurry, hoping for my last

opportunity to sit with Guruji in class and to say goodbye to him. I did not know that Sunday morning was always scheduled as a special day for the nearby villagers to sit with Shri Guruji in class for personal questions and to sing *bhajans* in his divine presence. When I entered the classroom at eleven that morning anticipating sitting near Guruji like usual, most villagers had already taken up all the spaces in the classroom. I could only squeeze in the very back of the room behind the locals who had come for their Sunday *satsang* (spiritual gathering) with Shri Guruji. Then Guruji entered the classroom, sat down, and addressed the villagers in Hindi or in the Punjabi language. I could not understand any word of it. By observing, I knew he was calling people forward who had not been initiated in *Kundalini*. I watched while several initiations were performed. The room filled with *shakti* energy and even in the back of the room where I sat this was palpable. Then the villagers asked their questions and I observed that he answered them with tender kindness towards each person. After class I noticed that people were going upstairs to the shrine room. I did not understand what was happening and by the time I decided to go upstairs to check, I was again too late to seize the opportunity to sit near Guruji in the front. My only choice was to take the last row for my last time with him.

To be in the company of the men and women from the nearby villages was an experience I will never forget. The scene could have easily been the same some two thousand years ago. Some of the women, their hair covered under thin silk or cotton shawls in various colors, were obviously very poor. I noticed how worn some of their *punjabi*-outfits (puffy pants with long dress-like tops and shawls) were. Men in old but clean *dhotis* with white tops or *kurta*-pyjamas and working-class women with prematurely wrinkled faces and hands and their children had gathered for their devotional singing *(bhajans)* to God, over which Shri Guruji presided.

When *bhajan* singing began, I was amazed that so far from

home I could sing the exact same tunes with these villagers with that same heartfelt devotion to God.

Shri Guruji entered the shrine room and sat down on a beautifully carved wooden ornate high chair with red upholstery. Above his head were the Sanskrit letters A-U-M, in silver, attached to the top of the chair, almost exactly like the one I had seen in Sai Baba's interview room. His matching footstool was covered with an arrangement of fresh flowers, offerings by his students (called *sadhakas*) in the ashram. Unaware Westerners may have thought this special chair to be a sign of overstated aggrandizement likened to the throne of a king or queen representing worldly power and ego. These types of chairs are, however, an accepted norm all over India as the chair on which a guru takes his or her seat. An ancient tradition, it symbolizes the divine status of the guru. Guruji, who was very modest indeed, just played it by the old rules of guru-ship as was expected of him in Indian culture. In later years it became clear to me how hard this must have been for him. But even an enlightened guru cannot ignore the tradition of his land and must accept it for the benefit of his students. It reminded me of the saying of Jesus in the Holy Bible in Matthew 22:21:

> Render therefore to Caesar the things that are Caesar's, and
> to God the things that are God's.

In other words: "Be in this world, honor the traditions or rules of this world, but know you are spirit."

Bhajan singing continued and I saw some villagers making strange body movements. All of a sudden a small beautiful young brown-faced boy began to wildly spin around the carpet as if in a trance. His movements went faster and faster until the whole carpet started swirling around him. It was a demonstration of the amazing power of *Kundalini*. I wondered whether some help was needed for this boy and looked at Guruji questioningly, but he sent me the message, "All is fine, I will take care!" I was deeply moved to witness these types of *Kundalini* movements for the first time. At the end of the *bhajans*, Guruji looked at me directly with his powerful eyes that penetrated my inner being, perhaps his way of saying goodbye to me, and in that look I received his benediction. Happy for what I experienced, but also with great sadness that I could not stay longer, I went back to my room to organize my luggage and wait for the taxi.

Chapter Fifty-eight

The Guru Watches

My taxi driver appeared. It was two in the afternoon. I felt a bit stressed because I did not have enough rupees to pay the taxi-fare to Delhi International Airport. Since Bombay I had not been able to exchange any traveler's checks and in the ashram I had just enough cash to pay for my room and board. The ashram was surrounded by vast farmlands with no bank in the near vicinity. Instead of going directly to the airport, I needed extra time in Delhi to exchange traveler's checks for rupees in a major hotel.

In one of Shri Guruji's talks, during the four o'clock class, he had said, "People who come here are often in bliss. Here they think of God, but as soon as they leave this ashram they fall back in their old patterns of thinking and behavior, acting from their ego-self and forgetting all they have experienced here." Hearing Guruji's remarks, I immediately thought, "Oh, not me, I will keep thinking of the Divine, even after leaving the ashram." My additional thoughts were, "How could anyone ever forget God?" I put a judgment on the unknown other, puffing myself up to be better than they. Little did I know that I would be tested.

I did not know my taxi driver Santosh very well. During our

drive to Delhi I tried to speak some English with him. He gave no indication that he understood what I said. In Bangalore, in southern India, Ali had been my driver for years. Even though his English was limited, he always knew exactly what I wanted and why. From day one with Ali, we had become friends. Ali used to go shopping with me or for me. He also would take a traveler's check as a payment for his services. He was never worried about being paid or not. As a Muslim, he said that everything came from Allah. "I am always at your service, Madam, anything you want I will do for you."

Before leaving Guruji's ashram, the canteen manager informed Santosh that he needed to bring me to a five-star hotel before going to the airport. He also advised me to pay Santosh a set amount of rupees, for going to and driving around Delhi including his return to Bhigaan. The manager explained, "Guruji wants the taxi drivers not to take monetary advantage of gullible western spiritual seekers."

We did not encounter much traffic in Delhi. It was early Sunday afternoon, siesta time, and the streets were rather empty. I did not understand Santosh, who strangely seemed to circle around Delhi as if we were sightseeing. He did not appear to be in any hurry. It took us quite some time before we arrived at one of the main hotels, the Imperial, where the doorman told Santosh straightaway that I could not get any rupees on Sunday and that all banks were closed.

We left, with Santosh proceeding in an odd sort of way, as if he did not know where he was going. "Do you know where we are going?" I asked. As always, he replied, "Yes, Madam," and to be truthful, I was not sure what he meant by it. I was getting tired and worried and thought I had a taxi driver who did not know his way around Delhi. We drove on, and I hoped we were heading for the next hotel. After some time, Santosh stopped at another hotel and instead of finding the main entrance, I was dropped off at the basement. I went inside and saw an escalator leading to an upper floor. The escalator did not work. I climbed the steps and came to a magnificent entry hall of one of the most astonishing stylish hotels I had ever seen. It was a Sikh hotel. I saw many men wearing the most beautiful Indian costumes with their heads wrapped in full turbans of all color varieties. I noticed a dining area with flowering tropical plants and palm trees and a large swimming pool in the background.

At the counter, a most gorgeous-looking receptionist in a deep red silk sari looked at me with her deep dark mysterious eyes and asked, "What do you want, Madam?" I explained, and showed my traveler's checks. "You are not staying at this hotel, Madam, we cannot give you any rupees," she said with a haughty smile as if she were a Maharani. Her head shook slightly from left to right, indicating that the conversation was over. I should have left, but instead I began to argue with her, begging at first, but when no answer came, I did get angry and told her that this is not the best way to treat or attract tourists. Oh, how furious I was. This dauntingly beautiful woman just stood there, like an ice-cold queen, completely unresponsive. I gave up, turned around and left through the front entry hall.

Time was flying away. "Do you understand my English?" I asked Santosh. Again he said, "Yes, Madam," but I was not sure whatsoever. I began to panic. "No more hotels, Santosh. Straight to airport," I screamed at him. "If you do not do so, I'll certainly miss my 6 o'clock flight!" We drove on and I had no idea where we were. Santosh pulled up in front of yet another hotel. I ran in, with some vague hope... Again I was told, "No rupees available." Back in the taxi, I knew I had to make a real strong impression on Santosh or I would certainly miss my flight. Again, now at the top of my lungs, I screamed, "No more hotels, Santosh, only airport!" He finally heard me. It was close to six when we arrived at the departure hall of the international airport. Santosh wanted his money. "I will pay you in dollars," I said. "I have dollars somewhere in my suitcase." He opened the trunk, and I began to unzip my large suitcase that had been difficult to close. My clothes spilled out, sliding down on the pavement. "Oh, no, no..." I stammered. I frantically searched through my belongings in hopes of finding my plastic zip-lock bag with dollars in it, but I couldn't find it.

A security guard came and said to Santosh, "You cannot park your taxi in front of the departure hall."

Santosh stared at me and said, "I must have my money now!"

"I will go in, to the bank exchange office," I blurted out. "Please help me close my suitcase." After pushing my clothes inside the suitcase, I sat on it and tried to zip it all up with Santosh's help. I now begged security to let Santosh wait for me so that I could fetch my rupees. I ran, while holding my traveler's checks tightly in my fist, to the exchange. Luckily no one was in front of me. Within minutes I received the needed currency. Relieved, I rushed out of the terminal to where Santosh was standing next to his old taxi. His face looked seriously grim and sad. I paid him the agreed-upon sum, but he looked even sadder as if it was completely wrong. I handed him another hundred-rupee bill, but he kept staring at me in a make-believe heartbreaking manner. "This is India, always begging for more from us Westerners," I thought. I took my luggage and turned around swiftly in the hope that I could still catch my flight.

During check-in at the Jet-Air counter I was informed that my flight was one hour delayed. I slumped down on an airport seat in the waiting hall completely out of breath from exhaustion, my heart pounding audibly. It had been quite an afternoon. I now finally had time to relax and reflect on all I had learned in Guruji's ashram. I realized how much frustration I had felt driving around Delhi and how I had blown off my anger at poor Santosh. Suddenly it hit me. I had been tested as soon as I left the ashram. I remembered Guruji saying, "As soon as people leave this ashram they fall back in their old patterns." "Oh my God, I failed his test!" flashed through my mind. The very instant that thought came to me, a gush of water struck me across the face, coming at me as if out of nowhere. Startled, I looked around. No one was sitting near me. I looked at the departure-hall ceiling, but there was absolutely no physical source from which any water could have appeared.

Only in India were mysteries of such transcendental phenomena plausible. The water certainly was a sign and symbol of purification or baptism. Deeply touched, I suddenly understood, "The guru is always watching, not like Big Brother, but as the everpresent divine Consciousness, always gently nudging us forward towards the light of deeper understanding."

Chapter Fifty-nine

Receiving Divine Grace

At the airport in Bangalore, Ali welcomed me with the good news that Sai Baba was in his residence in Whitefield, only a short drive away. It was four in the morning and I had traveled over fourteen hours since I left Guruji's ashram. Physically tired, but happy about my deep spiritual connection with Guruji, I was not eagerly looking forward to seeing Sai Baba.

Only by the sheer duty a devotee feels did I travel so far south to see him for the seventh time. The Sai Baba form had never been the focus of worship for me as it was for other devotees. My connection on the outer level had been at arm's length despite the interviews he had granted me, but on the inner level he represented my higher Consciousness. In contrast, my new relationship with Gurudev Shri Siddheswar Baba Maharaj (Guruji's official name, as was Dr. Goel) was in every respect personal on the outer as well as the inner levels. Alone with him in his classroom he had initiated me into the true path of *Kundalini*. While I was sitting at his feet he had answered my spiritual questions and given deep spiritual insights. Unlike Sai Baba, Guruji knew my personal name and took an interest in me as a spiritual seeker and always offered all the help I needed. I felt a longing, as well as a new belonging to Shri Guruji, but sensed extreme guilt to have such feelings after so many years of one-pointed focus on Sai Baba.

Ali took me to Kadugodi and stopped in front of the house of the Radhakrishnans, where I had rented a room in the past. I knocked on the front door. Mr. Radhakrishnan was performing his early morning *puja* and when he opened the door the sweet aroma of burning incense welcomed me. On the *puja* table, statues of Shri Ganesh, Lord Krishna and Baba were garlanded with fresh jasmine, while the tape recorder played the *arathi* (awakening song), whose reverberating sacred sounds filled the small concrete house. Mr. Radhnakrishnan finished his *puja* by waving the camphor flame in a circular motion in front of the statues. How auspicious it was to enter the house at the time of such devoted worship. The family was happy to see me and I was glad to hear that my old room with the lovely garden-view was available for rent. Mr. and Mrs. Radhakrishnan and their two young daughters helped me settle in. As soon as my bed was set up and my luggage arranged, I fell asleep under my rainbow-colored mosquito netting and woke up just in time for my short walk to attend afternoon *bhajans* at the Brindavan ashram.

As I sat down on the temple floor, it astonished me to feel the *Kundalini* rising up from my root *chakra*, softly rocking my body from right to left in the same manner as during my initiation by Shri Guruji. In prior years *Kundalini* had always disappeared before I entered Baba's ashram. The new experience pleased me because the soft shaking motions brought sweet joy to my inner being.

In a book entitled *Indian Culture and Spirituality*, published by the Third Eye Foundation, Shri Siddheswar's wisdom on *Kundalini* is quoted on page 108:

> When *Kundalini* is aroused by the mercy and the grace of the Guru/God, it is called 'Genuine' arousal of *Kundalini*. When it is aroused without the mercy and grace of Guru/God, it is called 'False' or abortive arousal of *Kundalini*.

Like Shri Siddheswar Baba, I too had suffered greatly from this abortive arousal of *Kundalini*. I believed that my own *Kundalini* awakening had happened without the grace of God. Nadia, a master of Huna healing, had first opened the pathway for the upward movement of *Kundalini* and as I continued the daily practice of *pranayama* and *lama yoga*, the combination may have accelerated the cosmic force to permanently escape from its slumbering position in the *muladhara chakra*. My genuine arousal of *Kundalini* finally took place by the initiation of Shri Siddheswar Baba, which undoubtedly was equivalent to receiving the grace of God.

With this grace I was able to experience *Kundalini* in the Sai Baba temple and later on in many other places of worship: other temples, churches, monasteries and congregations (*satsang*) of spiritual people anywhere in the world. Eventually I began seeing auras in places where spiritual people meet in addition to the divine light I had always known and seen.

With *Kundalini* moving freely though my body I knew a better time had arrived. I no longer feared what was happening inside my spinal column. I understood the sensations and involuntary movements of *Kundalini* to be beneficial for my life and fully accepted them. I was no longer on my own in the awakening process, but had the guidance of a fully realized guru to show the way home. That was the divine grace.

Chapter Sixty

Meditation Camp in Bhigaan

I signed up for the February 1997 international meditation classes at the Shri Siddheswar Baba ashram. Shri Guruji had led meditation camps in northern India for many years well before the Bhigaan ashram was established. When still holding a high position as an education officer in the Indian government, he answered his inner call to leave the material world and become a guru. After his full awakening this liberated soul received the gift to perform initiations to raise the *Kundalini*. He not only led the spiritual seeker into the *Kundalini*-awakening path but also gave higher teachings from his fountain of knowledge. His ashram offered meditation classes twice a year. Shri Guruji's teachings show how our backward journey to God, *Kundalini* awakening and meditation play a key role in reaching the goal of self-realization.

Guruji set the following meditation base guidelines for his students:

1. Be seated on the floor, if possible in lotus position; a chair can also be used.
2. Close your eyes.
3. Relax the body, part by part, beginning at the feet and go slowly all the way up to the top of the head.
4. When inhaling bring the awareness to the incoming breath.
5. When exhaling bring the awareness to the outgoing breath.
6. Stay focused on the breath and mentally chant the sacred Sanskrit mantra: *So* for the in-breath and *Hum* for the out-breath.

So Hum, in and out (also discussed in Part IV, Chapter Thirty-two, "The Beloved and I Are One"). Again, the meaning of the chant is: "I am He, He is I," or "the Beloved and I are one." Guruji said, "While doing the *So Hum* chant with focus on the in and out breath, bring the awareness slowly to *trikuti*, the third eye, between the eyebrows, and stay fixed at that point." Guruji further advised, "Say a brief prayer to your favorite divine image of your chosen God. Ask his or her help to stay focused in *trikuti*. Ask that you may see your sacred image. Ask with humility, 'Father, please, I am your child, help me.' Thoughts will come. Allow the thoughts to be there. Witness the thoughts and find their roots (the backward journey). Smile and understand, and be the objective witness. Continue to stay focused in *trikuti*." Guruji taught that it is safe to stay in *trikuti*, as the third eye is located above the awareness of the senses.

Yogis sometimes use other methods of meditation, in which focus on the crown *chakra* is practiced, but those methods are unsafe for most practitioners. Gopi Krishna, in his autobiography *Living with Kundalini*, wrote that he did meditate on his crown *chakra*, which brought him to full *Kundalini* awakening and liberation. According to Guruji this is a dangerous method that could lead to insanity. When the *Kundalini* force moves upward, all mental conditioning might be burned to ashes in one flash. This happens in the part of the brain between the sixth and the seventh *chakra*, where all human thought patterns are stored. Guruji strongly felt that Gopi Krishna, whom he knew personally, was, despite using this method of meditation on the crown *chakra*, saved by the grace of God.

Guruji recommended meditating one hour twice a day, morning and evening. If that time is not available, half an hour twice a day will suffice. Meditation preferably should be every day at the same time and place, but if this is not possible, Guruji strongly recommended meditating whenever or wherever possible.

Santosh picked me up from the Delhi airport. I felt a sense of unease when I saw him and immediately apologized for my angry behavior the year before. Santosh gave me a smirking smile. I figured he knew what I was talking about, but maybe this was only my imagination.

In the ashram I was happy to obtain a single room. The room was quite narrow, about five feet wide and twelve feet long, with tiled floors and whitewashed walls. Instead of glass-paned windows, permanent screens were installed. Inside the room the light-blue painted wooden shutters could close over the screens to shut out the cold winter air. An adjacent small room provided a cold-water shower, sink and toilet. My bed was a wooden cot like I had the year before. I placed my self-inflating air mattress on the cot and covered it with my permanent-press flowery-print sheets from home. During the month of February the ashram provided each room with heavy quilt-like blankets to overcome the cold at night.

The day after my arrival, the meditation camp would officially open at Guruji's house at a quarter to four in the morning. I carried my flashlight in the pitch-dark morning hours to find my way to *guru newas* (Guruji's house). It was extremely cold and I layered my cotton *punjabi* with a woolen sweater and draped the traditional northern Indian woolen shawl over it. In front of Guruji's house, a tent-material type tarp had been laid down over the brick road, where the camp participants could sit down on their meditation pillows. Guruji was standing on the verandah of his house waiting to give each participant his special blessing. When my turn came, Guruji touched my third eye and pulled *Shakti-Kundalini* to *trikuti* in the same way as he had done during my initiation the year before. I felt the guru's grace of higher vibration flowing into my being. As before he handed me *vibhuti* (sacred ash) with a cardamom seed embedded in it to eat. I left in silence as did the other *sadhakas* and walked back to my room to meditate. Guruji's way of beginning the camp had stirred profound feelings of sacredness in me.

Little by little I became immersed in an intensive two-week ashram program consisting of the above-mentioned meditation, chanting, *bhajans* and spiritual teachings. Ashram living in Bhigaan was like living in a monastery where, after days of spiritual practices, the mind begins to dwell solely on and in God. The sounds and words of *bhajans* and mantras stayed with me day and night. Sometimes the inner living essence of the *bhajans* woke me in the middle of the night. Most people who attended the meditation camp dwelt in the same mode. During my stroll around the ashram I heard some students reciting their mantras aloud or softly singing a *bhajan*. Wherever I walked in the ashram, my mind would immediately pick up the mantra or *bhajan* that floated in the air and I often would continue its tune. The ashram exuded vibrations of that higher Consciousness, and the heavenly atmosphere put me in states of constant joy.

Every day my spiritual connection with God deepened. Slowly I began to live just in the moment, "the here and now," realizing that deep beauty that is God. The ashram was kept silent to help keep the serious spiritual seekers focused within. Only some forty *sadhakas* participated in the camp. The ashram was a small and intimate place. Many times a day I saw Shri Guruji's small figure walking along the ashram-grounds spreading the divine light that radiated from this enlightened soul.

During our morning class at eleven we had the opportunity to hear a student's individual paper on a spiritual topic and listen to Shri Guruji's response from his eternal view.

When the office manager, Rachna, asked me to write a paper for the camp, I accepted and immediately decided that it should be about the well-known story of Adam and Eve. I had always been fascinated to know more about the inner meaning of the biblical stories from the point of view of eastern philosophy and my understanding of the mystical teachings. Rachna offered me the old-fashioned ashram typewriter and a small rickety table to type the paper in my room. Uncomfortably crouched over in my low lawn chair, I set out to work. "Write at least 2500 words!" Rachna said. Without any reference material or dictionary available, I typed down what I understood the ancient story of the beginnings of mankind to symbolize. With inspiration from my inner source my next chapter emerged (updated at a later time)...

Chapter Sixty-one

A Different Look at Paradise

The Book of Genesis in the Old Testament contains the well-known story of the creation of the world. In this story, God created Adam and Eve, the first man and woman. Adam and Eve lived in a place of absolute beauty, peace and harmony called Paradise or the Garden of Eden. Created by God, Adam and Eve are one with the mind of God or Cosmic Consciousness, who in Indian philosophy is none other than Lord Shiva himself.

The Bible story recounts how God tells Adam and Eve that they could freely partake of the fruits of all the trees in the garden of Paradise, except the fruit of one tree, which stands in the middle. This is the tree of the knowledge of good and evil, whose deeper mysteries can only be understood by God himself.

While Eve is standing near the forbidden tree, a snake approaches her, enticing her to eat an apple from this tree. After some deliberation, Eve falls for the snake's alluring persuasion and eats the fruit. Then Eve turns to Adam to entice him to eat of the apple as well. After they eat, they hear the sound of God walking in the garden, calling them. A first sense of guilt arises. They now feel transparent before the all-knowing and all-seeing *eye-I* of God and they try to hide from his presence. As a result of guilt, fear comes into being as Adam and Eve's consciousness begins to separate from the one mind in and with God. The first man and woman know for the first time wrong and they feel vulnerable. In shame for their actions they no longer dare to come face to face with God. The Bible says that before they answer God's call they put on loincloths made of fig leaves as a barrier to hide their disobedience. Their clothes symbolize the placing of a barrier between God and man, which ultimately is an illusion, as God sees everything and knows everything. The barrier is a block, but also a figment of Adam and Eve's imagination.

Then, when they face God, Adam blames Eve and Eve blames the snake. But the enticing snake is no other than *Shakti-Kundalini*, the female divine principle, which is also the creation of Lord Shiva. She is his *Shakti*, his consort or eternal companion. The snake symbolizes *Shakti*'s cunning rising powers and her alluring endearing enchantment. With the appearance of *Shakti*, the creation of the world is breathed into existence, as an illusion of being outside the cosmic mind of God, as if fallen from the Godhead itself. This is called the world of *maya* or illusion. Oneness or wholeness, the ideal of the *One Without a Second,* in which the first humans had been a part of their Creator God, seems lost. Adam and Eve fall into lower *chakra* consciousness, and become entangled in the web of *maya,* an illusion that makes them believe that they have been driven from the Garden of Eden.

The tree of the knowledge of good and evil, on the inner mystical level, is called the *sushumna*. It is the middle fine energy channel inside the spinal column through which *Shakti-Kundalini* rises upward until the energy channels *ida* and *pingala* find their balance, as earlier mentioned in Part VII, Chapter Fifty-two, "Kundalini Returns." In most mystical illustrations one can notice the serpent-like motion of *ida* and *pingala* moving through the five *chakra* points. The movements of these mystical energies resemble two snakes meeting at the sixth level of consciousness, the place where God resides.

My mystical teacher Earlyne Chaney, in her book *Kundalini and the Third Eye,* talks about the physician's symbol, the caduceus of Mercury, which represents the snake-like motions of *ida* and *pingala*.

> Esoterically this symbol represents the *Kundalini* force traveling along the spinal canal until it reaches the brow and Crown *chakras* at the top of the Head, resulting in unfoldment – enlightenment.

Christians in general talk about the fall from Paradise as the original sin, because the first man and woman disobeyed their Creator. In reality, this fall is the descent from the higher God consciousness to a more primal form of consciousness. *Shakti* represents the perishable nature, the impermanent form of Shiva, which is a temporary illusion. This is the fall from heaven to earth. Adam and Eve now become part of that illusive transient nature. They find themselves in separation from the harmony, the peace, and their amalgamation in the Godhead, which was symbolically the garden of Paradise. By falling for the snake's temptation, duality or ego is born, the development of a mind of limited awareness for Adam and Eve and subsequently for all their human descendants.

What seemed to be a disaster could not have happened without God's full knowledge. Had he not created the tempting serpent *Shakti-Kundalini* as his own counterpart? It is clear that God planned the fall from himself into a separate world of existence, allowing his creation of mankind to have a free will to co-create with him. Even though no longer *one* with God, the first men and women remain part of his divine plan, whose mysteries cannot be unraveled until such time as God will ordain.

I believe that in the Garden of Eden, Adam and Eve had only spirit or soul bodies. They existed only as pure light inside the cosmic mind or fountainhead of God. After the so-called fall, they acquired bodies of heavy and denser vibration, part of the frequency of the earth plane. No longer solely dwelling in God-consciousness, mankind could no longer look upon the face of God as they once had enjoyed in their home in Paradise. On Earth, God's brilliant light would blind them. In the *Bhagavad-Gita*, translated for the modern reader by Eknath Easwaran, Chapter 11, where Krishna reveals his divine form, unobtainable by the normal human eyes, Arjuna says to Krishna, "Your radiance is blinding and immeasurable." For the protection of humans, God had become invisible to the Earth man and woman in their new state of limited awareness.

That God punished the snake and made him crawl on his belly points to *Shakti's* descent into the first *chakra*, where the *Kundalini*, or serpent power, lies dormant until such time that the sacred *granti*-lock at the *muladhara chakra* will be broken. The *granti*-lock is like the cherubim described in the Bible with the flaming sword blocking the way to the tree of life after Adam and Eve were driven out of the Garden. For the human race, the snake or *Shakti-Kundalini* is not to rise again towards that higher Consciousness until the longing for God becomes so intense that it will shift the human attention from the entanglement in *maya* back to the light of God. This may happen with God's grace when human beings yearn for God with all their heart, mind and soul. This is difficult to achieve, but not impossible.

With Paradise lost, clothed in impermanent bodies, Adam and Eve and their descendants have to consume food to maintain these newly acquired bodies. They have to toil and work the earth to grow the crops they need to stay alive in their new environment. They have to build shelters for protection against the harsh elements of nature or becoming prey to dangerous animals. The humans have to multiply themselves because their physical bodies have but a short life span.

Even though Adam and Eve have fallen from the higher awareness, the memory of that beautiful blissful state of paradise subtly lingered in their hearts (mystically speaking, in their higher *chakras*) and in the hearts of generations to come.

During the tens of thousands of years in which souls were born again and again into human bodies, spiritual leaders appeared who had a stronger intuitive sense of that ultimate divine state of oneness in God. These men and women inspired others, thereby promoting religious thought. Some of them became priests, priestesses or prophets. The greatest ones amongst them started the major world religions. Each religion prescribed some mystical formulas by which Paradise could be regained.

In India, great saints and sages led the way by sacrificing themselves to the utmost extent to find the royal road back to

God. They did penance (*tapas*), renouncing the tempting nature of *maya*, which was enticing and binding them in the temporary impermanent world of *Shakti*'s creation. To find the ultimate truth many saints and sages focused with such determination and self-sacrifice that God himself in his mercy granted them liberation from bondage, taking them back to oneness in Him. "To these souls, the garden of Paradise opens with the cherubim releasing all locks back to the garden." They not only regained Paradise, but also were granted the boon of continuous realization in God. This is the realization of *tat twam asi* (*That* thou art, or thou art *That*), formulated as a central theme in the *Upanishads*, one of the holiest works in Indian philosophy.

Holy men or women and saints are relatively rare in earth's large population today. The majority of mankind seems to be looking for pleasure and happiness in the short term, in the world of *maya*. Most believe the material world they can see with their own physical eyes to be the true reality. The pursuit of happiness to obtain power and riches became a new religion. Paradise within the world of the senses equates to a paradise of ignorance in which humans murdered and plundered, robbed and waged wars. They broke all the laws that God had given through the words and writings of the saints and prophets. So strong is *maya* that even religion itself became entangled in this drama for power. Some religions proclaimed that God was exclusively theirs. People who worshiped other forms and names would be ostracized, persecuted or killed. From the misunderstandings of God's law and the real meaning of his Paradise, religious wars ensued.

The separate mind wrought after the fall of Paradise was never meant to become a sole separate entity, completely ignoring the almighty power of the creator God, of which it was a part. This secondary mind or ego was only meant to operate as a working mind, and to tune in to its source for direction and sustenance. This is written in the Lord's Prayer as "Thy will be done, on earth as it is in heaven," in the Hebrew Bible as: *"Sh'ma Yisra'eil, Adonai Eloheinu Adonai echad"* (Hear, O, Israel, the Lord

God is One), and in the Bhagavad Gita, Chapter 10:20: "I am the true Self in the heart of every creature, *Arjuna,* and the beginning, middle, and end of their existence."

In the Koran, Jihad as a holy war against the infidel was never meant to fight the unbeliever, but rather to overcome or wage war against the separate self in its limitations. Jihad literally means exertion. "We have returned from the lesser jihad," the Prophet Mohammed observed, following an encounter with the Meccans, "to face the greater jihad, to battle the enemy within oneself."

Despite God's word in the Holy Scriptures, the all too often self-serving interpretations or dogmas became a powerful tool to control people instead of pointing to the inner meaning of the scriptures. Manmade dogma is an aggrandizement of human institutionalized ego rather than a reflection of God, which has led to great suffering. Instead of cooperation, there is competition for power between people, tribes, and nations. In the twentieth century alone, such ignorance brought about the annihilation of about six million Jews, nearly three million gypsies, homosexuals and political opponents in the Hitler death camps; the purposeful starvation of about twenty-five million Ukrainians by Stalin; another twenty-five million Chinese purposefully starved by Mao Tse-Tung in China, as well as the many victims of his cultural revolution; the slayings of eight hundred thousand Tutsis by the Hutus in Africa; the Bosnian genocide. There is seemingly no end in sight. Every day, every minute, new atrocities from all around our world can be added to this litany.

The year 2001, 9-11, signaled the coming to the surface of an underground terrorist group called Al-Qaeda, whose motives focus on undermining and ultimately destroying western civilization. The group does not shrink from killing innocent people along the way to obtain their objectives. These terrorists use the holy Koran for selfish goals and aim to spread terror, hoping to cause a decline in the affluence of the western democratic states, where freedom is granted by parliamentary systems and constitutions. These terrorists recruit young men or women, and radicalize them to become suicide bomber-martyrs in a jihad for Allah. God, Allah, and the Koran as well as jihad are misused to promote the ego mind rather than the ideals of oneness in God. New groups of jihadis appeared under the name of ISIS and others that are striving to establish their own caliphates by means of terrorizing Islam itself and the West. Since 9-11 many devastating weapons and army units have been employed to root out the new evil but this also resulted in ever-mounting tragedies of loss of lives. The ego continues to look in the wrong direction for its self-fulfillment.

In Indian philosophy we see Lord Shiva often depicted with snakes around his neck. Not only does this mean that he is above the senses, where snakebites can do no harm, but it also symbolizes that Shiva is in control of *Shakti-Kundalini*. He is the one who calls on *Shakti* to no longer be enticed in *maya*, but to rise up from the bottom of the spine to the sixth *chakra*. This energy of the snake has been asleep in humans since the fall from Paradise, but by Lord Shiva's command (God's grace), *Shakti* will use her creativity in the ascension or upward journey. During this process *Shakti* shakes the conditioning of the human mind by cleansing the *chakras* and burning the karmas (wrong actions) of past and present lives. When *Shakti* brings the *jiva* (individualized spirit) back to Shiva, her cosmic fire frees all bindings to the illusion. Home again in God, our separate ego-mind will go through a transition to only serve in surrender to the infinite mind of God. This signals the end of duality.

Even though Guruji did not know about Al-Qaeda or ISIS in 1997 when I wrote the first concept of my paper for the meditation camp, he was well aware of the human ego bound in selfishness looking at the outside world for fulfillment rather than within one's own soul. Guruji's commentary on my Paradise paper was that Adam and Eve's Paradise was indeed perfect, but that they had, as it were, jumped from the sixth floor or the sixth *chakra* (*chakra* where God resides) down to the ground floor or root *chakra* (*muladhara*).

Ours is a time in which we witness increasing darkness, where morality or higher values are vastly disappearing. Yet I know that the true light can never be entirely extinguished. The light is still the magnet drawing in souls. The spark of light in each soul is still calling to know one's essence, which is God. Those with open hearts and sincerity who want change for our world have heard the inner calling, and God, as the light of the world, never ceases to respond. God has, in reality, never forsaken or abandoned mankind.

In the book *My Stroke of Insight* by Jill Bolte Taylor, Ph.D., the author, a brain anatomist who suffered a major stroke, began her new work of insight by experiencing the acute differences between the left and right hemispheres of her brain. After her stroke disabled most of her left-brain function, she received new revelations into the functions of the right brain as she went through the experience of right-brain awareness. She writes the following about her right brain or mind:

> My right mind is open to the eternal flow whereby I exist at ONE with the universe. It is the seat of my Divine mind, the knower, the wise woman and the observer. It is my intuition and higher consciousness.

I believe that even though humans mostly dwell in left-brain or separate ego-awareness, a shift to the right brain or mind is already taking place at this time. Saints and sages, artists, writers and composers have always had more ability to see the light of the right brain or mind. Modern-day spiritual philosopher Eckhart Tolle, the author of *A New Earth*, speaks of the change that is gradually happening, as people begin to understand themselves better and shift from the egoic-self to a more universal Self. The reconnection to the right brain, the connection to the universal mind of God, will be restored. A new human is in the process of coming to this new light of understanding, going in the opposite direction of Adam and Eve, who fell into duality.

The new man and woman will, once more, be *one* with their creator, now with the acquired knowledge of ages of human history as their cathartic process.

Chapter Sixty-two

Vision of the Divine Guru

I was lying down on my bed reciting the sacred mantra *Om Namah Shivaya*. It was afternoon rest time in the Siddheswarashram. I was in a very relaxed state. I closed my eyes and brought my awareness to *trikuti*, where beautiful floating swirling blue-purple lights instantaneously appeared.

I want to reiterate that these colors in my third eye were nothing new. They had been appearing since my fire initiation by Earlyne Chaney's hand in her bi-located ethereal form in Montana. Every time I meditate I am aware of these living colors of extraordinary hues of purple-blue. The translucent radiant blue-purple lights stay anchored and alive in my third eye no matter where I am.

The frequency of my soul essence vibrates in blue-purple, a ray out of God's infinite light. The blue-purple ray is my bridge or *antakharana* to my oversoul and God. My spirit travels by means of this bridge to the higher vibrations of consciousness.

I felt so serene lying on my bed in the ashram room observing my soul colors while still mentally reciting my mantra. When I opened my eyes, I noticed that the color was not only inside my third eye but also outside as an ethereal substance appearing in midair all around me. I continued *Om Namah Shivaya*, but abruptly stopped when I became aware of multi-millions of little specks of gold dancing in mid-air forming the body of Shri

Siddheswar Baba. I saw my guru floating in my room in a body of scintillating golden sparks.

The vision was of a short duration, but it gave me unfathomable joy and peace. The experience increased the deep love I felt for my guru, for it deepened my understanding that the form I saw represented divine Consciousness encouraging me on the path of self-realization. I asked Guruji later in class whether the vision was real. Shri Guruji replied, "We should always question a vision. But visions can be true. They are given by God in a form we recognize as divinity on our spiritual path." Shri Guruji himself had been given a vision of Sai Baba, which he considered to be a true vision. In his book *Psychoanalysis and Meditation* under his name of Dr. Goel, he writes on page 430 the following:

> At about one thirty in the morning, my blanket was pulled up by someone and I was woken up. To my great astonishment, I saw Shri Sathya Sai Baba standing near my bed in resplendent form.

I also believe that my vision of Shri Guruji was such a true vision, as I began to see him as my personal guru empowered with the energy of the higher Consciousness. I also knew that my first vision of my departed husband in 1985 was true. The vision of Harmen contained messages of love and appreciation for all that I had done, showing the continuation of his love from another dimension.

Shri Guruji further added that dreams about divine forms, be it Krishna, Rama, Buddha, Sai Baba, or Jesus, are always coming from the higher Consciousness and need no questioning. God, who is beyond all forms, can make use of our own inner sacred images to speak to us. Many people in the world have had visions of Jesus, Mary, the Archangels, or one of the many saints. One of these saints, Padre Pio, an Italian monk, could bi-locate to heal sick people on various continents of the world where he was seen in his ethereal form. The ethereal form looks exactly like the material human form. In most cases, the mind of the bi-located person will seldom retain the memory of having appeared elsewhere, because bi-locations take place through higher Consciousness, whose elevated vibration is of another dimension than the physical body. This is the reason why my guru did not have any memory of appearing in my room that afternoon.

In meditation with focus in the third eye, God will slowly reveal himself as light. As time goes on, the light will grow brighter as the Light is dawning and drawing all of us in.

Chapter Sixty-three

Mahashivaratri in Bhigaan

The ashram was getting ready to celebrate *Mahashivaratri*, a Hindu festival considered to be the most auspicious for transcending the mind and thereby finding liberation or self-realization. With the cosmic vibrations at its peak, Guruji would give a three-day special initiation for the students of the meditation camp. For me the initiations meant my formal dedication to God in the form of Mother *Shakti-Kundalini*, which Shri Guruji represented.

Guruji expected around one thousand *sadhakas* to come for the celebration. The ashram was small, and I heard from Rachna that Guruji himself had decided that I should move to another room. I was to share the room with another woman from the United States. As I realized that Indian *sadhakas* had to cram into small rooms with six or more family members and sleep "Indian style" (bodies in very close proximity to one another) on minimal bedding on the cold granite floors, I felt enormous gratitude for his gesture.

But after the luxury of solitude, sharing a room became more problematic than expected. I experienced personality conflicts with my new roommate, who expressed irritation with my Dutch mannerisms. "You remind me," she said, "of my upbringing by my German mother." I felt trapped in *maya* assuming that as long as the American woman and I shared one roof, I would not be able to go deeply into the spiritual silence I craved during this special festival. In my disappointment, I had forgotten God, and not my limited ways of thinking, was in charge. And above all, "Was I not preparing to surrender my egoic-limited-self to Him during the upcoming initiations?"

On the evening before the first *Mahashivaratri* initiation I had a hard time getting to sleep. Some of Guruji's *sadhakas* from the surrounding areas and Delhi were steadily arriving, creating a seldom-felt restless atmosphere in the ashram. The rooms were filling up to the brim. When the noisy conversations of a few late arrivals finally subsided, I dozed off to sleep. During that sleep, I had a profound dream:

> Two hands are holding my throat very gently and I wake up, but I am still dreaming... The hands are of an ethereal nature and belong to someone who is standing behind me. The two soft hands move downwards, softly touching all the major *chakra* points in my body. The hands and the being to which they belong completely merge into my body. I begin to feel divine love moving through my entire body. The intensity is building. I am losing my personal identity and I feel myself merging and totally dissolving into infinite love.

I woke up from my dream and felt the divine hands in my physical hands. I was in a state of complete oneness with something greater than the regular me. The feeling invoked indescribable joy, far beyond what ordinary words can express.

Part of the normal daily schedule in Guruji's ashram was the reading of a sacred text, the *Paath Durga Saptshati* out of the *Devi*

Mahatmyam, Glory of the Divine Mother (seven hundred mantras on Sri Durga). During these readings I had often been moved by the description of the hands of the Divine Mother in Chapter 4:27,

> O, Ambika, protect us on every side with your sword, spear and club and whatever other weapons your sprout-like (soft) hands have touched.

During our daily morning chant to the divine Mother, I had always imagined holding the sprout-like soft hand of Ambika-Durga, which is the same as *Shakti-Kundalini*.

Completely lost in immense love in which nothing else existed, I continued lying on my bed with my eyes closed. While I was floating in a divine river of love, the following thought surfaced: "These hands must have been Sai Baba's in the form of the divine Mother." The moment that thought flashed through my mind, a brilliant light appeared in the center of my head, like a gigantic multifaceted diamond. "Is that you, Baba?" I asked within. Another diamond-like star appeared in my head as bright and brilliant as the first one. Awestruck, in silent contemplation of what was happening, I suddenly realized that I had been the experiencer, the experience and that which I experienced, all at once. The moment that particular thought entered my mind, a third star of that same luminous brilliant light spread throughout my head, a confirmation of the truth of that thought.

The early morning light broke over the ashram and the *Mahashivaratri* festival began its first day. I realized that I had gone through the unique experience of absorption in divine love. In that state no other but God exists. Thoughts about my room-mate Ann had no longer any relevance. Ann had not particularly liked Shri Guruji, but when he had touched her head and third eye during the *Mahashivaratri*-initiation, she was stunned when a large lightning bolt appeared in midair, entering into her body with a tremendous force. Her doubts about him left and she realized who he really was. After that, we both had reasons to celebrate and we knew that the ashram was heaven on earth!

The sacred initiations had once more stirred in me the yearning for liberation. I felt it had to be the same as that supreme union, or the completion of self, I experienced in my dream. The only difference would be that the realization of *That* would be everlasting. I thought, "I am perhaps not ready for that as yet, and only God can know the exact time of my readiness to merge fully and forever into his light." After the festival was over, the experience of divine love did not abate, making it near impossible to leave Guruji's ashram. This time I could change my ticket so that I could attend the next meditation camp. This change would still allow me to have an eight-day stay with Sai Baba on the same round-trip ticket.

A new group soon arrived for the second meditation camp. I sensed a difference between the people arriving and myself. I vibrated on another level and the newcomers felt strangely worldly. I no longer felt any attachment to, or any desire for, that world. I remembered Jesus pointing to "our living in this world" without forgetting that we are ultimately spirit. It makes sense to be attached only to that which is permanent, one's own soul as a part in the infinite higher Consciousness. I had no doubt that I had, like others who live in monasteries, become more attuned to the spiritual way of life than the life in the world. I had gone through a major shift.

During the new camp a tarp was laid out on the lawn in the middle of the ashram. Here Guruji would meet with his students every afternoon punctually at four. I always made sure to sit right in front of Guruji's lawn chair, which was covered by an orange cloth. Most students would greet him with folded hands Indian style, their eyes meeting his. *Om Sai Ram* or *Om Namah Shivaya* was his greeting to us. "Any questions?" he would ask after he sat down. He knew many *sadhakas* by their personal name. If no one had a question, he often looked at me. "Ella, have you any questions?" He also knew that I was always able to come up with something to ask. I was so delighted to ask him anything, for when I looked at him and I started my question with, "Guruji –" I could, as before, feel the *Kundalini* rising up my spine. This rising of cosmic power to meet cosmic power, complete in Shri Guruji, gave ecstatic joy. Often I could taste the *Kundalini* in my mouth. I once asked Guruji whether this was a real experience. His answer was, "Yes."

Chapter Sixty-four

My Father

During my stay at the ashram I noticed an older village woman bowing down and touching Shri Guruji's feet. A thought immediately flashed through my mind that I too wanted to touch the feet of my Guru. "Please, Guruji, may I touch your feet?" I asked zealously. "Yes, but inside the classroom," he replied, shaking his head in affirmation... In Indian understanding, to touch the feet of a God-realized person is the same as touching the feet of God.

I went inside and kneeled down at the feet of my Guru, touching his feet and putting my third eye softly with all my devotion for God on his feet. For a brief moment in this mode of deep surrender, I felt as if I had reached the ultimate, the end and fulfillment of my yearning for God. When I sat down and looked at Guruji, he stated, "You have an infatuation with your father!" Shocked, I was instantly jerked out of my contemplation of God. Gone were my high feelings. "How could this be possible?" I had never had a close relationship with my father. I quickly decided that Guruji must certainly be wrong, but I nevertheless began to ponder what he said long and hard.

Soon my time at his ashram was up and as planned, I

traveled by plane from Delhi to Bangalore to stay near Sai Baba's ashram. In his temple during the many hours I had to sit and wait in *darshan* line, I read all of Dr. Goel's books I had bought in Bhigaan. I often reflected on Guruji's stern remarks that kept haunting me. "If the guru is God, he is that higher Consciousness and only speaks from that level; therefore," I reasoned, "the guru must always be right. What Shri Guruji said to me is perhaps something that God wants me to know." One night when contemplating once more my guru's comment, I fell asleep and received a revelation in a dream:

> I am watching a play that reminds me of *darshan* with Sai Baba. I am sitting on a chair in a row of chairs, each row elevated from the next, amphitheater style, so I could easily see the play on the stage. I see my father sitting some fifteen feet away from me to my left. He has his old-fashioned soft felt hat pulled over his eyes sideways, as if he does not want to be recognized. I can see that from under this hat he is watching me intently. His eyes are keenly observing all that I am doing, ready to notice my every move. It shakes me up. I immediately feel enormously guilty watching this play about Sai Baba. I know on a deep emotional level that my father is criticizing me.

When I woke up, I was flabbergasted. "Could Guruji be right? Did I have an infatuation with my father? What did he mean by infatuation?" My thoughts went back to my youth, as my father had looked so young in my dream. "Was I criticized by him during my upbringing and had I perhaps incorporated that judging part into myself?" I began to ponder this idea.

A parent is a powerful force in child development. Even after the child becomes an adult, parts of the parent remain as a figment of the imaginary mind with either positive or negative connotations. The parent, in my case my father, was held in my mind as a censor, not necessarily representing the real outer parent, but that part that a child may presumably adopt as an inner judge for its own good.

A year later during my second meditation camp in Bhigaan, I again thought how that critical part within myself was still present and most likely holding me back on my spiritual journey. I wondered if Shri Guruji could shine more light on this potential problem. After all he was the one who had made me aware of something that apparently needed looking at.

From the first day I met Guruji, I had been impressed by his humility, wisdom, wit and honesty. He did not create an impression of himself that he was higher than any of us and yet Guruji had more powers than he let us know. He was simply too modest to make a display of himself. I peeked once in a while at Shri Guruji when he sat on his guru throne in the shrine room during our evening bhajan singing and noticed that he was in some kind of trance state of higher awareness. Perhaps I was in a trance too as I could see a liquid transparent energy of divine love flowing from him, especially to those *sadhakas* who had asked him in class for help with their problems. Seeing this was quite blissful, like divine nectar, and yet I realized that I was unable to look at him for a longer period of time as his powerful radiant light energy affected me in a way I did not readily understand. But I had an innate sense that by focusing my eyes on Guruji, from his higher perspective he would help me with my unresolved dilemma as he was doing for the other students.

One night, during devotional singing, I decided I had to take courage to look directly at Guruji while he sat on his throne wrapped in a large off-white Indian blanket covering his orange *kurta*-pyjama. Strangely, whenever I lifted my head to look at him, I found that I was only able to do so for a very short period of time. Whenever Guruji looked back at me with his powerful eyes, I immediately had to cast my eyes downward. I came to the realization that I was extremely afraid to look at him for longer periods. It suddenly dawned on me that it was not Shri Guruji himself, but my own inner part representing my father of whom I was really afraid. I was frightened to be with my guru and to be criticized by my father for it. It was my judging father sitting right inside of me, watching my every move. I began to feel enormously uncertain as to what this "judge inside" might think of me, or do to me.

I remembered my father's raging disapproval when I had placed a small vase containing an orchid next to a picture of Sai Baba in the bookcase of the guest room several years ago, and what intense emotions this had evoked in me. I now understood my deep inner problem of having an extreme fear of my father, who was seemingly well established as the critic within. "I must overcome this fear by facing it head on," I thought. I again began to look at Shri Guruji, trying to hold my gaze for longer periods. I forced myself to keep my eyes fixed on him but this gave rise to the most unbearable agony. My effort to continue staring could be likened to climbing a high, treacherously steep mountain without taking any break. My heart was throbbing wildly. After a while I noticed that Guruji knew what was internally going on with me from his cosmic perspective. He was kindly and with great understanding encouraging me with his eyes to look at him, but this made me even more nervous. I was looking the fear for my father straight in the face. I kept focusing on my guru's eyes to will myself with all my might to overcome this intense angst. It took all my courage and all my determination to over-come the overwhelming, almost paralyzing fear that I was not strong enough to persevere. I continued gazing at Shri Guruji till I succeeded in making full eye contact with him. Suddenly all fear left... At that moment, I felt completely drained of energy even though I knew I had won an enormous psychological battle.

After *bhajans*, I walked back to my room and sat down for meditation to reflect on what had occurred within me. Suddenly I started to cry... Floods of tears were flowing from my eyes. This lasted for ten minutes. It was as if I was cleansed of the criticizing judge within, for good. Suddenly the weeping stopped and I began to laugh and was soon roaring with extreme laughter. I could clearly see my conditioning regarding my father from a very early age on. I was transcending the bindings of imprison-ment by my inner critic, and tears of release and happiness were flowing. I realized how it had restrained my own freedom and development to reach God.

After all, Guruji had been correct. The infatuation had been for God the Father, for which I was severely criticized by that part within me that corresponded to my birth father. I was in love with God, and my father (inside) tried to stop me due to the fact that I had incorporated him as my inner critic. I realized that I had seen the Divine at work through the form of Shri Guruji. I knew I had received a huge release in my process of deconditioning on the *Kundalini* path to enlightenment.

Chapter Sixty-five

Kundalini Movements

In a soul response to Guruji's radiant energy, *sadhakas* were falling into deep trance states, their upper bodies moving in circular motions in a variety of ways. I saw a young woman from Switzerland, who sat on my left during *bhajans*, slowly sliding down to the ground while her head turned upward towards the ceiling. She stayed in a state of complete motionless statue-like ecstatic rapture. Her eyes looked empty as if consciousness had left the body. At the same time, other *sadhakas* shook their heads back and forth, from side to side, or up and down, sometimes quite violently. I observed a woman with her eyes fixated towards the ceiling in a staring gaze that lasted for half an hour. Guruji's fully enlightened presence stirred and re-ignited the cosmic force of *Kundalini* in his students, whose bodies responded by making strange jerking movements with arms, hands, legs, spines and heads, sometimes accompanied by utterances of sounds or words that could not be readily understood.

These movements and sounds happen involuntarily. The motions cannot be stopped and the body is compelled to go along with the *shakti*-force. The divine purpose of this mother *Kundalini* power is to bring the *jiva* back to Shiva, bringing the soul home to reunite with the unbound Consciousness.

Guruji, in class, once reported that he had seen a village woman who partially took on the form of Mother Kali, her tongue elongated and protruding out of her mouth. I also heard that one *sadhaka* in the past, in a *Kundalini* state, thought he was a monkey and as such jumped from tree to tree in the ashram. Without being familiar with these *Kundalini* movements, one can be quite shocked observing them.

I remember when a bit over-assertive tall middle-aged woman from Sweden, a psychiatrist by profession, came to visit a friend, but with a keen interest as well to learn what was happening at the *Kundalini* ashram. After attending her first *bhajan* session in which she observed the various *Kundalini* movements, this woman stood up and remarked unsympathetically, "This is an insane asylum." Shocked and intellectually unable to comprehend what she saw, she quickly left the ashram to continue her travels through India. I had sympathy for the woman because I understood that without knowing anything about *Kundalini*, the movements and trance states look, at first glance, extremely bizarre.

In my own body I sensed subtle motions of *Shakti-Kundalini* that were undetectable to others. I felt as if I was attached to a magnetic force, which was pulling the *Kundalini* toward the crown *chakra* in a circular motion, causing feelings of bliss, nausea, dizziness and also pressure inside my head.

This power is so intense that by writing the words now on this paper I experience the force of Kundalini *and my head suddenly shakes and trembles. The power is of another dimension and its frequency opens me up to higher Consciousness. Pressure builds in my crown* chakra *and I feel the* Kundalini *rising up through my throat. For a moment I just feel the* kali *forces of* Shakti, *and a sense of enormous gratitude wells up from my heart* chakra.

Guruji said that some people make the violent movements when the *shakti* path is obstructed. All a *sadhaka* can do is surrender to the cosmic force and not inhibit the movements. Trying to stop them may cause pain.

When I first met Shri Guruji in May 1996, I noticed that his legs, in sitting position, were shaking most the time. Guruji explained, "These types of *Kundalini* movements will cease. There is no need to worry about them." When we met again in 1997, the involuntary leg movements of Guruji had fully disappeared.

I already wrote that Guruji explained that there are two nerves near the crown *chakra*, called *dwesha* and *raga*, on which the whole personality of the individual is situated. These nerves are the center of the ego and mind. Once these most basic nerves are displaced from their original position, they cannot be put back.

One can be reborn while in this human body either through many years of meditation or the arousal of *Kundalini* by a guru. In this rebirth, supreme mother *Kundalini* acts as the mother in place of the birth mother. Supreme Consciousness as Lord Shiva acts as the father in place of the birth father. The individual *jiva* acts as the child. Not only will the old nervous system be completely dissolved, but a new nervous system will also be created through a slow process. This new system contains all spiritual knowledge. After this second birth, one lives in the world as a son of God or a messenger of God, or even as God himself.

The teachings of Shri Siddheswar Baba have helped me understand that in my life these nerves near my *Brahma-randhra* have fallen twice: the first time when I experienced a nervous breakdown during the movie *Back to the Future* and the second time after my session with a hypnotist, resulting in another nervous breakdown. Both breakdowns were immediately followed by *Kundalini* activities and symptoms.

It is interesting to note that when my first nervous breakdown took place in the theater, I could only see the screen and was no longer able to engage in the drama displayed on it. This event literally relates to a chapter in Professor N. Kasturi's book entitled *Prashanti, Pathway to Peace*, in which he explains that the screen in a movie theater is like the unchanging world called *nitya,* and the projected picture on this screen represents the changing world, *anitya.*

Eckhart Tolle says the same in his book *Stillness Speaks.* He talks about the field of alert stillness in which the phenomenal world of forms appears. The screen is still and stillness, unmovable and yet the basis of all.

I had connected with this screen, but at that time could not fully grasp what was taking place and what the message was for me. With the screen I could have found that self-realization I was longing for, but I realize I was not ready for that great blessing. My understanding of the screen was still viewed by my mind and intellect, narrowing the phenomenon of what was taking place. When the nerves broke at my *Brahma-randhra,* my ego-self, fearing its final destruction, began to fight to get back to that state this limited-self called "normal." The screen, figuratively speaking, scared me. Had I removed all fear of my new situation, the light of understanding would have flooded in and taken me Home. Instead, I remained in an in-between state, which I often referred to as an altered state. My own frightful thoughts became the biggest roadblocks to my final goal. But mother *Kundalini,* once awakened from her sleep in the *muladhara chakra*, constantly creates new possibilities of homecoming. I believe that it was her power that ultimately directed me to Shri Guruji to grant me healing from an abortive *Kundalini* arousal.

Chapter Sixty-six

Merging with My Guru's Guru

Guruji fulfilled all my spiritual desires. I wished I could have stayed with him forever. At the end of my six weeks' stay at my second meditation camp, I lived in a state of full acceptance of all that is. Still, underneath this blissful state, I was aware of feelings of obligation to pay my respect to Sai Baba, the guru of my guru. I shared this notion with other devotees, but Shri Guruji never told us we were under such obligation. Unfortunately, I never asked him directly. My time in the ashram was ending, and I needed to get ready to use the eight days I had left on my airline ticket to see Sai Baba, before returning back home to the United States.

Before taking leave of Shri Guruji, I asked for a personal interview. I waited outside and sat on the tarp on the lawn in the center of the ashram. Guruji came and sat down on his lawn chair. With reverence, I asked him, "Are you my guru?" I had been wondering whether I was meant to live for longer duration in the Bhigaan ashram to find God-realization. Guruji answered, "Ella, the guru is within you. He is *always* with you." He also added, "Come to India three months out of the year and sit with an enlightened saint." He did not mention himself, but to me the Siddheswar-ashram was the only place, away from home, where I really wanted to be.

When I arrived in Bangalore, Syed Ali took me to the Ashraya Hotel to spend the night. I felt radiant. At early dawn the next day Ali picked me up and dropped me off at Patel's Guest House. A room was available, and with the help of Ali and the Patel boys, I was able to move in quickly. The luscious tropical flower gardens surrounding the guesthouse gave me a sense of beauty and serenity. I was pleased to have a quiet room to continue the *sadhana* (spiritual practices) I had learned in Guruji's ashram.

In the afternoon I dressed in my blue *punjabi* to make the short walk to Sai Baba's ashram. I received favorable seating in the Ramesh Hall, sat down and waited for *bhajan* singing to begin. Suddenly the door on the back left side of the podium opened and Swami appeared in his flaming red-orange robe. He sat down on his ornamental chair that stood in the middle of the podium. As

I sat close to the podium, I could see his facial expressions clearly. In the shrine room in Bhigaan, I had learned not to be afraid to look one's guru straight in the face. I also understood the benefits of usinng the outer guru's form to find the guru within.

In my new way of spiritual resoluteness I fixed my eyes on Sai Baba's face and gazed at him and felt myself slowly flowing into his form until we became one. The barriers between us completely disappeared. I was aware he knew me and knew who I was. It felt exceedingly intimate and tears of joy were flowing inside my spiritual heart. For a moment I became breathless and felt my heart merging into his, and I realized that I was having a heart-to-heart spiritual experience with Swami. He talked to me inside and at the same time from where he was sitting on the platform. I saw him weeping with joy at the same time that I wept with joy. I saw tears streaming from his eyes. His intense look made me smile as he continued to look at me directly. He smiled when I smiled. Words are not enough to express the depth of connectedness I experienced. I do not remember anything else afterwards. I must have gone back to my hotel with my mind in a complete trance state.

In the night following this spiritual experience I became violently ill. I vomited all night and suffered all the other nasty symptoms of dysentery. Weakened, I staggered to the door and struggled to get the door lock unbolted and the door opened. I had forgotten about the monkey families that lived on the rooftops who would love to come and steal any food they could lay their hands on. All I could think was, "I am not going to make it through the night." I wanted the door open so that my dead body could be found in the morning and not after the eight days had gone by for which I had paid in advance. I crawled on my hands and feet over the brown painted cement floor to and from the bathroom as the need arose. I reached for my acidophilus tablets in my bag and swallowed several to boost the flora of good bacteria in my intestinal track. I kept cleaning the mess I was making by using antibacterial cleansers I always kept handy while in India. Exhausted, I lay down on the cold concrete floor for some time. When I regained enough strength I moved and managed to raise myself into my bed. Completely worn out, I quietly stretched out on my back under the mosquito netting and fortunately dozed off to sleep.

I woke up in the early morning still extremely weak. I felt alone, and thought, "If I had died, no one would have known." A next thought arose: "This type of thinking is false. God, as Sai Baba, always knew where I was." As I recalled the beautiful oneness with him the prior day, a beautiful dazzling diamond-white light appeared in my third eye making my whole body shake by its intensity and confirming my thoughts to be correct.

Thanks to Guruji I had been freed from the highly critical father-part inside me. It had allowed me to fully focus on Baba's form as a representation of higher mind. Since my *Kundalini* awakening, I paid homage to Sai Baba in a different way, as my diminished egoic-self had been placed in the hands of Shri Siddhweswar Baba as my guide to realization. I remember Guruji saying in class, "Anyone who comes here and is touched by me will not be able to run away from me, for I have come to liberate that soul. It is my duty as a guru."

I also remembered his departing words: "The guru is within you and always with you." It did not matter really which form I would choose, be it Sai Baba, Shri Guruji, Shirdi Sai Baba, Krishna, the Buddha or any other form. God uses all forms and paths to bring a spiritual aspirant closer to him.

To my surprise, sick as I had been with dysentery, I was able to go for *darshan* that morning. The feelings of oneness with Sai Baba did not return during my remaining week with him. It did not matter. "My cup (had) runneth over" and there was simply nothing more to add.

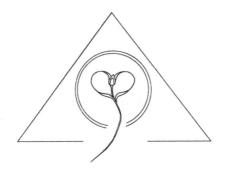

PART VIII

Stumbling Blocks

Chapter Sixty-seven

Obstacles on the Path

I came back to the United States in early spring with my inner light glowing and determined to go back to Guruji in October to attend my third and fourth meditation camps.

While pondering what to choose as a spiritual topic of writing for the fall meditation camps, I received a subtle inner prompting that it should be on fear. "How strange," I thought. "How can I write about fear without actually going through the experience?" It was early summer and I could not have guessed that my spiritual journey would soon be facing obstacles. It all started when I was looking for a document in the attic. Suddenly, while hopping down the stairs with some boxes, my left knee twisted, making climbing up or down the stairs difficult. After several weeks of favoring my left leg, my right leg began to hurt and I became frightened. My paper entitled "Fear on the Spiritual Path" was in the making.

For the next months, I struggled with knee pain, trying various modalities in the alternative healing field without any relief. Desperate to get well before my trip to India, I decided to consult with a medical doctor specializing in sports medicine. This doctor, rather than looking at my knees, did some spinal adjustments. When he was done he announced, "All will be well in three days." But after three days I was still hurting. I phoned my doctor, who enthusiastically said, "Come right over! I will give you injections that will cure your pain immediately." With that promise, I hurried to his office.

Upon my arrival Dr. P said smilingly, "There is a new German method to alleviate pain of the knees by injecting procaine into the abdominal nerve plexus." On his examination table, he poked around in the lower abdominal area and then left the room. Within minutes he reappeared, rolling in a whole surgical table heaped with instruments to perform the procedure. Frightened, I asked the doctor where he planned to inject and why there were so many tubes lying on the table. "I know my anatomy and this new direct way of healing," he said, going forward. Within ten minutes it was all over. When I got off the table, the doctor was dancing around me asking, "How is it? How are your knees? Is the pain gone?"

I answered, "No, it is not gone, and something strange is occurring that I cannot quite explain."

"Take a week and you will be well," he said.

Within the week, instead of pain relief, I began to have unbearable abdominal pain. The pain around my knees suddenly became a minor issue. When I revisited the doctor I exclaimed, "I am in excruciating pain in the abdominal area where you put the shots," while looking him straight in the eyes.

Dr. P said, "I am sorry!" His next comment was, "You are re-experiencing appendicitis attacks. The shots brought on a change in your nervous system, laying bare old memories of pain." I was eight years old when my appendix had been removed, and it distressed and surprised me to hear that my present pain related to that time. The doctor suggested, "I will give you more shots of procaine into the abdominal area totally free of charge!" Shocked, I declined the offer, opting for other opinions and possible solutions.

Besides my pain, *Kundalini* intensified. I felt nauseated, could not hold down food, lost my appetite and experienced dizzy spells.

Kundalini would rise and shake me, causing more pain. I realized that on the *Kundalini* path physical pain is experienced more intensely than in people not in that awakening process. *Kundalini* had given me the spiritual gifts of bliss, knowing and seeing beyond the physical realms, but also oversensitivity to all things. During my reality shifts, *Kundalini* also brought the subconsciously held fear regarding pain to my awareness. Fear is augmented when the mind imagines a future with accelerating pain scenarios, which in turn throws the psyche into more anxieties. With an active *Kundalini* this is experienced even more dramatically.

In my calmer moments of reflection I seriously wondered whether my pain reaction to the shots could imply karma. *Kundalini* is known to bring up the karmas from past and present lives in an ever-increasing manner. If this were the case, I was not doing well in the practice of being the objective witness, as I had no equanimity whatsoever. Besides the pain, I began to experience cold spells. I remember lying down on my deckchair in the hot summer sun covered by heavy blankets, wearing woolen socks and my teeth chattering from cold. I obviously needed help. I went to my regular doctor, who sent me immediately to the hospital, expecting internal bleeding. He ordered a CT scan, but no evidence of any bleeding or damaged organs was found. "I cannot do anything for you!" my G.P. said. "You will have to put mind over matter!"

Despite all the turmoil and agonies in my life, I nevertheless miraculously managed to hang onto a clear-thinking mind and an innate ability to sense beyond the normal. I also had an incredible determination to get well. After two months of inner questioning, I just knew, as did my husband, that there was no better place to bring my problems than to the feet of my *Kundalini* guru, Shri Siddeshwar Baba.

Chapter Sixty-eight

Back to Guruji's Ashram

After all my travel plans were set in motion, I felt it was a huge mistake to travel first to Puttaparthi to see Sai Baba. Looking back it still surprises me that I could have had such determination of spirit to make that long trip in severe pain and in altered states of *Kundalini*. I arrived in Puttaparthi during the Paduka festival (festival of the blessing of sandals representing the feet of the Lord, to be used in *puja* rooms). The ashram was packed to the brim with devotees. All the rooms in the ashram were taken, but fortunately some kind women devotees invited me to share their hotel room at Sai Towers with me. As Sai Baba was sought out for healing by devotees and non-devotees the world over, I too entertained some vague hope that I might receive healing. But things turned out quite differently.

On the morning of the festival, Sai Baba appeared before his crowds of devotees riding triumphantly in a pure golden chariot modeled after those of India's ancient days. I had never seen such a display of wealth except with the royalty of Europe. Most devotees were jubilant to witness the golden chariot and believed it signaled the dawning of a "New Age." I thought, "Would God, in order to bring spiritual revival to humankind, need to display such wealth in such a poor country?" I began to question Sai Baba's validity as an avatar. My secret hope to find healing in the Puttaparthi ashram also began to shatter. "This is no longer my ashram," I thought. "I need to go north and be with my true guru, Shri Siddheswar Baba." The enormous crowds, the miracle stories, and the huge display of wealth began to take its toll on me. As my physical situation worsened, I called my husband, desperate and uncertain as to where to go from here.

Jon said, "If you come home, Stanley (the dog) and I will take care of you, but going to Guruji might be your better option." I chose the latter.

It was monsoon time. On my flight to Delhi I peeked from my window seat through the breaks in the huge cloud formations below and became mesmerized by the endless green patches of land and hills soaked in complete dampness beneath me. At the Delhi airport, Santosh was waiting, ready to take me for the two-hour drive to the Siddheswar ashram. During our ride I re-entered altered states and my abdominal pain increased. The situation was at its peak by the time I reached the ashram.

I was glad to be greeted by Munish, a Guruji *sadhaka* I knew from a former meditation camp. This time he was the accommo-dation officer in charge and took me to my assigned room. He asked me how I was doing, and I said, "Not very well, I feel sick and do not know whether I will be able to stay."

Munish's reply was, "You have come to the right place, as there is nothing so bad that Guruji cannot fix it." His remark sounded like music to my ears. "This is definitely my true ashram," I thought.

I forced myself to set up my room and check in with the administration to pay for the camp. By the time I saw the administrator, Rachna, I was in such a lost state that it did not seem to matter whether I lived or died. "Are you paying for one meditation camp?" Rachna wanted to know.

"I do not know," I said. "Perhaps I can only stay two days as I feel so sick. I may need to call my husband to come and take me home. Please, let me talk to Shri Guruji personally," I pleaded.

Rachna answered, "I will ask Guruji, and let you know as soon as possible." Despite high anxiety levels, I managed to have a reasonable night's rest. Rachna appeared at my door in the early morning and reported, "Shri Guruji can see you privately in two days, after morning class." I had no idea if I could hold on that long. My situation felt dire and every minute of the day became a huge psychological struggle to keep myself from going over the edge of no return. I felt an isolation that was absolutely unbearable.

In the canteen I recognized Dr. Klaus T from the prior medi-tation camps. I mentally forced myself to join him at his table with some vague hope to divert my mind. At the canteen table

I was introduced to another gentleman, Gerry, who had just arrived from the United Kingdom. Gerry spoke about his healing practice in Britain, which involved the energizing of the higher *chakras*. I felt prompted to tell Gerry about my ordeal and added, "In two days I will have a private interview with Guruji, and if you agree I will seek his permission to have your *chakra* treatments." While still in conversation with Gerry and Klaus, my pain level dropped. I was able to relax slightly. Later on I learned that Gerry sent healing energy as soon as I mentioned my pain. But the pain came back full force the next day. The mere fact that Guruji would see me the morning thereafter kept me alive.

After class Rachna called me to meet Guruji on the lawn in front of his house. "Ella, what has happened to you?" he said, looking concerned. I related my story about the procaine injections, my plunge into a life with pain, altered states of *Kundalini*, and my high anxiety levels.

"Oh," Shri Guruji said, his eyes full of compassion, "this should not have happened to you." He continued to tell me that the real problem was that the practice of medicine is no longer a healing art. "Doctors are commercial, selling their wares for high fees. As patients, we have to be extremely aware and careful when we see a doctor in this age of moral decline. Always, when you see a doctor, pray that God will help you, pray that this doctor will do the right thing for you. Always ask God like that," Guruji said. His words had a soothing effect on my psyche, like balsam on a wound. "Come, sit closer to me, at my feet." I was already sitting at his feet but moved forward even further. Shri Guruji put his hands on my crown *chakra*, rubbing his divine energy into it. While Guruji was doing this work on me I felt changes occurring inside my head. My head was moving in his hands and I was able to surrender to the higher states of consciousness. I do not know how long he worked on me. After my time of sitting with him was up, I asked whether Gerry could work on me during the camp. "Yes, let him work on you, that healer has much *shakti*," Guruji replied. The shift on the inner level made it possible as well as desirable to stay for the full period of the meditation camp.

Gerry began his healing work by energizing my higher *chakras* (from the heart *chakra* up to the crown *chakra*) with his divinely charged magnetism, and gradually my pain level dropped. By activating the higher *chakras*, Gerry had brought my awareness above the senses of bodily existence, where pain is not registered. By the end of the meditation camp I was free of pain and able to keep my original schedule to stay for another ten-day camp. Many students including Gerry left and a new group of about twenty-five people arrived from the United Kingdom.

Within days of the new meditation camp my pain returned. There was a fresh influx of healers from Britain who kindly offered all sorts of "hands-on healing" help to me. I was touched by their love, but the daily healings brought pain relief for only a short duration.

At this time I presented my paper entitled, "Fear on the Spiritual Path." Pain and fear are part of our collective human experience, bringing up feelings of powerlessness, hopelessness and desperation. Instead of surrendering to the will of the higher Consciousness, doubt and fear held me in their clutches, which undoubtedly kept manifesting the pain in my body. Doubt causes fear, and both come from ego and live in ego. The ego mind does not want to give up its acquired territory, and its whole existence feeds on all the restrictive thoughts, which never lead the spirit back to God. We all have the power of will to change negative thoughts into positive ones, which in turn will expand our awareness of God, allowing rays of his light to enter. In God-awareness the ego will be subordinate, a tool to act out the divine plan.

Can doubt ever be helpful? Doubt can be of use when it is doubtful of a negative. Doubting a negative can become a positive. Not letting doubt be the only consideration leaves room for the intuitive self or inner voice to be heard. This happens in silence and always comes from the higher Consciousness. Byron Katie, a self-realized woman, makes this point clear in her teaching method designed to awaken other souls, entitled *The Work*. The book *The Awakening West* records a conversation between John Lumiere-Wins, one of the authors, and Byron Katie. In a reply to the question posed to her whether she had any suggestions or recommendations for those who are experiencing a desire to awaken, she states:

> Catch a belief, write it down and ask, "Is it true? Can I know that it is true?...
>
> And lastly ask, "Who would I be without that belief? Then just be still and know.

Byron Katie is saying to her students that doubting belief systems is helpful on the spiritual path. Turning belief systems around and looking at the beliefs from different angles will help spiritual aspirants to become the seer rather than the ego. The seer or witness is always the higher-Self looking.

Guruji's response to my paper was positive. It brought up questions and the sharing of experiences of other *sadhakas*. Afterwards two of Guruji's lady *sadhakas* came to talk to me. They shared their own private experiences with severe long-term pain linked to revealed actions in prior lives. Through them I learned the truth about karmic suffering, as well as the ultimate release from the bindings of karma. In eastern philosophy karma is the word for action, which can be good or bad. Action that takes place has a reaction, as cause always has an effect. Actions that take place in a person's life cause a reaction in this particular life or in the next life. Actions from prior lives can have a consequence in today's life. To give an example, "If you are dishonest and steal from someone, chances are that you will undergo the same situation in this life or the next. But karma is not based on revenge, as 'an eye for an eye,' but is for deepening a person's understanding of his or her action."

In my own life I believe that the death of my first husband

Harmen was karmic. I came in this school of life to learn and grow deeper in the understanding of love. Harmen's sudden tragic loss affected my soul and person forever and brought me to realms of love far beyond the physical. The event was perhaps written in the blueprint of my life created before I was born.

Most souls come into birth to overcome some karma. This karma, the urge to seek deeper understanding, also keeps us in the bondage of reincarnation. The karmic bindings can be removed one by one, through suffering, or through having good things come our way because of good deeds in the past. After the *Kundalini* awakening, *Shakti* brings up these karmas faster, which causes life to intensify, helping the sufferer to clear the way to liberation. After liberation karma plays no further role. Liberation is the end-goal and freedom for the soul. It forever releases the *jiva*-spirit from the wheel of reincarnation. A realized soul can choose to come into birth again to help elevate humankind with the teachings on higher Consciousness.

Chapter Sixty-nine

Screams in *Kundalini*

A young woman in her late twenties from a Scandinavian country suddenly appeared in the middle of our meditation camp. I noticed her strange behavior in the shrine room when she approached Guruji, and immediately knew that she was not well mentally. Another student who knew her told me that earlier in her life she had her *Kundalini*-awakening intentionally induced by taking illicit drugs. This method is extremely dangerous and can easily lead to insanity. It is like any abortive *Kundalini* state, an awakening without the grace of a divine Guru. Sometimes even a Guru cannot make such a person whole again, because of the karma involved. Shri Guruji was as helpful as he could be, but the mental state of the woman deteriorated rapidly. Her bizarre behavior often reminded me of Ophelia in Shakespeare's *Hamlet*.

Help was needed. Guruji called the best psychiatrist from Delhi to come to the ashram for consultation. During the day two other medical doctors, participants in the meditation camp, and Guruji himself attended to the young woman's special needs. Besides insanity, the woman suffered from severe anxiety attacks. As I had suffered the same, I felt the deepest love for her. Most students took turns around the clock to stay with the young woman, as she could not be left on her own. How well I remembered my own fear of insanity during my ups and downs in *Kundalini*. By observing a woman who had slipped over the edge, I thanked God that I had not gone there. I knew full well that my initial *Kundalini*-awakening had also been abortive with all the dangers this entailed. I felt I had slipped through the eye of a needle.

The whole camp became involved in this challenging case of mental breakdown. A sum of money was quickly raised to buy a plane ticket for the young woman and a *sadhaka*- countryman to accompany her back home. It was an intense time at the ashram. The mentally ill woman did not want to leave the ashram, nor India.

One evening, I was strolling around the ashram grounds with June, one of the healers from England. June was a powerful healer and a wonderful spiritually evolved human being. She had spent much of her daytime trying to bring relief to our "mental woman." From where we walked we could hear the *bhajan* singing in the shrine room on the other side of the ashram. Instead of *bhajans*, we were clear that it was more important to discuss the matter of the young woman, which had become a new focus in the ashram. The sacred and melodious sounds of the singing accompanied us while we circled around the small ashram.

I began to notice brilliant sparks of divine light everywhere, and *Kundalini* shook my body whenever these intense penetrating lights presented themselves. I told June about it and also mentioned that I was experiencing increased physical pain. "Let us immediately go to your room," she said, "and I will do a special healing on you." In my room June asked that I sit down in my chair so that she could begin her particular method of energy transfer. When I was seated she said, "Tune in to the Divine or Shiva." I followed her instructions, and at that very moment of connecting with the divine in the form of Shiva, involuntary screams upon screams exited from my throat. The screams were so intense that June could not proceed with her healing work. These screams were beyond my control; they just happened and their raw violence hurt my throat.

The next day during breakfast in the canteen I overheard *sadhakas* talking about the loud screams they heard the night before. Everybody in the ashram had noticed, but attributed the screams to the unfortunate insane woman. I decided to tell the ladies at my table that it had actually been me who had been screaming so deafeningly and that it was part of my *Kundalini* expression over which I had no control. Later on I asked Shri Guruji about these screams that come through me involuntarily whenever I tune in to divine vibration or divine light that connects me to the higher levels of consciousness. Guruji said, "Be the witness," as his only comment.

At a later time, by re-reading the book *The Kundalini Experience* by the psychiatrist Dr. Lee Sannella, I found in Chapter 8: "Summary of Signs and Symptoms," under Motor Phenomena:

> The movements are spontaneous. These automatic movements also include spontaneous crying, laughing, screaming, and whistling.

I had experienced the deep crying, laughing, and screaming in my *Kundalini* process, and was delighted to know these symptoms were well documented in the work of Dr. Sannella.

Chapter Seventy
Kundalini and Sex

In addition to aforementioned symptoms, I feel that it is necessary to add the possibility of experiencing severe sexual yearnings and trials like the ones Swami Muktananda, a *siddha* yogi, describes in his book *Play of Consciousness*. In Swami Muktananda's meditation, the divine Mother appears and allures him sexually to draw out all the hidden unconscious desires he did not even know he possessed. I found the same theme in Irena Tweedie's autobiography and liberation story, *The Chasm of Fire*, wherein she reports a paroxysm of sex craving. She writes to have experienced:

> A wild howling of everything female in me, for a male. The whole body was sex only; every cell, every particle, was shouting for it; even the skin, the hands, the nails, every atom…

> …A fire was burning inside my bowels and the sensation of heat increased and decreased in waves. I could do nothing. I was in complete psychological turmoil.

I too have experienced such tremendous persuasive sexual callings. To my understanding this phenomenon happens on most spiritual seekers' journeys, because we absolutely must fully acknowledge and come to grips with the forces of sexual power in the world as well as in ourselves. Kahlil Gibran in his work *The Prophet* writes on *Pleasure*:

> Often times in denying yourself pleasure you do but store the desire in the recesses of your being.

All those dedicated to the spiritual life, monks, nuns, priests, *sannyasis* or *brahmacharyas,* etc., have encountered the powers of sex either in this or in many previous lives. For some of these spiritually dedicated people the denial or renunciation of the sexual creative forces has in some cases unfortunately led to the opposite, a secret misuse of the human sexual impulses, thereby hurting others in the process. The vow to celibacy is perhaps an unnatural method to control the base instincts in humans. Without a more integrative understanding on the topic, the road to the light could be lost, resulting in more darkness of soul.

India is a land that has often acknowledged these sexual forces, as one can see, for instance, in the temple of Khajuraho, which is known, as are others, for the profusion of erotic scenes that adorn it. Maybe the *maithuna*, representing the sexual union, seen on temples in Hinduism as well as Buddhism, also forces men and women to have an honest look at themselves in the life of a householder as well as in the life of the ascetic, to realize what influence such powerful forces have caused or are causing in their lives. Sex to many is to enjoy the physical wonders created by God, the procreation force or the force of creation.

Sometimes I hear the question, "Could it be that on the path to liberation we have to free ourselves in the end from the pull of these earthly forces to the higher call of heaven's spiritual powers?" I do not wish to answer the question, since it is a personal one for all to ask and probe. But I am certain that on the spiritual path, the spiritual aspirant must confront these physical forces of creation that are so deeply embedded in us. We need to feel them, experience them and witness them in order to fully understand their implications, and I believe that only then the royal road to God can fully open to the ultimate knowledge. *The Katha Upanishads*, Part II, 1:3 states:

> That through which one enjoys form, sound, smell, taste, touch, and sexual union is the Self. Can there be anything not known to him who is the One in all?... That which enjoys the honey (rasa) from the flowers of the senses is the Self.

But the sexual *Kundalini* symptoms can be most frightening and overpowering as it was for Baba Muktananda and Irina

Tweedie, and as it has been in my own life. Muktananda and Irina Tweedie received help through their guru-guides, who directed them on the inner channels to meditate and focus deeply inward to regain their states of equanimity.

Another way to cope is to use *Kundalini's* ethereal energies of the sexual drive, called *ojas*, to achieve the higher states of consciousness. These sacred *ojas* must be raised up the spine towards the heart. Then, by further meditation, the essence will move toward the higher *chakras*, bringing an inner orgasm to the brain where these energies unite between the pineal and pituitary glands. Through this union temporary illuminating bliss may be reached. Practicing the upward movements of *ojas* as part of meditation is one of the keys to have a revelation of higher Consciousness. The science of these tantric methods can be found in books on this subject. I again recommend the book *Kundalini and the Third Eye* by Earlyne Chaney and William L. Messick of the Astara mystical school. Not all disclosure on this topic is given, as secrets around these sacred methods are often reserved for the spiritual seeker who has achieved and is thereby initiated in the knowledge of certain levels of the hidden mysteries. Staying celibate or practicing tantric sex for couples are also options to be considered.

Shri Ramana Maharshi in the book *Teachings of Bhagavan Shri Ramana Maharshi in His Own Words*, page 95, gives, regarding celibacy on the spiritual path, the following answer to a student about the topic of *brahmacharya,* which in India is considered celibacy on the spiritual path:

> Brahmacharya means living in Brahman; it has no connection with celibacy as commonly understood. A real Brahmachari is one who lives in Brahman and finds bliss in Brahman, which is the same as the Self. Why, then, should he look for other sources of happiness? In fact it is emergence (away) from the Self that is the cause of all misery.

To the question, "Can a married man (woman) realize the Self?"
Shri Ramana answers:

> Certainly. It is a question of fitness of mind. Married or
> unmarried, a man can realize the Self, because the Self is
> here and now.

In my own life of moving through this intense process, I call
upon the wisdom of my higher inner teachers and have found,
through dreams and inner promptings, that they are aware of my
struggles in these so private dilemmas. Recently my teachers of
higher Consciousness have lighted up new pathways to find the
key that best fits my personal process of becoming. Through their
guidance I have found that sex need not be the forbidden fruit for
a spiritual seeker, but may instead be a true helper on the way to
a more integrated awareness. In my understanding, when in the
sexual encounter the activation of the sexual impulses combines
with the essential soul-love that flows from the spiritual heart
to give to the other, it becomes a force divine in which mystical
experiences spontaneously happen, as it has for me.

And after all, this is the same as what Shri Ramana Maharshi
concludes, that Brahman has to be part of the equation, and I
like to add, "as it is to any situation in our lives."

Chapter Seventy-one

Going Home to Turmoil

After attending two meditation camps I extended my ticket
home for two more weeks. I still experienced physical pain,
but following my interview with Guruji no longer suffered from
altered states. The ashram was filled with the higher vibration of

light and had I not been married, I would have preferred to stay on with Shri Guruji for as long as he would permit.

Participating in the prescribed spiritual practices and residing in the sacred monastery-like atmosphere drew God nearer and worldly desires gradually melted away. Soaked in divine Consciousness, I sat with Guruji in *Kundalini*-bliss in which I transcended my body and in such moments I did not feel pain.

The day before my departure to the United States I had a dream warning me that going home was not going to be pleasant.

> Dream: November, 1997:
>
> Jon is driving our family car, a white Honda Accord. I am sitting next to him in the passenger seat. Jon is speeding. I am scared. Jon makes a turn. A grassy knoll appears on the right side of the road. Because of the speed, the car hits the knoll, turns upside down and falls into the ravine that lies beneath it. The car lands in water filled with mud and gets stuck in it. In the next scene Jon and I are present in a room. I am begging him to call our car service to have the car pulled out of the ravine. Jon does not want to cooperate with my ideas. Then I look at myself and notice that I have a beautiful purple-blue jacket on, but there are mud stains on it. I tell myself, "At least I can take care of my own jacket. All I have to do is to send it to the cleaners."

The dream troubled me and during breakfast on my last day in the Bhigaan ashram, I said to my fellow sadhakas: "My life at home is going to be in trouble and it has something to do with my husband!" I tried hard to forget the dream and forced myself to keep an open mind and to look forward to reconnecting with Jon, whom I had not seen since September that year. It had been three months.

Jon picked me up from our local airport. Before we reached home I told him about my agonies and pain during my stay in India. Surprisingly, his reaction to my painful story was loud almost sardonic laughter and nothing else. I felt an immediate sense of alarm. Jon had always been the most gracious of husbands, as completely dedicated to me as I was to him. He had been supportive of whatever I wanted to pursue in life, much as I had been supportive of his pursuits. Jon, over the years, had played the role of househusband. He preferred staying home, taking care of shopping and meals, and writing symphonies or other musical scores. I was the one who handled the finances to make sure we had the monies to fund all that was needed for the family. Our marriage had been unusual but solid as a rock. We were both deeply spiritual and Jon wholeheartedly followed in my spiritual footsteps wherever they led.

Because of his response at the airport, a wave of enormous uncertainty came over me and I knew it was true that my dream warned me that my marital relationship was shifting and that extreme emotional upheaval was at hand. I wondered if I had been away too long to know where Jon was in his experience of life. It was clear that his image of me had changed, and he could no longer communicate except in complete bursts of anger thrown against me. It was as if a shadow side of his personality had come to the foreground. I felt completely powerless.

Looking at the troubles at hand, I discovered that Jon, after a failed recording session of one of his best pieces of music, suffered from the deep emotional wounds of rejection. A subsequent rejection of a formidable piece of his art entered at the Mayor's Art Show pushed him internally over the brink, and he felt like a complete failure. Having grown up with a mother who constantly told him that he would be a failure, Jon began to reconnect with the label his mom put on him and then began to see me as "the mother" that was still sitting inside his own psyche. During my time in India, he had the time to ponder his life, wondering whether I should stay a part of it. He felt he had been a kept husband living in a golden cage and that it was time to break away and destroy the life he had known, and become his own man on his own terms. How much it reminded me of Nora in the Danish play of Henrik Ibsen, *A Doll's House,* to which he often referred, as he too saw the world as a play in which he wanted so badly to be the actor on his own self-made stage.

Jon's work foremost consisted of creating music, and secondarily art and design. In his heart and mind lived the eternal sounds of the higher spheres of consciousness and it was there that he found his God, the destiny to his soul's yearnings. He had been struggling for years to have his music recognized, and his art seen. Upon my return from India, Jon was ready to move on an idea to settle in a tiny eastern Oregon high desert town to establish an art gallery. He dreamed that as the owner he would have control of an outlet to sell his art and music. Overwhelmed by proposed plans for implementing his way through life and all the risks this entailed, I was not ready yet to come with him to sustain his ideas and make them mine as well. My struggle was still with finding a way to heal my physical pain and to know God.

When my husband disappeared to stay, as I later found out, in a guesthouse in his favorite town to write a new play, I fell apart, emotionally, physically and spiritually. All that Jon and I once had held in common seemed to have evaporated in thin air. I hardly made it through that day. With Jon's departure, all the intense sorrows of my prior experience of losing a husband came back to haunt me indescribably. I felt wounded. After weeks of enormous inner uproar, it became clear that all I could do was to look at myself and clean up my own act, as shown in the dream in India, by having the mud stains on my blue-purple jacket cleaned. If the stains represented karma, by reflecting on past actions and the motivations behind them, I realized it was important to at least stay honest with myself. "And, did not the seeing of the mud on my jacket expose it to the light of God, and was that light not like 'the cleaners' to which I had to bring my jacket?" I understood that it was no longer by my own power that things would change. I simply had to surrender.

My physical pain increased and I consulted with a well-known doctor in Eugene. After a few months of physical observation, this doctor said, "On the line between life and death you are sliding down quickly. I cannot do anything for you! Do not look anywhere, do not go anywhere, and do not see anyone else for this problem. You simply cannot be helped!" He looked at me in an unpleasant way and said, "Lift up your leg." Surprised, I did what he asked. The doctor continued, "You can still lift your leg!" Then in a mocking voice, he added, "You are taking it very well." I stared at him in disbelief and left his office for good.

The next day I was on the road with Jon, who had come back home after his short disappearance. We were mentally in disarray and heading for the coast hoping for a day of relaxation. During our ride it suddenly dawned on me that my doctor had closed the door on the healing I was seeking. I wept and felt terribly abandoned by this medical man and also realized there was no one else to turn to.

At the end of March, I received a phone call from my sister that my mother had suffered a severe stroke. She insisted that I come to The Netherlands at once to see my mother before it was too late. The call happened after I made plans to give Jon a belated "surprise birthday party." He had turned seventy when I was in India and the party was scheduled to take place in two days. Torn whether to be part of Jon's party or to see my mother, I dutifully booked a flight to Amsterdam. My son David, who had arrived from The Netherlands for a short vacation in the United States, promised to handle Jon's surprise party in my absence. I was saddened that again the road was blocked to show Jon the deep love I held for him.

At my time of arrival at my mother's bedside in the hospital, she had slipped away into a coma and was not responsive to anything. A bleed had affected the speech center in her brain, which meant that she would never speak, read or write again. My sister and I visited daily, hoping for a miracle that she would perhaps open her eyes and recognize us.

Chapter Seventy-two

A Glimpse of Light

Shortly before my sudden departure from the United States, my friend Annette had phoned. Annette was an angel who always stood by me through my unusual life trials. She often mentioned a superior healer in The Netherlands she had known for years. When she heard I was about to leave for my home country, she had urged me, "Ella, please, see Ton Borgesius. He, for sure, is the one who can help you with your pain."

At my sister's house I called Mr. Borgesius several times, but his phone kept ringing. I wondered if I had the wrong number or whether the healer was still in practice. I tenaciously kept trying. I must have made some fifty calls, when one day, to my utter amazement, Ton Borgesius picked up the phone. As I began to tell my story he interrupted and said, "Write me a letter fully explaining what is going on with you. I will call you back after I have read your letter." I gave him the phone numbers of family members where I might be staying. In my letter I narrated my story about pain, procaine injections, and *Kundalini*. I did not hear back from Mr. Borgesius and as my time in The Netherlands was limited, I consulted with a pain doctor instead, hoping to find a different approach. Unfortunately, this doctor's diagnosis was that I could not be helped. Devastated and alone with my problem, I thought it best to let go of all expectations. Needless to say it took me yet again by total surprise when one morning Mr. Borgesius phoned me at my niece's house to set up an appointment with him.

Ton Borgesius lived in Hilversum in the province of Utrecht. I took several trains to get to his town. I climbed the steep stairs of his small villa that led up to the waiting room and immediately recognized something in the house that took me back to my childhood. Maybe it was the mood the antique Dutch furnishings exuded: the dark wood coat rack, a faded Persian rug against the wall, the thick woven Persian rug on a small round table in the middle of the room. An old large Dutch upright clock with its muffled tick...tick...tick...only hinted to time in a room where I felt that time stood still... Except for the ticking clock, the waiting room radiated an atmosphere of tranquility and deep silence. Through the window I noticed beautiful Dutch red-tiled roofs of the neighboring red brick houses with their lovely gardens. There was a genuine wholesomeness as well as a touch of austerity to be felt in the house. I could have just sat there for hours, as the silence contained a calmness that was healing.

Mr. Borgesius, slightly grey-haired, dressed in a neat suit and tie, appeared and invited me into his consultation room. He was in his late sixties, tall, and very unassuming. I sat down on a chair in an old-fashioned-looking study room with a large bureau, four chairs, and walls lined with bookcases. Ton Borgesius sat down on a chair next to me. He spoke in a very soft but reassuring voice, while applying gentle healing energies through my upper *chakras*. After fifteen minutes of working on me and talking to me, he said quietly, "I am able to make you well!" His kind remark touched the core of my being and I felt a glimpse of light returning to my life.

Ton had a colleague who practiced acupuncture in the adjacent consultation room in the house and suggested, "It is best that you be treated every week. I will work on you first, and afterwards you should have an acupuncture session with Mr. van der Vet."

I will never forget that first meeting with Ton Borgesius and eagerly began to look forward to my weekly healing sessions, which were helping me physically and spiritually. After I told Ton by the end of April 1998, "My departure date is coming up," he had a meeting about my case with his colleague and together they decided that it was important for me to stay on for at least three more weeks. I agreed and phoned Jon. In my absence his surprise birthday party, which included hired musicians singing lyrics from his musicals, had been a success and had given Jon a glimpse of my continued love for him. "Jon," I said, "I am on the right track of healing with Mr. Borgesius, but I need another three weeks of sessions before coming home."

Jon understood that the extra time was also needed for my family while my mother was still in a semi-coma. Jon sounded upbeat when he said, "Great, Ella, this will give me time to write a new piece of music for you!"

During my stay in The Netherlands I found a book called *Kwan Yin, Over het hoger bewustzijn* (translation: *About The Higher Consciousness*) authored by Ernst Verwaal and Robert The Tjong Tjioe, which speaks about the higher states of consciousness. I read the book wherever I traveled and meditated on its contents. This book explains perfectly how God sees his plan from a higher or all-dimensional view and how from that view all creation is perfect. I was not surprised to notice a statue of Kwan Yin on the antique bookcase in the consultation room of Ton Borgesius. Ton did his healing work from those higher vibrations and most of the time dwelled in higher states of consciousness where he gained access to the souls' records, called the *akashic records*. He was a true mystic.

During all the weeks of my visits with Ton, I discovered that we did not just have a casual healer-patient relationship. One time, after a healing, back on the train to the town of one of my relatives, my spirit felt pure love flowing from him to me and I became spiritually attuned to him. It was as if an invisible line of light between him and me had been established. This line would never extinguish. He became my Dutch guru, counselor and friend. I was overjoyed.

Ton told me that we had been close friends in a former life in which we had been Roman Catholic priests. Because of that friendship he never allowed me to pay for his services. Besides working on me during my visits at his house, Ton sent waves of radiant light from higher Consciousness through the ethers literally pounding my higher *chakras* on a weekly basis. When this energy entered my body I felt overcome with the flow of intense magnetic frequencies that came in through my crown *chakra*, wherever I happened to be, on a plane and back home in Oregon. That light of higher Consciousness was slowly beginning to heal my body. Ton represented the light of God and through him the spots on my dream-jacket were being removed. He also strengthened me emotionally and spiritually to handle and endure whatever was to come up in my life.

Today, as I look at problems with pain, I know that bringing the awareness to higher Consciousness, rather than the ego or body consciousness, can alleviate pain. This was the way Ton Borgesius worked on his patients. Ego or body consciousness is impermanent with boundaries, but the higher Consciousness is permanent without boundaries. To go from the bound to the unbound is the healing. This can happen by praying to God, reciting mantras, singing God's glory or having sincere competent healers pulling the energies from the lower to the higher *chakras*.

Chapter Seventy-three

Saying Goodbye

The time came to say goodbye to my mother. She had been hospitalized for more than one month and remained in a sub-coma, but was breathing on her own. She had a feeding tube in her nose and they had put her on a computerized air mattress. I bought a bouquet of pink long-stemmed roses for her in the hope that she could smell their soft sweet fragrance.

I felt extremely sad when I saw her, and believed it was the last time I would lay my eyes on her. Tears welled up in my heart and soul as I looked at my mother. Ton Borgesius had told me that I had a strong spiritual connection with my mother. This sounded strange, since she had never spoken much about spirituality, and yet I claim her to be my first spiritual teacher. As I wrote before, she only taught me two prayers: a child's prayer and later, the Lord's Prayer.

My mother had a liking for the theosophists in her younger years. When I grew up she mentioned the names Annie Besant, Madam Blavatsky, and Krishna Murti, whose teachings had been important in her life. I realized that at a higher level of consciousness we had never been apart.

I remember my last phone conversation with my mother in February of 1998. My father had been admitted to the hospital for observation and my mother was concerned he might die. It was the first time that my mother revealed her private thoughts about life and death and the hereafter. She said that of all the things she had experienced in her life, the worst had been the tragic death of Harmen. She said that she had been very fond of him. The best thing that had happened to her was an experience she had while she was hospitalized some years ago. Then my mother recounted the following story:

> I was in my hospital room on my way to the bathroom when I suddenly fainted and collapsed. As I lost consciousness, I became aware of a beautiful serene white light that enfolded me and I experienced total peace... Slowly a long row of people dressed in white clothing became visible. A man, radiating with white light, stepped forward out of this line and walked towards me stretching out his hand as a sign of welcome. I felt a deep peace and joy and wanted to step forward to shake hands with this shining man in white, when a screeching voice of a nurse spoke in my ear and said, "She is coming back, she is regaining consciousness!"

My mother did not want to come back as she was in a state of complete peace and beauty of spirit. The voice of that nurse was the worst voice, she said, she had ever wanted to hear. What happened to my mother was like an out-of-body experience, well documented in our days in books on death and dying. I have no doubt that when her physical body became unconscious, she traveled temporarily out of her body to the higher realms of consciousness. During the meeting with "the people in white" my mother remained connected to her body through her silver cord. The silver cord is a vapor-like string that gives the spirit the freedom to leave the body during sleep or during severe illness or in accidents. All humans travel to the various levels of conscious-ness while asleep. Sometimes there is a memory of meeting divine beings, or of being taught in the great halls of learning on the higher planes. Most of the time we forget these nightly encoun-ters, but nevertheless are influenced by them. Through intuition, which is tuning in to the soul essence, we often act according to the instructions received in the night. During these night flights, the silver cord can stretch as far as it needs to go. Only at the moment of physical death will this silver cord be severed, when the spirit permanently leaves the physical realm. The *New English Bible* talks about the silver cord in Ecclesiastes 12:6–8,

> For man goes to his everlasting home, and the mourners go about the streets. Remember him before the silver cord is snapped – before the dust returns to the Earth as it began and the spirit returns to God who gave it.

I was ready to leave my mother's hospital room. Tears were welling up in my eyes as this was the final moment of my last farewell and I did not know whether she knew I was there at all. My son David was with me during this goodbye visit to my mother, but he never spoke or interrupted the intensity of what took place. There was only complete stillness.

Without any words spoken while we were waiting at the tram stop, I knew that my son understood what was going through my heart and soul. Quietly he held my hand.

Chapter Seventy-four
Meeting Ammachi

Within a few weeks of my return from The Netherlands, Annette invited me to come to California to attend the yearly offered public program of Mata Amritanandamayi, also known as Ammachi. Ammachi, a well-known Indian teacher, on tour in the United States, held her *satsang* in her ashram in San Ramon, California, near Annette's home. I never met Amma in person, but recalled memories of a mystical experience of ecstatic union with her while listening to her voice on a *bhajan* tape.

During my stay in The Netherlands, Jon wrote a new piece of music, but upon my return he fell back into another dark depression. He exclaimed, "I want to be alone, please go away."

Understanding that Jon really needed this, I accepted Annette's invitation. I arrived at San Francisco airport in the late afternoon and was welcomed by Annette, who was waiting with her car. We crossed the Bay via the San Mateo Bridge, went for a quick burrito dinner, and set off for Ammachi's ashram in San Ramon, called the M.A. Center.

Darshan of Ammachi is considered a divine blessing and comes in the form of compassionate hugs for all who come to see her. In the *darshan* hall, Annette and I sat down on the pillows we brought along and waited our turn to meet Amma face to face. Several hours went by while musicians played devotional Indian music. I noticed many people weeping with joy when they emerged from Ammachi's "divine embrace." At last our turn came, but when Amma took me into her loving arms, it surprised and disappointed me that I could not feel anything special, either emotional or spiritual.

The next morning, I told Annette that I had a strong intuitive feeling to buy a bouquet of flowers for Ammachi before going back to the M.A. Center. This feeling had something to do with my mother, who was still in semi-comatose condition on a hospital bed in The Netherlands. Upon our arrival at the ashram, the devotee-in-charge told us, "You are too late for line-up for Mother's *darshan*."

"But I have these flowers for her," I stammered...

"Keep them for tonight's *darshan*," she advised. Saddened, I sat down in the *darshan* hall with Annette. We sat in silence and watched how Ammachi worked with the people that came to her. Her apparent love for them impressed me. I noticed a man on a stretcher who was paralyzed from the neck down and on life support. His stretcher was wheeled onto the podium where Ammachi was sitting. This afflicted man apparently was only able to move his eyes. His eyes were shining with light and completely fixed on Amma. I saw her connecting with this man... She was kissing and caressing him while softly speaking to him. I noticed the difference this made in this man's aura. This beautiful special event took place right in front of my eyes. It gave me the urge to continue to watch Amma and to stay focused on her at all times. Suddenly my *Kundalini* started moving in a way I had not experienced before. My head suddenly shook fast and uncontrollably. My consciousness shifted into bliss as I recognized the divine light in Amma.

After *darshan*, I was still holding my flowers. Devotees began lining up on both sides of the aisle in the hall where Ammachi was expected to walk from the podium towards the exit doors. A car was waiting outside to take her to the M.A. Center house on the hill. I decided to join the rows of gathering devotees with the flower bouquet in my hand with some faint hope I could still offer the flowers. An official appeared and sternly reprimanded me, saying, "You are not allowed to stand in this greeting line to offer flowers while Amma is leaving the hall. It is against the rules."

I did not know what to do, but somehow could not help but remain in the line with them anyway. I saw Ammachi descending from her platform. All devotees' eyes were on her as she passed through the lines. Ammachi was touching her devotees' hands on both sides of the aisle while walking towards the door. I prayed to her and asked her in my own Dutch native language to accept these flowers from and for my Dutch mother. I thought of my mother in her semi-comatose state from which she may never wake up. "These are a gift from my mother" (*Dit is van mijn moeder*), I said in Dutch inside myself over and over again.

All of a sudden, Ammachi stood directly before me. She took the flowers from my hands and embraced me over and over again, while I was saying to her (in Dutch), "*Het is voor mijn moeder*" (It is for my mother). Ammachi kept hugging me. Her bodyguard tried to push me away, but Ammachi held onto me, and said, "My darling daughter, my darling daughter," and again, "my darling daughter." Tears of happiness started to flow from my eyes. Then Ammachi gave me some chocolate candy "kisses" as *prasad,* a special blessing, and proceeded to the waiting car. Many of her devotees came running towards me and crowded around, asking, "Who are you?" They told me that what had happened was incredibly special, as Mother (Amma) never accepted flowers after *darshan*. All I could say to these devotees was, "It was all for my mother."

Chapter Seventy-five

Major Change and Challenge

In the fall of 1998, I made another trip to The Netherlands. It was a surprise visit to be at my son's second master's degree graduation at the University of Amsterdam. Again, it gave me the opportunity to visit my mystic-healer and friend, Ton. Thanks to him, my pain level had gone down quite a bit and this time I could thoroughly enjoy being with my son David.

My mother, to everyone's surprise, had regained

consciousness and was moved to a nursing facility. When I entered the nursing home, I ran into my mother, who was "alive and well" walking through the hallway. In that very moment, a radiating energy of love burst forth from my spiritual heart... Unfortunately, due to the damage of the stroke to my mother's brain, she remained unable to speak, read, or write. I sadly realized I would never hear her voice again, or have any conversation with her. My father, age ninety-one, lived in a retirement home nearby. His new task was an afternoon visit to my mother. Every day in the nursing home family room, they were holding each other's hands in silence, and that silent gesture embodied a love of seventy-two years.

I came back to the United States feeling joy about my son's accomplishment and my mother's revival. I resumed my spiritual practices. One day as I looked at Shri Guruji's picture, I became aware that soft golden hues surrounded his image. "He is very happy," I thought. "He is radiating in a new dimension of golden light." Shortly thereafter, I had a dream in which Shri Guruji appeared:

> Guruji is standing on top of a high stairway. I am in the Bhigaan ashram, but this staircase is higher than the usual stairs leading to the shrine room. Guruji looks at me and I look at him with folded hands. I lift my hands to my third eye and then over the very top of my head to pay the utmost respect to him. It is something that I had never done before in real life or in any dream. I know I am greeting the divine most-high in Hindu fashion.

The dream's meaning became clear when I received a phone call from Annette, who lived in the Sai Baba ashram in India at that time. She said, "Ella, I have sad news for you, but thought it best if I were the one to tell you." She continued, "The news is that your Guruji suddenly died on the third of October." Deeply shocked, I realized that my soul in a dream-state had been aware of his passing, which allowed me to pay my respect and say my final goodbye. The dream also revealed that Guruji had reached the highest state of *samadhi*, called *maha-samadhi*. I clearly understood why his photo was glowing with such immeasurable hues of golden light. I felt overcome by a sense of deep loss, inexpressibly painful. My guru was gone and gone were my dreams of feeling my *Kundalini* rise in his presence, creating ecstatic moments of bliss.

I remembered the last time I had seen him. I had prayed to receive a sign from the higher Consciousness that he was indeed my guru. I was sitting at his feet during that last class before my departure. I was in some kind of a trance when I saw an ethereal fluidic essence in the colors of a transparent purple-blue emerging from his body. This fluidic essence flowed slowly from his body into my body and being. It was then that I knew that my prayer had been answered and that I had received the grace and ultimate initiation of my guru. I went to see him once more, and found him in front of his house drinking chai-tea. I thanked him for his teachings and kindness and said my goodbye. His last words to me were, "Be happy."

For a while, I lived in denial of the truth of his passing. I had to digest the finality of the situation and meditated on the death of my guru. Slowly, I began to feel him inside stronger than ever before. "Was he, my sweet guru, not always inside as Shri Guruji himself had said over and over again?" The guru is not the form we see. Behind the form is the eternal Consciousness, which has no form, birth or death. I heard his words as soft ethereal whisperings saying, "Go inside, I am there, do not waste time, reach your goal of self-realization!"

Yet a desire to go to the Bhigaan ashram to honor him and pay my last respects at his graveside became intense. "What better time to go than on his birthday," I thought. No sooner had I thought that than a letter arrived from the board governing the ashram to inform me that a statue of Shri Siddheswar Baba would be installed on his birthday, March 25, 1999. I was invited to come.

Chapter Seventy-six

The Guru Lives

Early March 1999, I left for Delhi. After one overnight at the Ambassador Hotel, Santosh picked me up at the crack of dawn. When I arrived at the Siddheswar Baba ashram, Munish gave me a room in the Shirdi Sai Block across the fields from the new shrine room, where Guruji's body was entombed.

Shri Guruji's tomb, called his *samadhi*, was built of white marble. His remains rested underneath the podium of a large, newly finished shrine room. The floor of the temple consisted of white marble squares, which added to the serenity and transcendental atmosphere of this holy place.

After Guruji's death, the board of directors drew up new plans to develop the ashram's appearance. At the entrance of the ashram, a new small temple housed a four-armed Ganesha sitting on a small bench, clad in a neatly draped yellow *dhoti,* and bedecked with golden wrist and arm bands, as well as a heavy golden necklace and a golden sacred thread. This God with the elephant head is known as the deity that removes obstacles and, as such, is prayed to before all other Gods in Hindu tradition. The head of the statue wore a bejeweled golden crown with a red and golden aura surrounding it, depicting divinity. Another statue was put up on top of the ashram water tower, the highest point in the ashram. It was Lord Shiva in lotus position with snakes draped around his shoulders, and a large *lingam* on top of his crown *chakra,* a center part of his glowing golden aura. This statue was accompanied by a golden trident, which represents the trinity of Brahma, Shiva and Vishnu. Besides these two newly installed statues, the most important was a life-like colored plaster representation of Guruji himself sitting on top of his *samadhi*, which like the other two, would be inaugurated on his birthday.

In contrast to the years when Guruji was alive, few Westerners showed up for the meditation camp. I believe I was the only foreigner who had actually signed up for it. Two *sadhakas* of the Third Eye Foundation of Togo, Africa, joined later, as did some Guruji students from Delhi and the surrounding areas. The meditation camp started with the usual schedule as set by Guruji. After early morning *omkar* (the chanting of AUMs), the participants assembled for *nagar sankirtan*, the singing of *bhajans* around the ashram grounds, ending at *guru newas* (Guruji's house) with the singing of the *arathi* morning song and the *sarva dharma* universal prayer that acknowledges all world religions. Struck by inexpressible sadness, we just stood there...and in that moment realized that we would never see Guruji's door open again and see this so modest and yet so powerful guru come out to give us his special blessings.

Every day during the camp, I meditated at the graveside and focused on my guru, who had given me such treasures, spiritually speaking, and with whom I had hoped "to sit" for many years to come. I was witnessing my own psychological pain, even though I was convinced that somehow the high spiritual vibration remained present as if "he *is* still living."

God uses many forms through which the higher essence of his light can radiate out to lift up all mankind. God himself appoints the guru to be a guru, as had been the case for Shri Siddheswar Baba. I like to reiterate that after years of inner prompting, Guruji had given up an important post with the Indian Government to become a spiritual teacher to help others to reach the goal of self-realization in this life, or the next. Shri Guruji activated the *Kundalini* in more than ten thousand spiritual aspirants, which, I believe, makes him the most important *Kundalini* guru of our times.

The following story illustrates how Guruji immediately continued his spiritual work after he took *maha-samadhi*. Just days before his passing, a Baba devotee, Carmen, who was staying in Sai Baba's southern Indian ashram, was reading Dr. Goel's *Third Eye* book. Most of her life Carmen endured the mysterious ups and downs of an early *Kundalini* awakening, and she yearned to receive the divine grace of the *Kundalini* Guru. Following a strong urge to visit him straight away, everything fell quickly into place to travel to Bhigaan. On October 2, 1998, Carmen arrived at the ashram and met with Shri Guruji. His first words to her were, "I have been waiting for you." The next day, while hoping for initiation, she instead found Sathya Narayana, the cook of the ashram, weeping in front of Guruji's house and was told that Guruji had just taken *maha-samadhi* (which meant, he had passed away). Some *sadhakas*, who spoke to him earlier that morning, said, "He looked radiant." Carmen went through the immense shock of the mysteriousness of the death of a guru she had just met the day before. The day after the funeral rites, Carmen returned to Baba's ashram in southern India where in a dream Guruji appeared "alive and well" and initiated her into the path of *Kundalini*, a final blessing of his divine grace.

This event, like many others, revealed that the power of Shri Siddheswar Baba would never diminish, as it remained part of God's eternal Light. From the source of that Light the Guru still takes care of his *sadhakas*. *Sadhakas* and others who experience *Kundalini* symptoms may well find peace praying to the image of Shri Siddhewar Baba for help on their journey back to God.

Chapter Seventy-seven

Guruji's Statue

In the temple, I again sat down at the *samadhi* of my guru when no one else was around. I tuned in to the statue still robed in a dark-red velvet cloth and noticed that light emanated from the covered form. This light grew in strength and began to move over the podium. The orange curtains that hung on each side of the podium took on light-blue ethereal hues. I just sat there, observing the living light-form of Shri Guruji, and knew he "is present."

I began to make daily visits to the shrine and every single time that same golden light appeared. I recognized that this was a place where the unbound eternal Consciousness was manifesting itself as a moving form of light taking on many different shapes. When I closed my eyes I saw the same light as I saw with my eyes wide open. At the same time, I heard the eternal sound of *Om (A-U-M)* in the deep silence.

A *pandit* arrived at the ashram to perform a three-day *puja* to sanctify the statues during the birthday festival. This *pandit* was the teacher of an ancient Vedic school where the sacred Indian scriptures are taught. Three young students and an assistant came with him to help with the complex rituals that had their roots in the ancient rites that would invoke divine vibrations to the statues and the grounds of the ashram. The *pandit* had a beautiful strong singing voice and his recitation of mantras resounded everywhere in the ashram, lifting our spirits godwards.

Guruji's birthday came. I filled two Indian copper vessels with flowers from the ashram grounds. I knew Guruji had been fond of these flowers. He once told us in class, "I still dream, and sometimes I dream about the flowers in the ashram." I put the flower bouquets on his tomb while the students of the Vedic priest were building a large platform from bricks and colored sands laid out in ancient patterns. In the center was an open space for the ritual fires. By now hundreds of people were arriving from Delhi and the nearby villages to take part in the special birthday celebration, and soon the ashram was packed.

On the birthday itself, when I stepped out of my room to resume the continuous festivities in the temple, I was offered a spoonful of holy water from a vessel carried by Munish. After I took a sip, it was explained to me that the water was a run-off from the ritual bathing of Guruji's statue. The water looked cloudy, because it had been scraped up from the top of the tomb where *sadhakas* had been standing in their bare feet. For a second, my Western mind panicked with the thought that I could become seriously ill as the water obviously contained bacteria from all those bare and likely dirty feet. I asked the doctor from Togo, Africa, about it. The doctor, who was a dedicated Guruji student, assured me that no harm could come from it, as it was truly holy water. "The high cosmic energy of Guruji is certainly in the water," the doctor explained.

I then understood that in such water bacteria have no means of infiltrating other systems as the higher frequencies immobilize all that is of a different vibratory level. With this new clarity, I also finally could appreciate the many miracles of other holy waters that had appeared during the history of mankind. I like to refer, for example, to the waters described in books about Lourdes in France, the place where the Virgin Mary appeared and where a source of water sprang up from where she had stood. Lourdes since became a place of pilgrimage to millions of Catholics. In the baths of Lourdes sick pilgrims with oozing wounds or infectious diseases are all submerged in the exact same water. It is a well-known proven fact that no one has ever fallen ill by taking these baths. Indeed this water has healed pilgrims, sometimes physically and other times spiritually, even though not all pilgrims are healed in Lourdes.

After accepting the spoonful of water as a blessing, I entered the shrine room. Many *sadhakas* were standing next to Guruji's just unveiled statue on his *samadhi* participating in the last ritual, the washing of the statue. I was asked to come forward and take part in the ceremony. With hesitation I put my hands on the statue of my guru, and the contact with Guruji's life-like image evoked enormous emotions in me. I softly washed Guruji's head, hands and feet. When I touched his hands, they felt like living hands.

For most people it was a joyous event, but tears were flowing from my eyes. I wept for the loss of my guru, but also felt the greatest of love. Traditionally, Indians make much noise during festivals as a different way of coping with emotions. As I had to grieve my way, I left the new shrine room to sit by myself in the old classroom where we used to meet with Shri Guruji at four in the afternoon. No one was present and I just sat down for a while in total silence looking at Guruji's chair, remembering how he used to sit there with us. Slowly a hue of golden light became visible in the room. While I was in deep reverie, my senses recognized the subtle fragrance of *amrita,* the divine nectar of the Gods. Other people came in to meditate. I needed to be alone, and left to go to the upstairs old shrine room. I sat down for meditation and tasted the thick honey-like substance of *amrita* in my mouth. I believed this was a special blessing from my guru on his birthday.

After the birthday, times became less blissful. Various well-meaning *sadhakas* wanted to be in charge by stepping into the shoes of their departed Guruji, to run the ashram. I did not agree with the new direction and felt that some women were ordering me around. This put me at odds with them.

It was early dawn on my departure day, when an enormous reverberating roaring sound woke me up. The sounds reminded me of a locomotive rumbling through the ashram. My cot shook from left to right, and back, and the lock on the door rattled violently. My first thought was, "Is this *Kundalini* or an earthquake?" With no time to lose, I jumped out of bed. I ran to open the door to stand under the doorway in what I thought to be a safe "Californian earthquake-style response." I looked over the ashram grounds, but there was no one in sight. Again I thought, "Am I imagining things and is this really an earthquake, or *Shakti-Kundalini* after all?" But it was a real earthquake, and I did not know if I was going to live through it... I stood in my door opening silent and alone, ready to die, while reciting all the powerful mantras I knew, *Gayatri, Om Namah Shivaya,* and *So Hum.* An incredible feeling of peace overcame me and I felt I was standing in the presence of God. The earlier words I had and the friction I had felt with some women *sadhakas* vanished into nothingness, as it dawned on me that we might soon die together. Suddenly, I felt a deep connection with them and an immense love began to flow through my heart. No longer frightened by what may happen, I went back to bed. I fell asleep and was again woken up by the shaking of my cot. It was an aftershock, but as I was still experiencing feelings of total peace with whatever was to happen, I turned over and got back to sleep. Early next morning, I realized that the earthquake caused a shift inside me, reconnecting me once more to higher Consciousness. I was able to say my goodbyes to everyone in the ashram with love flowing from a heart filled with joy.

Chapter Seventy-eight

Blessings for Writing

I flew to Bangalore, and was surprised to find Ali waiting for me with his new air-conditioned car. My face was still full of smiles from the shift in consciousness that happened during the earthquake in the Bhigaan ashram. We drove to Whitefield, where I could rent my former room at the Radhakrishnans' home, in Kadugodi. The traffic in the area had quadrupled during the last year and visible black slimy exhaust gases from diesel-run cars and trucks were causing serious pollution. After a few days the fumes began to affect my throat and lungs and I came down with bronchitis. While I sat waiting with many devotees for Sai Baba's *darshan* in the Brindavan temple, I noticed black smog rolling in from the street into the temple area. By now, I was coughing constantly, and sometimes a sympathetic woman devotee would gently tap me on the shoulder to offer her favorite cough medicine. The lung condition exhausted me and my strength began to fail.

In an effort to escape the smog as much as I could, I moved into Patel's Guest House, seeking comfort, a good bed, a hot-water shower and a private toilet. I was getting older, and even though I was willing to be an ascetic, the harsh Indian climate, the threat of dysentery, the mosquito attacks and the pollution were all taking their toll on me.

I joined three devotees I knew from prior years to form an American group of four. It was Sunday the eighteenth of April. I intuitively sensed that part of my mission in life was to write books, but there was still some hesitance to truly believe my inner message. I yearned to speak about it with Swami to check with him if my hunches were true. I also wanted to ask my friend Annette, but on my way to her room I ended up in a conversation with her Australian roommate. I communicated my frustration over not ever getting Swami's attention during *darshan*. The Australian woman, to my surprise, said, "I know of a very Indian way to get Swami's attention. Offer him a letter and place two cloves on top of it. One clove is meant for Lord Ganesha, the remover of obstacles, and the other is for God. I am sure by doing this, Swami will see you!"

My last day in India arrived. I woke before five in the morning. I washed my bed sheets and clothes to have plenty of time for line drying on the rooftop of my hotel before packing. In the afternoon I was to leave India and fly to The Netherlands for a ten-day stay. Suddenly I noticed it was getting late for morning *darshan*. I quickly draped a woolen shawl around my *punjabi* and ran into the chilly morning air towards the ashram. In the temple I settled down on the dark marble floor in my small air-inflated chair. I looked around and realized that I was on the exact same spot Sai Baba had turned his back on me two weeks earlier. I wondered whether my last *darshan* would turn out the same way. I began my meditation but was interrupted by extreme coughing fits. Several women were turning their heads toward me. My coughing was unstoppable and I felt I was going to suffocate. I reached for my purse to find the little plastic bag with cloves, Mrs. Gupta, the Reiki grandmaster, had given me to suppress the coughing. I was ready to put one clove in my mouth when I suddenly remembered what Annette's Australian roommate had told me. Forgetting the coughing, I took one clove in my hand, and prayed to Lord Ganesha to remove all obstacles to have an interview. I then took the second clove in my hand, and prayed to God to have an interview. I placed the two cloves on a letter I was to personally deliver to Swami for a Canadian devotee. I was anxious, but expected nothing. I sang my spiritual song in my mind and imagined the song entering Sai Baba's lotus flower house. While I was holding onto that image, the *seva-dal* in front of me moved away and suddenly I sat in the first row. My cough intensified. A box with double-strength cough medicine appeared. I took one pill and found relief. At that time, Swami was leaving his lotus flower house. As he came closer, I held the letter with the two cloves on it in my hands. Baba moved towards me, looked with surprise at the cloves, picked them up, energized them and put them back into my hands. All this happened very quickly. He took the letter. I did not want to ask for an interview, because I had done that in the past, most unsuccessfully. But before he turned his back this time, I blurted out to my own amazement, "Swami, I am leaving this afternoon!"

"Leaving!" Swami said. "Where are you from?"

"Oregon, United States, Swami."

"How many of you?" he asked.

"Four, Swami."

"Go, go in!" he said.

I picked up my chair and my woolen shawl and ran with Annette and Elly, followed by her son Jacob, toward the gate that leads to Sai Baba's house.

When Swami reappeared from *darshan*, he invited us into his house. He seated our group of four, up front, at his feet. "How are you, Sir?" he asked me.

"Very well, since I am here with you," I answered.

For the next minutes, Swami materialized many objects for the Indian devotees who were also called in for an interview. There was also a group of nine Danes, who were the first to be called for private interviews in the inner interview room.

I was sitting in the main room and felt my *Kundalini* rising in a most blissful way. My body was swaying. The *shakti* made me feel perfectly happy and it was easy to forget everything. I forced myself to think and get ready for my personal questions. After I was done mentally rehearsing my questions, I thought, "Well, Baba may not even speak to me." I began to pray to him, "Swami, I know you may not speak to me, but please at least let me know about writing. If you want me to write come straight toward me, and touch me on my head as soon as you come out with the Danes." I waited. After some time, Swami reappeared with the Danes. He walked straight toward me and touched me on the head.

My prayer had been answered, but if given the chance, I would ask again in a person-to-person talk. When our turn came to go into the inner interview room, Swami addressed me first by saying, "How are you?"

"Very well, but I do have some questions, may I ask?" He nodded and I said, "What about writing, Swami?"

"Yes, write, write, write," he said, while touching my head again.

"I wanted permission," I said.

"Permission given!" he replied, accentuating the word permission.

"Will you help write through me?" I asked.

"Yes, yes, but all is already in your head! I will help!" Again and again he touched my head. Then he asked, "When are you going home?"

"This afternoon, Swami," I answered.

"So soon," he said, putting real emphasis on the soon. For a while Swami leaned back in his chair and became quiet. Then he bent forward towards me and said, "I will be coming home with you."

After Guruji's death, I accepted that staying with Sai Baba was the same as being in the presence of my real Self, the Self that is always directing my life. I had no more doubt that I was to write. Then another question came up for me. "Would I ever come back to India? Did he want me back?"

While leaving the lotus flower house I had to pass by Swami, who was standing on the small bridge leading to the ashram. I stood before Swami and looked deeply into his eyes and said, "Swami, do you want me to come back to India?"

"Write, write, write," he said, tapping my head again.

PART IX

From Form to Formless God

Chapter Seventy-nine

Mahashivaratri 2000

Early in the new millennium I came to India again. I like to reiterate that Guruji, before he took *maha-samadhi*, had said to me, "To find liberation in this lifetime sit with a saint in India, three months out of the year." He had not mentioned himself, but at that time I was certain that Guruji would always be that saint. Now under the changed circumstances, I came to believe that only Sai Baba could fulfill Guruji's advice to sit in the higher vibrations. As there was still a housing shortage in Baba's ashram, I made plans to buy a flat in Puttaparthi to make it easier for me to come back to India any time.

During late fall of 1999, the marital situation with my husband underwent severe up and down swings. Shortly before my departure to India, Jon told me that he was going through a personality change. He said he needed to materialize his dream to establish an art gallery in the eastern Oregon town he had so often talked about. He wanted to do the remodel of an acquired property alone and during that process sort out his own mental state. Jon also wrote to me in a letter, "I am beckoned by a force over which none of us have control. I am entering a forest of my own making where brambles and undergrowth need clearing and trimming or else I will die." Jon's need was to reflect on his life as a composer and his disappointment of not having been performed as much as he would have liked. His self-confidence was ripped apart even though I always considered him "a true genius composer." On top of it all, Jon was increasingly worried about the beginning symptoms of a lung disease that brought on severe coughing spells. My trip to India in 2000 not only had his wholehearted consent, but his wish was that I stay away for one whole year. My ticket had an April return on it and I decided to leave that as it was for the time being. Jon promised to see me in India toward the last weeks of my stay whenever that may be...

During all the years of my marriage I had come to know Jon as an unusually selfless person. Others always came first and he served everyone. He lived by the famous prayer of Saint Francis of Assisi.

Lord, make me an instrument of your peace:
where there is hatred, let me sow love;
where there is injury, pardon;
where there is doubt, faith;
where there is despair, hope;
where there is darkness, light;
where there is sadness, joy.

O divine Master, grant that I may not so much seek
to be consoled as to console,
to be understood as to understand,
to be loved as to love.
For it is in giving that we receive,
it is in pardoning that we are pardoned,
and it is in dying [to self] that we
are born to eternal life.
Amen.

Maybe his little self (ego) was not ready to surrender to the higher Consciousness and be born to the eternal life (liberation), because he announced to some friends that he was on an ego-trip in which the world had better dance to his tune. He became quite narcissistic, a turning from yang to yin (dark shadow side) where he had to face the dark night of his soul. I accepted the fact that there was nothing I could do but leave the situation in divine hands. I no longer recognized the person I had loved so much and yet still loved.

That year, there were rumors in the ashram that Sai Baba would materialize the golden lingam during the upcoming *Mahashivaratri* festival. The lingam (*Brahmanda*) is the symbolic form of the Godhead and holds five elemental substances, which compose the creation of the world. In Hindu belief, only a God-man can materialize a lingam, as this act constitutes the creation of a new universe and only God has that power and knowledge.

After an absence of many years of producing a lingam, Sai Baba, in 1999, had graced his devotees again with this most extraordinary sacred creation. In his discourse during that prior *Mahashivaratri*, he announced that whosoever witnessed the golden lingam emerging from his mouth was granted liberation in this lifetime.

This year, devotees anticipated a repeat of the same grand event of manifestation. No wonder that the crowds were swelling, hoping to be freed from the bondage of birth and death. But I was not one of the believers in this type of *moksha*. I was more concerned about the large groups of people that were gathering, knowing full well the dangers such large crowds might pose. I knew I had to be in these crowds as part of a choral group that was to perform Shiva songs for the auspicious Shiva-night celebration.

On the morning of the festival around ten in the morning, our choir-members and hundreds of other devotees put down our pillows in the street in front of the bookstore and sat down. By lining up this way, the devotees hoped to be able to reserve a space later on in the temple. But no one knew precisely how the festival was going to be organized. Around noon there was a sudden rush of devotees toward the stairs leading to the line-up next to the Poorna Chandra hall, Sai Baba's living quarters. It became an instant stampede. I wanted to wait by letting people go ahead of me. Some friends did the same while others climbed the stairs calling me to join. As soon as I moved forward up the stairs, my body became squashed, followed by a heavy blow against my tailbone. Shocked, I pulled away and with difficulty managed to get down. I wanted to go home to my rented room. I placed my shoes in the sand and stared in disbelief at the pushing and shoving of multitudes of women that did not reflect in any way the *Love All, Serve All* doctrine of the Sai movement. My friends in the choir motioned again to come back up, gesturing to me they would help. Again I tried, but soon we were hanging on each other's shoulders like the blind leading the blind. My tailbone felt bruised and I was in a state of high anxiety. The force of the collision of these multiple bodies produced enormous heat and it nauseated me. Perspiration began to flow from all the pores of my body. With great effort, I reached the top of the stairs where the ashram security was in control. As I sat down on my pillow, my body started to tremble and shake. I had trouble breathing and lost consciousness. I regained my senses when a woman threw water over my face. I began to cry. It was the cry of a soul witnessing the insanity of crowd behavior.

I slowly recuperated and took notice of my surroundings. I was sitting in the middle of a long line of devotees with my choir-members. The whole area filled up with bodies tightly packed against bodies. "Move Madam, move Madam, *Sai Ram* and sit tight," echoed the *seva-dals* like a new mantra. When the time came to go into the temple area we were lucky that we received favorable seating close to the podium where Sai Baba was expected to appear in the afternoon. I decided to stay. Slowly the compound filled to the brim. The numbers must have been well over ten thousand. Western and Indian devotees who did not get a space and many villagers surrounded the temple-compound on the outside. The huge crowds soon became rowdy, and when I heard them shouting and screaming, it sent chills up my spine. I sat for many hours without water or food. I noticed that some women did leave their tight spots to go to the Indian toilets on the outside. By the time they returned, other women had taken their spaces. I saw fights between the so-called civilized western women arguing about these tiny sitting plots. Few seemed to remember the spiritual teachings. I became quite frightened.

Finally, around four, Swami appeared. The *shakti* energy suddenly rose. I felt the *Kundalini* rushing to the top of my head. After introductory speeches by Baba's students and professors, Swami stood up behind his lectern to begin a discourse in his Telegu tongue, which Professor Kumar, his interpreter, translated into English. Around seven the discourse ended. The festival started with the singing of the well-known *bhajan*: *Prema Muditha Mana Se Kaho, Rama Rama Ram, Rama Rama Ram, Rama Rama Ram, Sri Rama Rama Ram*...(translation: with the heart that is full of love, repeat the name of Ram). Rama was the avatar king of ancient days and is prayed to by many Indians. The Rama-Ram mantra calls upon the eternal all-pervading Conciousness. Mahatma Gandhi, whose mantra was Rama-Naam, said that he hoped to say this Rama Ram mantra in his dying moments, and even though he could not speak after being shot, that mantra undoubtedly always reverberated in this great soul.

No wonder that the high vibrations of this mantra revived me after almost nine hours of sitting. I was full of enthusiasm to join the crowds with the singing and the clapping of the rhythms. With Guruji we often sang the Rama bhajan before he came to the classroom. By the time he entered, I was in a most high state of awareness and the colors of purple-blue would be visible inside and outside my physical being. Remembering this, I thought of my guru and was subtly directed to pay full attention to Sai Baba. I became completely focused on him while the *bhajans* were in progress.

All of a sudden, I noticed that Swami's upper body was swaying in strange convulsions as if he needed to throw up. A dark-colored lingam appeared from his mouth. No one responded, which surprised me greatly. "This seems to be the divine moment people had hoped for," I thought. Swami placed the lingam in a cup on the table before him in a casual manner. Early that morning I had asked inside, "If I am meant to write about the lingam, show it to me so that I can report on it!" Now that I had seen the lingam, I wanted to leave. I looked behind me, but devotees were packed in so tightly that it looked impossible to find a way out. All I could see was an ocean of heads. I hesitated, turned around to the podium, and again paid full attention to Sai Baba, who by gesturing was asking for water. It was quickly supplied and he drank of it several times.

Suddenly a flash of silver-colored liquid propelled forward from his mouth, which materialized into a silver lingam. Again the crowds did not seem to notice anything. Swami put this lingam in another cup, next to where he had put the dark-colored one. It mystified me that no one noticed. I expected Swami to leave as soon as two lingams had already been manifested. I saw that he drank again from his cup. The *bhajans* were in full swing. I continued focusing on Sai Baba and observed that he was in pain. With empathy, I began to associate with his pain and convulsions. It was as if I lived his experience.

Unexpectedly, a stream of liquid molten gold shot forth from his mouth and solidified in the air into a large golden lingam. At the exact moment of the birth of this golden lingam, my own body shook wildly from left to right. It was *Shakti-Kundalini*. My body felt as if it were delivering this golden lingam at the exact same time it appeared from Swami's mouth. It all happened in a split second. Sai Baba stood up and proudly held the golden lingam up in his right hand for all to see.

The crowds went wild. People in the rows behind me stood up, pushing forward. Rows of bodies were rising and falling, resembling the waves of the ocean. I felt myself falling. There was no longer room for my feet. I became one with the masses. Bodies began to fall on top of me. I was trampled under. In a sense it was as if this was happening in slow motion. It felt unreal. I stared death by trampling straight in the face. Up and under I went, as if drowning. I recited my special mantra, because I thought I would die. Then I screamed, "God please help us."

Sai Baba was standing ten feet away, smiling proudly as he was showing the golden lingam, while the crowds were in imminent danger before him. He did nothing to contain the situation. He just stood there. In that moment I realized that I was not really asking him for his help, but the help of the invisible God of Light, the true "Love All, Serve All" God of the universe. That was after all the one who knew all things and was always on my side.

I felt myself falling again and then noticed my friend Annette about ten feet away. Annette, a tall woman with a lot of physical strength, was not falling, even though her body swayed back and forth. I called out to her. Annette moved towards me and put her arms around me to prevent the other bodies from pulling me under... She released me when the crowds fell into a somewhat calmer mood. I wanted to leave at once if I could, but Annette wanted to find her purse. I did not want to risk our lives for it and urged her to come away with me, but she stayed behind. I did not know where my belongings were nor did I care. My chair and pillow were lost and my large shawl was missing. Miraculously my small purse was still hanging around my neck.

I turned around facing the crowds and saw a vast sea of glimmering eyes lit up by the temple chandeliers and caught in a hypnotic trance of a collective "wild desire" to see the golden lingam. As I was growing increasingly frightened, I began to question why I was there while I struggled towards the exit facing this hypnotized crowd. I fell several times while trying my best to squeeze through the masses without hurting anyone. I saw only three other western women trying to get out. "My wise sisters," I uttered to myself. Outside the temple-gate, crowds were still everywhere and it took quite a bit of pushing and shoving to find my way out of the ashram. I was exhausted and my heart felt weak.

At last I arrived at my favorite restaurant, Sai Towers. The niece, son and daughter of the old Maharaja of northern India (royalty from before India's Independence in 1948) were having their evening meal.

"Ella, you look pale," one of them remarked, noticing that I was not properly dressed because the large shawl I had been wearing had been lost in the stampede. For a moment I felt naked, as I by now was accustomed to the Indian rules of decency.

"Please," I said, rushing to sit down at their table, "I am in desperate need of something to drink and eat, I am in a state of total collapse." I quickly motioned the waiter I knew to come. With a worn-out whispery voice, I began to order two pineapple juices and a large dinner, when Herendra, the handsome well-known prince, who was wearing his impeccable white turban, interrupted my order and said, "We have our dinner already on the table, eat, drink, take whatever you like." I drank and ate to my heart's content, and then recounted all that had happened on the temple grounds. My friends had been dining and speculating that if Sai Baba would materialize a lingam, it would happen in the early morning hours. They sadly realized that they missed what they believed to be the greatest opportunity of their lives, namely the promise of self-realization.

Chapter Eighty

Doubts

Back in my flat, my exhaustion helped me to fall asleep, but soon the ringing sounds of the alarm clock rudely woke me just a few hours later. It was eleven-thirty at night and time to get up for the midnight performance. Still worn out from the stampede, I nevertheless dutifully draped myself in my special white silk sari with a broad golden border. I put on a silver chain with a Shiva pendant, symbolizing this auspicious Shiva night.

I walked to our meeting place in the back of the temple. Thousands of devotees had left and lining-up in our waiting area was unexpectedly easy. At the performance time, a *seva-dal* appeared, ushering us to a space near the table where the three materialized lingams were on display. We sat down on the temple floor. When a lady in my choir pushed me and yelled, "Get out of my way! I want to see the lingams!" I felt quite irritated, but moved, thinking, "This is all wrong. To be liberated from the cycle of birth and death has little to do with seeing the lingams, but more with loving your fellowman." The promise of liberation made by Sai Baba reminded me of the sale of indulgences issued by the Pope in the late Middle Ages, then a sure ticket to heaven. Again I felt quite out of place, but when our voices filled the temple area with the sacred Shiva *kirtans* (songs, often in Sanskrit, depicting God), the powerful words softened my heart and my judgment faded...

The next morning the ashram was humming with discussions about the festival. I heard that devotees had counted forty-seven stretchers carrying injured bodies to a nearby hospital. I asked other devotees how *Mahashivaratri* had affected them and heard that most had feared for their lives, but they reasoned that through the experience of imminent danger they had been released from old karma. When I recounted that I had witnessed three lingams emerging from Swami's mouth, it caused tremendous negative reactions. It took me by surprise and it dawned on me that I was dealing with spiritual jealousy as well as spiritual competition. Maybe the seeing of the lingams was seen as a special divine gift and as such a devotee on the receiving end was supposedly better than others. Fortunately, I met a Swedish woman who sat near Swami during the event who saw exactly the same as I did, which convinced me I had not been dreaming.

At this time, I began to take a more critical look at Sai Baba. I asked myself, "Did he actually affect the lives of his devotees in a positive way?" He had said, "My life is my message." "What did we know of his life?" Twice a day he gave *darshan* and presided over *bhajans*. Few were called for interviews to get a closer look at him. But Sai Baba's goodness could perhaps be recognized in his water projects for many poor villages, or the building of free hospitals. But it was by charitable donations of devotees that these projects were possible. Many doctors gave large sums of money as well as their own free services, based on their conviction that Sai Baba was the guru of gurus or God's living form on Earth.

I recall a time when I sat reminiscing the advent of the avatar in the entrance hall under the great dome of the Super Specialty Hospital, an awe-inspiring palace-like building. I looked at the huge crystal chandelier hanging from the center of the ceiling. "A gift from Italian devotees," I heard. Pictures of Sai Baba were displayed on every wall. The sounds of spiritual music reverberated through the hall. I truly sensed a higher presence. Suddenly I was confronted by a *seva-dal* who said, "Leave at once, Madam, your time is up." I had not known there had been any time limit in sitting in this magnificent hall. Saddened, I wondered where that God feeling had come from. Was it Sai Baba or my own inner Self? Again I realized that the God-spark within me was projected onto the image of Sai Baba. I reasoned that this was in principle true for all devotees, but out of that inner spark of God should come only good.

Other things were getting my attention in Puttaparthi. I was living in a small flat, a seven-minute walk to the ashram entrance. On the way to the ashram I had to pass through a narrow street with small bazaars on each side. In one of the shops I befriended the shopkeeper, a young boy, and learned from him that many young children in the village were often forced by poor parents to work in shops, restaurants or construction. I regularly saw small-sized young boys carrying loads of steel construction material on their heads toward the numerous high-rise construction sites. I frequently ate in a downtown hotel, where a small smiling beautiful boy of eleven was our waiter, carrying a heavy load of dishes to our table. When we tipped him generously it brought beaming smiles to his little face. I was pained by the burdens these children had to bear and felt that something had to be done to improve their conditions.

Puttaparthi was Sai Baba's town. If Sai Baba was the avatar, the townspeople's lives should reflect the fact that they were living in close proximity to the light of God. In an effort to understand more about the situation I visited Professor Bordoloi, who was my landlord and also taught at the Sai Baba College. I asked him if child labor was permitted under Indian law.

"Child labor is not legal in India," was his response, "but in Puttaparthi we are experiencing one of the highest rates of child labor in the country."

"Why doesn't Baba do something about it?" I asked. The professor shook his head. I said, "It should become a Sai project to stop child labor!"

The professor advised me, "Speak with Swami's right hand man, Mr. Chakrvarti. He is the man who has daily contact with Sai Baba."

Hoping to be a helpful devotee, I set out to look this important man up in his ashram office. But his door was locked and guarded by a *seva-dal*, who demanded I write a request for a meeting by stating my name and purpose. I scribbled the information on a piece of paper, whereupon the *seva-dal* said, "It will be up to Mr. Chakrvarti to grant or deny you access." A week of waiting ensued. I became weary and assumed that child labor was not a priority at this point for Sai Baba. I finally gave up and figured, "This is India after all, a land full of problems, and I, as a westerner, cannot presume to bring changes about. Such changes must come from the Indian people themselves encouraged by Sai Baba. But," I reasoned, "a model town should at least be the outcome of Baba's teachings in action."

My next step was to meet Mrs. Ravi, a businesswoman with whom I had corresponded about the purchase of a flat when I was still in the United States. She had mailed brochures of an apartment-project under construction of which she was the general contractor. The property was described as one of fine quality that people interested in meditation would favor because of its quiet setting near an old orange grove at the outskirts of town. Before I left for India, Mrs. Ravi had phoned me to advertise her project and recommended that I send a down payment to reserve a well-located flat for me. I consulted with my Bombay business friends about the idea, and they strongly advised to hold off on any down payment. "See first for yourself if the flat suits your purpose" was their sound advice.

Mrs. Ravi owned a large hotel in the center of Puttaparthi. I took a rickshaw to the hotel and asked the receptionist if I could see her. I was taken to her office on the main floor, where I found a large woman in a sari shouting at the top of her lungs at her servant. She did not notice my arrival and continued her hollering, which I quietly observed from a distance. Her acting out showed me that Mrs. Ravi was an authoritarian and unkind woman and it gave me a sort of forewarning... "Can I trust someone like her?" was the thought that flashed through my mind. After she finished venting her rage upon the poor servant, she turned around and, noticing me, sat me down with a phony smile. Then she gave me her sales spiel of the flats under construction.

"But why is the purchase price so high compared to other flats?" I questioned. Again she emphasized the quality of workmanship, the superb quiet location, and added that some of the proceeds would go to an orphanage she was about to establish. Mrs. Ravi handed me some new brochures. I left and took a rickshaw to the property. The building site was near the end of the main road where the traffic was heavy and noisy. I heard that nearby a new railroad station was to be constructed shortly.

After I had checked the site, I investigated further by talking to permanent western residents in Puttaparthi. I learned from them that Mrs. Ravi's project was overpriced and that I should not trust her. It made me feel sad knowing that she was a graduate of Sai Baba's College in Anantapur, whose graduating students were believed to be honest and trustworthy people that would effect positive change in Indian society. Life in and around the ashram was not at the high level I expected and I felt dismayed by my findings.

Chapter Eighty-one

Personal Pain

One afternoon while I was resting under my mosquito netting, Annette knocked on my door with a telegram in her hand. "From your husband!" she said. The message read that Beverley had passed away from cancer. I had to sit down to take in the enormous blow of having lost my closest friend and confidante of twenty-four years. When I left for The Netherlands in December 1999, Beverley had not been feeling well. When I called her from Amsterdam in early January, she told me, "Ella, I have been diagnosed with cancer, but will fight it with all I have!" Knowing Bev's enormous inner strength and determination made me think she could beat the cancer. After my arrival in India, I phoned her several times, but she had become too weak to speak with me. I nevertheless kept hoping that I would see her again.

A few days after the emotional impact of losing Bev, I received a letter from Jon, whose writing was most disturbing. Before I left the United States, we had reconciled our marriage, but his vague terminology showed that he was still contemplating a possible different life than was last discussed. I remembered that he had said that he was going through a personality change and the letter did show a change of character. With deep anguish over a possible loss of my husband and a pained heart over the death of my dearest friend, I threw myself into the dark abyss of despair.

I no longer looked to find a house to buy. When Baba left Puttaparthi for his Whitefield ashram, I immediately followed him. In nearby Kadugodi I rented a large room in the best hotel hoping that Jon might still keep his promise to join me in April. I realized that I first needed to figure out where I actually stood in my marriage on an emotional, spiritual and psychological level. "If only I could have Swami's advice in an interview," I thought because I believed he really knew what was best for both of us. But I was not called in.

One afternoon during *bhajans*, I decided to look intently at Sai Baba's form as a representation of my inner guru to find the answers. While making the connection, I spoke inside, "Do you want me to give up my husband? Is this God's will? And if so, where must I find the courage to do it?" I saw Baba staring at me. I spoke inside again, "If this is God's will, I must give him up! Through death, I have already given up one husband. Must I now make a second sacrifice? Am I being tested?" I felt severe pain in my heart region while continuing my eye contact with Swami. The connection grew in intensity. Tears were flowing from my eyes, because to give up Jon was too hard to bear. While sitting on the temple floor, I sank into deep contemplation and my consciousness shifted. I heard the sounds of deep silence and in that silence was deep peace. The outside world disappeared, and only peace in silence existed. *Bhajans* ended, but I remained seated experiencing the peace beyond all understanding. It took hours to come back to my normal state of reality.

The experience did not resolve what I should do. I thought, "My deep love for Jon, despite all the negatives of last year, has not abated. Even though I love him, I might have to give him up for a higher purpose of both our souls." As so much was at stake I began to look for help in other directions than what my own intuitive self was whispering all along, namely to stay with him.

I decided to talk with Dr. Gupta, the clairvoyant sweet-mannered professor I had come to know the prior year when he had done a psychic reading for me. In that reading he saw that I was a *rishi* in the ancient times and that in this life my mission was to write spiritual books. Through Dr. Gupta's wife, Rama, a Reiki grandmaster, I had received my Reiki mastership initiations. I had gotten to know the Guptas quite well and trusted them.

Dr. Gupta welcomed me with big smiles and guided me to the back room where in the past we had sat down for readings. The atmosphere was of an extraordinarily high spiritual vibration, perhaps due to *pujas* performed in the small temple in the back of the room. I opened my purse and pulled out my husband's letter. Dr. Gupta took the letter and held it in his hands for some time. He seemed to go into some kind of trance.

"Very bad, very bad," he said, giving the letter back to me. "The vibrations in this letter are definitely not good. Do not worry. Your husband can never leave you. You have been together for more than three hundred years. No matter what is happening with your husband now, no matter what he thinks, all will turn around again and he will be with you, no doubt about it." I was happy with his conclusion, but had no idea how this might come about.

For many years I had heard about Little Heart, an enlightened woman from Australia, who had written a small book about her enlightenment. I heard that some devotees consulted with her about their problems. I read two of her published little books and even though they were spiritually intriguing, her writing did not completely convince me that she was enlightened. I, nevertheless, decided to see her. Little Heart's modest house was located in the southern part of Kadugodi, a ten-minute walk from the ashram. The neighborhood represented the real India with dusty roads and potholes, flowering trees and strong-smelling open sewers. Westerners did not come very often to her part of town. I climbed the several narrow hand-made cement stairs before knocking on her glass front door. A tall gray-haired woman dressed in a somewhat colorless sari opened the door, and welcomed me.

Little Heart had the eyes of a mystic like Guruji, but with a much sturdier look about her. In Guruji's face I had seen the joy of enlightenment, which I did not detect in the Australian woman's face. Inside her house, she seated me on a small sofa.

Her flat was clean with good vibrations and taste. I noticed colorful blue cooking pots in her small kitchen next to her modest living room. The rooms had a touch of western living. There were beautiful plants everywhere and freshly cut roses on the table. Little Heart, who appeared to be a gracious, open-minded woman, began to tell me her stories in relation to Sai Baba and her life in Australia. Her stories were phenomenal. She lived permanently in this small flat she owned. Little Heart, after one hour of talks, looked at me deeply and said emphatically, "You have to leave your husband. Do not wait till you get home. Send him a cable to not pick you up from the airport." Little Heart had also left her husband and there was no doubt that she truly believed I had to do the same if I sought enlightenment. I felt stunned by the intensity of her remarks. I deliberated on what she said and went back to see her for two more sessions. Every time I spoke with her, her advice remained the same, "Leave your husband and do not delay it."

One Sunday afternoon, my friends Jaya and Hari invited me for a special Vedic ritual at a nearby temple of a woman saint. We took an auto-rickshaw and arrived around four in the afternoon. In the garden area in front of the temple, offerings of ghee and incense were being made into a sacred fire while ancient mantras were being recited. The sage's temple, which was also her residence, displayed statues of various Gods that were garlanded with fresh fragrant flowers. At the feet of the deities were the offerings of broken coconuts. My *Kundalini* moved gently through my body in oneness with that Vedic realm of higher vibrations. We were offered a simple vegetarian meal of rice, dal, and some curry on a paper plate, and I was certain it was safe to eat in this type of environment.

The woman sage intrigued me. She was an older woman with long white hair knotted in a bun at the back of her head. She wore an orange sari, a sign of renouncing the world. I felt a liking for her and decided to seek her advice regarding my marital problems as I yearned for divinely guided counsel. I asked one of her followers if we could meet privately. The devotee disappeared to see the sage and when she came back reported, "You have permission for a five-minute talk!" and showed me where to go. I sat down with the sage in the front of the temple while people were thronging to get a glimpse of the deities around us. I came directly to the point and explained in a few words the situation between my husband and me. After a few minutes of silence, the sage spoke with her penetrating eyes looking at me and said, "You must leave your husband!"

Her straightforwardness shook me to the core of my being. My sacred vows "for better or for worse" some twenty-five years ago were based on divine guidance: the dream with Harmen's message to choose "the most humane person" and the minister's confirmation of that dream, as well as the revelation of the depth of Beethoven's "Ode to Joy" in his *Ninth Symphony* all told me that my choice had to be Jon. "Had my marriage to Jon not always been for a higher spiritual purpose? Or had that purpose already been fulfilled?" Such were my thoughts. I began to weep profusely and could not stop. Through my tears, I asked the old sage if I could come back the next morning to allow time for a more extensive talk. She agreed to see me at nine in the morning, the following day. Jaya, Hari and I left the temple. Outside the gates, we waited in silence for our rickshaw driver to drive us back to Baba's ashram. The sandy road was lined with flowering bougainvillea, flamboyant trees, and coconut palms. As I took in the beauty of the surroundings, I suddenly began to weep for a second time. My depth of sorrow, besides the possible loss of Jon, also related back to the deep scars in my heart over the loss of Harmen.

The next day, I sat alone at the feet of the woman saint. I had time to explain more about my life as well as my spiritual endeavors. The sage heard me, but again advised, "You must leave your husband at once." I begged her to see it differently. She shook her head and looked at me long and hard and said, "Well, if you wish to wait till you arrive home, you can give him a second chance." With that statement, our conversation was over. The rickshaw driver was waiting and I was driven back to my hotel room while my mind was twisting and turning from the daunting advice I had received so far.

There were three weeks left before my departure to the United States. It was siesta time. I was lying down on the bed in my hotel room trying to get some sleep, but sleep would not come. I had been analyzing my life and the direction I ought to take for many weeks. Little Heart and the woman sage told me to leave my husband. In India, only Dr. Gupta had said, "All will be well. Your husband can never leave you." In The Netherlands, before leaving for India that year, I had visited my Dutch mystic healer and friend, Ton Borgesius. Ton, who could look into my past lives and karma, told me that my karma with Jon was over. Ton said, "Ella, you are free to leave him, but if you stay, there will be many spiritual treasures in store for you."

I rolled around under my mosquito netting hoping to get all the thoughts in my head to calm down. It was hot in the room. The ceiling fan was making buzzing sounds, but this did not help in cooling the dull hanging heat in the room. It dawned on me that within one hour it would be time to get up for afternoon *bhajans*. Suddenly a thought hit me like lightning. "It is all about courage. I do not have the courage to divorce my husband. I am attached to him like a little child clinging to its mother. I must cut the cord! This is what God wants of me now." With these thoughts racing through my mind, I lifted the mosquito netting, rolled out of bed, and rushed to my table where I had my pen and paper. I sat down in my chair and started to write a letter to my husband.

"Dear Jon," I wrote. "After many months of contemplation I have decided that divorce..." The precise moment I wrote that word *divorce*, a huge unexpected rainstorm rose and swept across my table. To my utter amazement the force of this storm bent the tall tree outside my window all the way down to the ground, hitting the flowerbeds three stories below. Gushes of torrential rain cascaded though the open glass shutters over my paper, erasing the words I had written. My mind shut down in bewilderment, while I managed with all my might to close the shutters against this great force. I opened the door to the balcony on the other side of the room and sat down on the floor behind the screen door, shivering in my nightgown while watching in awe the display of a nature so violent and yet so beautiful.

I remained on the tiled floor for a while trying to recuperate from the intensity of the event. I watched the rain sweeping across the balcony, and it dawned on me how I had always been carried in divine hands, and that God had clearly spoken, ending my personal dilemma about giving up my husband. I simply had to wait and not come to any final conclusion. No letter was ever written or sent.

Chapter Eighty-two
"Not Now"

I came to India in the beginning of the new millennium not only to sit in the higher vibrations but also to promote my draft manuscript called *Drawn to the Light,* a report of my spiritual journey thus far. Every day I carried the manuscript to *darshan* in the hope that Baba would bless it or talk to me about it in an interview. One day as I was seated in the second row, Baba walked close by. I felt an inner force compelling me to push forward through the first row to show my writings to him.

"This is for you!" I surprisingly heard myself say very loudly.

Baba looked at my neat stack of papers held together in a transparent folder. He held up his hands in a blessing and made a loud and clear statement, "Not now!"

His remarks mystified me. I nevertheless wanted to move

forward and submit my manuscript *Drawn to the Light* to Sai Towers Publishers. Sai Towers accepted the manuscript, and informed me that I would hear back from their team of editors. In the meantime their editing department kindly offered that I could type any revision to the manuscript directly into their computer. Besides going for *darshan,* my new routine was a daily walk to the publishing house to do further re-edits. The work helped me to stay mentally focused and to keep me from drowning in emotions of heart-wrenching despair over my situation with Jon.

When Sai Baba said, "Not now," he could have meant not that very day, and therefore I thought it wise to still take the manuscript along to every *darshan.* I kept anxiously hoping for an interview, but this did not happen. My conclusion was that whether or not Sai Baba showed an interest, if Sai Towers agreed to publish, I would return to India later that year with my final revisions.

My last day arrived. I got up at five in the morning. I was early, which gave me time for contemplation. In our women's part of the group only Annette, Jaya and I remained. Our friend Elly was seriously ill with cancer and could no longer attend *darshan.* She was a Polish-born woman of forty-five, small with short brown hair and a beautiful saintly face. She had been a judge in her country before moving to the United States. Already a year earlier, Elly had told us that she suffered from breast cancer, but this was never properly diagnosed. Annette and I had urged her to consult with a medical doctor, but Elly categorically refused. Swami was the only doctor she cared to have. When I went to say my goodbye to her, she could not see me because of the pain. That last *darshan* my thoughts went out to her... I missed Elly's sweet personality, which had given harmonizing energy to our small group. I wondered if I would ever see her again.

The temple filled up quickly on the women's side. I was reading a new book about Babaji of the Siddha Kriya Yoga tradition, brought to the West by Yogananda. My contemplation on the text put me in a meditative mood as Babaji is of that same vibration as the cosmic vibrations of Shri Guruji. I sat in silence with thousands of other devotees for one hour. Then a soft murmuring sound went through the waiting crowds, a sure sign that Swami had left his lotus flower house. I could see him as he walked towards the Temple. Right then, the sound-system started playing *Ave Maria*, the song so dear to me. I had never heard it played in the ashram before and considered it my farewell blessing. Swami came nearer, and it looked for a moment as if he was going to talk to me, but at that suspended moment in time he turned his back towards me and I knew my last *darshan* was over.

I left for Bangalore with my friends Hari, his wife Jaya, and Annette, my mind still filled with the melody of my favorite song. My friends invited me for a farewell lunch at the famous Oberoi Hotel. I had become accustomed to eating simple Indian meals in the ashram canteen. In contrast, the Oberoi menu represented the refined sophistication of ancient India, in which maharajas and maharanis had found some of their earthly pleasures. I immensely enjoyed the sight of the doorman, his white turban crowning his olive-brown face as he stood dressed in his colorful red colonial style gold-buttoned outfit at the hotel entrance, as well as the hotel's tropical gardens with cascading waterfalls and outdoor terraces. For a moment I felt like royalty drinking in the delight from an abundant fountain. The time came to say goodbye. Little did I know that I would not return to India or set foot in Sai Baba's ashram again...

On the plane to Amsterdam the melody of *Ave Maria* kept softly reverberating in my mind. It assured me in a subtle way that the divine is always near.

Chapter Eighty-three

Resurrection

After twelve hours of travel, I arrived in Amsterdam. The six-hour layover before my next flight to the United States gave me the opportunity to meet my son, who still resided in Amsterdam. How thrilled I was to find David waiting for me at the Schiphol airport that Saturday morning at six-thirty. We took the train to Amsterdam Central Station and wandered about the old completely empty streets in the brisk morning hours. When a *warme bakker* shop (a bakery with hot bread right out of the oven) opened, we sat down to have a *koffie-verkeerd* (coffee with creamy milk) and some delicious Dutch bread hot from the oven. Here I drew David into a serious conversation regarding my marriage to his stepfather.

Almost twenty-five years ago I had accepted Jon's marriage proposal. David had also welcomed the idea of having a stepdad, even though we were both still in the depth of sorrow over Harmen's passing. Without much knowledge of spiritual teachings in those early days, I understood already that "life is love and to love gives life, but also that love never dies."

During most of the years of my marriage, Jon had been that "most humane person" Harmen had pointed to in a dream, leading to my remarriage. Altruism was the essence of his character, which was now hiding behind dark clouds, the demons perhaps of the karmic makings of many lifetimes, of which only Jon and God had knowledge.

Now I asked again for the input of David's thoughts regarding Jon. It soon became clear that we both held feelings of gratitude and love towards him. David understood that I would do anything to save the marriage, but that it was clearly not entirely up to me. Much depended on where Jon was in his life story, spiritually, mentally and emotionally. I had been gone for more than four months and had not the slightest idea what was happening in Jon's mind and soul. I certainly had feelings of foreboding, because of the confusing contents of the only letter I ever received from him while in India.

On the last leg of my journey, on the flight from Seattle to Eugene, I again reviewed my thoughts relating to the situation. My truth, spiritually speaking, had to be that "If Jon wanted to continue his life's journey without me, it would be more harmonizing to let him go without any resistance on my part. In my journey to the light, I should not hinder or harm another soul on the road to their freedom of soul." But while in thought ready to let go, I also reasoned, "Was it not God who gave me a sign to continue with Jon, as the sudden erasing of the word *divorce* by a torrential rain storm indicated?"

Confused and exhausted from thinking, worrying and too much advice, I finally landed at the small airport in Eugene, Oregon, where Jon was waiting. After a curt greeting, he brought me the news that Eddy, Beverley's husband, had died one month after his wife's passing. On top of all the other thoughts that were racing through my mind, I could not take it in completely. When I arrived home, I felt a strong urge, as of old, to pick up the phone and dial Beverley's number to say, "Hello, Beverley, I am back!"

Eddy, a university professor and composer, had been a close spiritual friend and a secret Sai Baba admirer, who read all the Baba books in our library. Eddy also had a keen interest in the writings about out-of-body experiences, and the possibility of life after death. "Eddy now finally knows" was all I could think. Beverley had been a pianist by profession and had not at all been interested in the Sai Baba phenomenon. Nevertheless, every Thursday, she had donated armfuls of freshly cut flowers from her garden to adorn our *puja* room for our weekly Sai *satsang*. That was typical Beverley, a gracious down-to-earth woman with strong opinions and a heart filled with true warmth. I stared the loss of these long-time close friends in the face and realized that I could not reach out to anyone for moral support.

I was also tremendously pained when Jon, who had been

living in eastern Oregon during my India trip, said, "I do not wish to stay at the house tonight. I will be somewhere else." Jon had put a vase with fresh-cut flowers on our dining room table, and yet had other plans that did not include me any longer. It all seemed quite unreal to me. The shock of losing my friends and not having a husband with whom to share my sorrow overwhelmed me. Physically tired and emotionally distraught, I sobbed through the night. Our home felt empty, ice-cold, impersonal and eerie like a haunted house. I paced back and forth, then from floor to floor not knowing what the next day and future would hold. I finally went to bed, but too much was on my mind to get to sleep. Exhausted, I finally saw the new daylight breaking. Even though dawn had arrived, I had no idea where it would lead me. I was deeply troubled and could no longer pray. Alone, I had to face whatever God had in store for me that day.

It was Easter Sunday, the day of the resurrection of Jesus from his death on the cross. But I was not thinking about the biblical meaning of Easter that morning. All I knew was that I stood at a major crossroads in my life. I went to church in a frazzled state and could not take in what was preached that morning. "The Lord has risen, yes, he has risen indeed," I heard. To me the Lord as the light "*is* always risen." He is in and above us all as our guiding star. The light of my own soul and its connection to God was far from visible that morning, as I felt sobering clouds hanging over my head. I was to meet Jon after church for talks and I was scared – I realized that the tremendous tension in the marriage had come to its climax. Only divorce or reconciliation was now possible, nothing in between.

Jon wanted to meet at a restaurant for discussions, but after some persuasion agreed that we would have more privacy at home. We each drove our own car to the house we had lived in for decades. I found myself standing at the dining room table staring at the colorful bouquet of flowers Jon had put there the day before, as he had done so many times during our marriage. Then I looked into his eyes as he was standing opposite me. I remained silent.

"I want a divorce," he said.

"Oh my God, it is all over now," flashed through my mind.

I felt as if a steel dagger slit through my heart, sending chills up my spine. I wanted to fulfill his wish and make it short and said, "Okay, but there are some papers on my desk upstairs I want you to sign. I want you to know that after signing those papers, I never need nor want to see you ever again." I ran upstairs to fetch the papers pertaining to taxes and other legal matters. I rushed with the paperwork down the stairs to the middle floor where Jon was still standing in the same spot, ready to leave. I put the paperwork on the dining room table with a pen for Jon to sign, when I suddenly remembered the presents I bought for him in India.

"Wait a minute," I said. "I have some presents I want you to have before you leave." Again I ran upstairs and opened my suitcase pulling out the gifts I had selected for him. I knew he was still standing at the dining table furiously chomping at the bit to leave my house and life for good, and hurried down to at least hand him my Indian gifts.

Without looking at him, I put several items down on our dining room table. First, a brown-golden Ganesha enameled in copper, floating in lotus position in a circle of royal blue; his right hand upheld the divine light and in his left hand the trident, symbol of the divine trinity. Above his third eye in white light appeared a golden crown *chakra* as a golden temple depicting his divine status. I was not focusing on Lord Ganesha, the divine remover of obstacles, when I slowly stacked one present on top of the other. I handed over my gifts in a trance-like state as a final act ever to perform for Jon. I still remember the gift of two high-quality cotton sheets bordered with purple flowers and leaf motifs meant for our bed, but that I now needed to let go off, as I would never see my husband again. The stack on the table grew and I topped it off with ten white cotton handkerchiefs Jon had asked me to get, specially made for him by an Indian tailor.

Now, I felt I had completely let go of Jon – nothing was said. Jon still stood there looking at the stack of presents on the table. Then his face changed, and he bent over and began to weep uncontrollably. He could not stop, and I had to hold him in my arms as he was telling me how much he loved me and that he could never live without me. There was no reason for me to say anything. The avalanche of gifts was like that torrential windstorm in India wiping out the word *divorce* forever. This was still the day of Easter, or the day of resurrection, which also represents springtime and renewal. For us, the light had triumphed over the darkness in which we had dwelt for almost two years. No doubt it was the hand of God on that symbolic day that saved our marriage.

During my stay in India, Jon had been busy with remodeling a charming 1948 cottage in a high desert town, a three-hour drive from Eugene. His original plan to convert the little house into an art gallery still needed much work. I felt a new exhilaration of creativity flowing through my veins and was eager to help make the necessary changes to the cottage and hire outside help where needed. I spent most of the weeks following Easter with cleaning, painting and redecorating, while Jon remodeled two bathrooms. Our combined efforts paid off and soon the place was ready for its final touches.

In June, with our twenty-fifth wedding anniversary nearing, I proposed a two-week vacation to California to celebrate. When we heard that Mata Amritanandamayi was in her ashram in San Ramon, we planned to see her.

Chapter Eighty-four

Our Sai World Crashes

After a few hours patiently waiting in line at the M.A. Center in San Ramon, California, Jon and I received the *darshan* of Amma's silent embraces. Again as in my prior visit, Amma's famous hugs did not invoke anything spiritual in me and this was the same for Jon. Nevertheless we were deeply moved by the devotional atmosphere that was palpably present in the *darshan* hall where we watched how others wept with joy when they emerged from the hugs of this world-renowned spiritual leader. We held Amma in high regard as she too represented to us the mother aspect of higher Consciousness. Like Sai Baba we had placed her on the pedestal of divinity and with this faith I eagerly hoped for a special spiritual blessing for our twenty-fifth wedding anniversary from her. After I asked an Amma volunteer for a chance to speak with her, the two of us were guided to sit down in the back of a long waiting line for that purpose. When our turn came, I handed my written request to Amma's interpreter and we sat back in silence... Then Ammachi turned her round smiling brown face towards us and made eye contact with her deep dark, somewhat mysterious, eyes. She spoke in English and said, "It is a great accomplishment to be married for twenty-five years in our type of world." She then continued, "I give you my blessings for the continuing years of your marriage." For us this blessing came straight from that higher abundance of light in which Jon and I sought to find our own God-Self.

The event put us in a happy mood. We celebrated our silver anniversary with a dinner at Il Fornaio, an Italian restaurant in Walnut Creek, a town relatively close to the M.A. Center. We stayed on for a few more days in this delightful town and took pleasure in strolling along the aesthetically pleasing malls lined with large terracotta pots filled with flowering shrubbery. We sat, talked and meditated on sculptured benches next to one of the downtown's elaborate fountains.

In a relaxed mood we continued our vacation with a trip to Shasta where we spent the night in a motel at the foot of the magnificent snow-capped Mount Shasta (14,000 feet), resembling Lord Shiva's abode on Mount Kailash in the Himalayas. In this conspicuous spiritual place, we bought a purple-blue leaded glass lamp to commemorate our twenty-five years' union. The symbols of the decoration on the lamp shade conveyed a subtle message telling us that light had returned to our relationship and that beauty of spirit surrounded our marriage. Once again, we felt deeply united. All was well…

On our arrival home we found a letter in the mailbox. I was sitting at my desk in the living room opening it. The envelope contained a letter from Mrs. C, who with her husband and son had occasionally visited our Sai Baba Center. Her letter told of two shocking experiences her fifteen-year-old son Jacob had endured in two consecutive private interviews with Sai Baba in the early fall of 1999. Her letter included a copy of Jacob's four-page handwritten report describing, step-by-step, the gruesome facts of how Sai Baba manipulated him into engaging in sexual acts. At the end of the first interview Sai Baba implored Jacob, "Don't tell anyone! Don't tell Mother! I will give you another interview tomorrow!" In the next private interview, the following day, Swami offered Jacob three thousand rupees and continued sexually molesting him. Shocked, I suddenly remembered what my own eyes had seen in the inner interview room in 1989. It validated that despite my denial then, I truly had witnessed the beginnings of a sexual approach. No wonder Sai Baba had come rushing forward to shut the drapes in front of my eyes that had seen too much.

I felt something shifting inside me… Mrs. C's letter and Jacob's detailed notes sounded credible to me. I figured that a fifteen-year-old could not possibly have dreamed up such accusations. It also occurred to me that it must have taken some courage for a young man his age to reveal these intimate sexual details. The appalling news made me speechless for a moment. I slumped over in my chair covering my eyes as if I did not want to see what I had read. The foul deeds of a man we had believed to be like a God on Earth were taking their toll on me in every cell of my being. My mind became still and I gazed into nowhere as if in a trance. I was only aware of the pounding of my heart. I again picked up Jacob's four-page testimony and read it once more to make sure that I read it correctly. Jacob's report clearly showed that he could not foresee how Baba set him up and lured him to submit to his sexual advances. The sexual acts were an unmistakable case of pedophilia in which an underage victim is seduced into sexual acts by a predator. Pedophilia is a criminal act, punishable under the laws of many countries in our world today.

After I read Mrs. C's letter and Jacob's notes to my husband, we stared at each other. I heard Jon softly muttering, "Well that is that!" We both knew what it meant... As my mind was taking in the information, it dawned on me that the world we had known for the last fifteen years had come to an end.

At that moment the doorbell rang. It was my friend Sally, a Unitarian minister and spiritual friend with a sympathetic interest in Sai Baba and his movement. "Something has happened, Sally," I said. "I want to read you a letter and some interview details we just received in the mail." Sally sat down as I read Jacob's notes to her. The graphic descriptions were hard to read aloud and I stopped several times to catch my breath.

After I finished, Sally stared at me in disbelief. "When are you going to take the Sai Baba pictures off the walls?" was all she could say.

"Give me just one day," I replied with a sigh. "They will be taken down tomorrow." The Sai Baba photos hung on virtually every wall of our house, especially on the ground floor where the Sai-temple was located.

That same afternoon, I received an e-mail message from Sai Towers Publishing House in India that read, "We are unable, at this time, to publish your manuscript." It struck me how timely this was. I was delighted, realizing that my writing could have been construed as propaganda material supporting a possible pedophile. I suddenly remembered my father's study notes in the Sai Baba book he had given me years ago on which he wrote, "This is propaganda material."

My first impulse was to share the distressing news with my close Sai Baba friends Yody and Linda. I got on the phone. To my surprise they already knew the damaging facts and other serious allegations that were posted on the Internet. Linda also revealed that Sai Baba had inappropriately approached her son Michael in a private interview in 1988. He did not tell his mother then, but when Linda, years later, wanted to take her younger son to see Sai Baba, Michael finally spoke of the incident. Linda told me that she had written a letter about the sexual incident regarding her son to Dr. Goldstein, the chairman of the Sai organization's western hemisphere. Dr. Goldstein promised Linda to personally talk to Sathya Sai Baba about it, but never followed suit.

I began reading the allegations that were posted on the various websites. I also like to refer the reader to an outstanding website: exbaba.nl and its links, where Jacob's report of the two interviews can be found under his own name, which he did not permit me to reveal in this book. I also want to draw your attention to two other reports on the Internet.

One is of David Bailey, who was a professor of music at the Sai Baba College for five years. As his students came to trust David, they came to him to reveal their anguish and pain of being sexually exploited by Sai Baba on many occasions. They asked for help. David and his wife Faye, then still staunch as well as famous devotees and part of the inner circle of Sai Baba, took the enormous courage to do an investigation into these matters, which resulted in a full report on Sai Baba's "shady ungodly side" in a document called *The Findings* (published around 1999). I furthermore especially found the information given by Dr. Naresh Bhatia, once the head of the blood bank of the Super Specialty Hospital in Puttaparthi, astonishingly gruesome, as it tells of a seventh grade male student who after an interview with Sai Baba cried for several days. Dr. Bhatia was called to investigate, and found that the boy had been sexually penetrated via the anus. The child was taken to Bangalore and re-examined. A second medical opinion confirmed the sexual abuse.

The many worldwide allegations on the websites convinced me that Sai Baba was definitely not who he said he was, namely the avatar, an incarnation of the Godhead himself.

Chapter Eighty-five

Taking a Stand

The Baba pictures came off the wall, including the new oil painting of Sai Baba, Jon's best portrait work. Jon burned this excellent piece of art in the stove of his studio. How devastated we both felt! We left the organization we had served for fifteen years for good.

Above all else, I now needed to find out where the local Sai officers stood regarding the allegations. The center president, a close friend, admitted that he and the other officers knew of the copied handwritten notes of the fifteen-year-old boy's molestations. A long dialogue ensued in which my friend surprisingly made the following statement, "Ella, the accusations are either all rumors or something that Swami does, of which we simply do not have the right understanding." He continued, "Do not judge Baba's actions, and do not question Sai Baba." I was further informed that the center officers had requested Dr. Goldstein to ask Swami personally about the alleged crimes. Sai Baba responded by saying, "Swami is purity itself," and that remark was sufficient for our local officials to embrace their spiritual leader once more without further questioning. When other conscious-minded high-ranking officers worldwide were asking questions, the Sai organization responded by simply forcing them to resign.

Then the legendary words "Swami is purity itself" became the new dictum for the Sai organization and under that mantle nothing changed and Sai spiritual business went on as usual without any proper investigation. "Do not read the Internet" was Baba's next remark in a public discourse to his devotees regarding the allegations. Some devotees who stayed the course with him began a war against ex-devotees by placing vile judgments on the ex-devotees following Sai Baba's own example when, in another public discourse, he coined them "Judases."

My next step was to make contact with some of Sai Baba's

victims in Sweden, The Netherlands, Germany, Australia and the United States, to verify for myself the validity of the alleged crimes. I e-mailed and made phone calls to the victims, their parents and friends. The misuse of victims like Conny Larsson of Sweden and Alaya Rahm of the United States was heart wrenching. Conny Larsson, a known Swedish actor and film star, has since written a book called *Behind the Mask of the Clown,* with the subtitle: *Truths, Sex and Sects,* revealing the sexual abuse he had suffered at the hands of Sai Baba. In my opinion these victims had much to lose and little to gain from going public with their revelation of Sai Baba's intimate sexual ploys.

I felt the inner call to stand up, not only for the children, but also against the apparent cover-up of the alleged crimes. A proper investigation into the sexual allegations did not seem forthcoming. With all my heart, I wanted the Sai organization to live up to its own high standard of spiritual teachings and in that vein I wrote a letter that asks for reflection on, as well as clarification of, the alleged sexual abuse of their leader. My letter also specifically asked for a worldwide investigation and suggested that if Sai Baba was the avatar he would undoubtedly welcome a comprehensive investigation to clear him and his organization of any wrongdoings. My letter was read and signed by seventy-five distraught ex-devotees I had gotten to know through the Internet. On August 1, 2000, I mailed the letter to Dr. Goldstein with copies to nine high-ranking officers of the Sai organization in the United States. One month later, I received my letter back from Dr. Goldstein, unopened. Only Dr. John C. Evans, President of the Sathya Sai Baba Council of the United States of America, wrote a response letter showing the position the organization was taking, based on *Advaita* philosophy.

In his response, Dr. Evans took refuge in the philosophy of *Advaita* to explain away the concerns of seventy-five highly spiritual ex-devotees. *Advaita* teachings are based on the great Indian philosopher Sankara, who lived A.D. 788–820. Sankara taught that the entire world of phenomena is ultimately illusionary, since its existence resulted from the false imposition (*maya*) of qualities on Brahman. This is the *Advaita* philosophy of non-dualism, where God or Brahman is undivided, the *One Without a Second.* To understand the teachings one has to transcend the duality of the phenomenal world and enter a world of higher Consciousness and from that elevated point "all that is" stands revealed to be only Brahman or God himself. The world based in Brahman is Brahman. Sankara has and can be easily misinterpreted. By giving quotes of Advaitic teachings by Sai Baba as well as a contemporary Indian teacher Ramesh Balsekar, Dr. Evans suggested that the alleged crimes of Sai Baba have no real existence as far as the Sai organization was concerned and needed to be seen as illusions of the mind. I wholeheartedly disagreed with such a point of view.

Another equally great Indian philosopher, Ramanuja (c. A.D. 1017–c. A.D. 1137) is perhaps easier to understand than Sankara. Ramanuja argued against the position seen during the ages as purely Sankara's, and stated that the phenomenal world is real as it is the creation of God himself. To Ramanuja, *maya* is not an illusion, but came into being as a result of Brahman's intention to become the many. Human beings are then part of the body of Brahman. But both philosophies, when talking about the Real or the Self, are ultimately based in Brahman (God).

Following the latter philosophy, all people are a creation of God living in God's dream of himself. "In that dream we have the choice to play our roles as officers of spiritual organizations responsibly, to make sure that no harm can come to anyone, especially the children."

To understand the ancient scriptures that state that God is beyond evil, I like to point to the Svetasvatara *Upanishad,* which makes it even clearer that in this world of illusion there is evil, which obstructs the light of God. It states in Chapter III:20:

> The Self [which is God], smaller than the small, greater than the great, is hidden in the hearts of creatures. The wise, by the grace of the Creator, behold the Lord, majestic and desireless, and become free from grief.

The interpretation of the word "majestic" in the above-quoted Upanishad in a *New Translation by Swami Nikhilananda,* Volume Two, is explained as follows:

> The unique majesty of Atman [the soul] consists in the fact that it does not expand or contract by association with upadhis [the ego or ignorance], great or small. It does not become holy through a man's good action, or sinful through his evil action, because its association with upadhis is illusionary and not real. **But evil action creates a barrier and hinders a man from beholding Atman, whereas good action removes the barrier.**

In other words man has to stand on the side of good and against evil and this is of course also the basis of most religions. The cover-up and denial of lots of evidence by the Sai organization made it clear that it was time to move on. Even though saddened by these circumstances, I also found it refreshing to return to the God of transcendental light, the light I had always seen and experienced long before I ever knew about Sathya Sai Baba.

Chapter Eighty-six

The Sai Baba Cult

I need to inform my reader that Sathya Sai Baba is no longer a threat for young men, as he passed away on April 24, 2011. He was eighty-five. His prediction that he would live till the age of ninety-six did not materialize.

But there are still cults in this world often headed by charismatic teachers who lead their followers astray. Out of great concern, I feel the need to expose the still existing Sai organization and tell the remaining devotees that they are caught in a cleverly spun web of deceit. I also want to give my fellow ex-devotees and the public at large insights into how cults happen and how to avoid the traps set by cult-like organizations.

In 2000, I had reached out to groups of ex-devotees who, shocked by the loss of their spiritual leader, experienced a deep sense of grief. While reviewing the despicable facts that came to light, we sustained each other in our moments of sorrow. We had believed that Sai Baba represented the light of God. Even though deceived by him and his organization, we had also misled ourselves by surrendering our own God-given discerning faculties of mind to him. "How was it possible that we gave away our personal power?"

I found the answer to that question after reading one of the works of an enlightened Spanish nun of our Lady of Mount Carmel, who later became a Roman Catholic saint. Her name is Theresa of Avila. In 1577 Saint Theresa wrote a book called *The Interior Castle*. In her book Saint Theresa explained the five different levels or rooms in a spiritual aspirant's journey to the ultimate goal of union with God. She calls these levels the five dwelling places. In *The Interior Castle, The First Dwelling Places*, Chapter 2:15 in *The Collective Works* of St. Theresa of Avila, St. Theresa writes, talking to her sisters in the convent:

> Remember that there are few dwelling places in this castle in which the devils do not wage battle. True, in some rooms the guards (which I believe are the faculties) have the strength to fight; but it is very necessary that we don't grow careless in recognizing the wiles of the devil, and that he not deceive us by changing himself into an angel of light. There's a host of things he can do to cause us harm; he enters little by little, and until he has done the harm, we do not recognize him.

Harm was done not only to the young boys, but also to the souls of devotees. "Had Sai Baba not deceived well-meaning people into claiming that he was the Cosmic Christ and had this falsehood not impeded their spiritual journey towards the light?" I believe that the negative forces, the so-called devils of Saint Theresa, often consist of ignorant erroneous group talk and thinking. In cults, the spiritual leader and his close entourage take the followers in by humanitarian slogans that sound appealing, even touching the human heart. A spiritual leader may be a wolf hiding in sheep's clothing. This can be very dangerous. In the history of mankind we have seen this happen over and over again in other movements of faith.

I would never have believed that I would ever call the Sai organization a cult. When I was a member, I never saw anything seriously amiss. When my husband and I joined the movement we could see no wrong in singing songs to God. The weekly *satsang* was free of charge and the organization never solicited funds from the devotees in the centers. We could see no wrong in volunteering in soup kitchens and nursing homes or other humanitarian projects in our community, as was recommended. And of course there is nothing wrong with studying the ancient scriptures of India on which some of Sai Baba's teachings were perhaps cleverly based. And yet these seemingly positive ideals can nevertheless lure you into pathways that lead the spiritual aspirant astray, as Theresa of Avila already knew in her day.

I also have to confess that for years, before receiving Jacob's notes, stories of improper sexual conduct by Sai Baba had occasionally come to my attention... I seriously blame myself for not having paid closer attention to them, including what my own eyes had seen in the inner interview room in 1989. Already in the early seventies, the author Tal Brooke, in his book *Lord of the Air* (later republished as *Avatar of Night*), called for public awareness as to what was happening behind the curtains of the interview room in Puttaparthi, where Tal himself had been sexually molested. The power of Sai Baba, not only spiritually, but also politically, was so strong that Tal's book became officially forbidden reading in India and the Sai organization certainly tried to constrain devotees from reading his book.

In the past, as a devotee, I had taken the position, as did many, that the rumors of Sai Baba's sexual misconduct had been misconstrued and were likely an initiation into the pathway of *Kundalini*, the road to self-realization. When I stayed in the Shri Siddheswar ashram, Guruji once told us that there was another "yogi method" to arouse *Kundalini* in which a guru touches with his thumb the nerve clusters lying between the perineum and the testicles, thereby raising the *Kundalini* with his yogi-powers. Guruji said, "As a rule I do not practice this method!" What young Jacob recounted in his interview report was definitely not that type of *Kundalini* rousing.

A year after our Sai world crashed, I got back in touch with a bright young man from Germany I met in the Shri Siddheshwar Baba ashram. I informed him about the sexual molestations of young males by Sai Baba and mentioned that some devotees still believed that these activities had something to do with *Kundalini* rousing. Guruji's student (*sadhaka*) then revealed his personal story of the "other kind" of *Kundalini* arousal to me, as described hereunder:

> I went to Guruji and asked him to initiate me in *Kundalini* "in the other way" he had once described in class, different from the touching of my third eye and the top of my head. It seemed to me that my *Kundalini* was still not moving perfectly. Guruji kindly told me to come inside. He asked me to lie down on the floor. I was fully dressed. No feelings of sexuality were present. Guruji told me to take hold of his thumb and to put it between my perineum and genitals. This is what I did. It took a few minutes. It was absolutely not sexual.

Sathya Sai Baba's death has set him free from ever having to face the alleged crimes in any court. I believe some devotees will defend him now more than ever before, as he remains their legend on which they base their faith in God. Shortly after his death, various newspaper articles revealed that the funds of the Sai Central Trust were estimated between $5.5 and $9 billion. The organization still keeps silent about the allegations, but the difference now is that several reliable newspapers have given information about the sexual allegations and have also pointed to monetary irregularities. A revealing documentary, *Secret Swami,* includes interviews with some of his victims. It was broadcast by the BBC in the UK on Thursday, June 17, 2004, on BBC Two, and still can been viewed on the Internet.

I advise all spiritual aspirants to stay critical and alert on the spiritual path, and to not be afraid to watch or investigate their guru in order to avoid falling into a potential spiritual deception.

Chapter Eighty-seven

Analysis of Sai-Miracles

Devotees of Sathya Sai Baba came from Hindu, Catholic, Protestant, Jewish, or Buddhist backgrounds and other religions. What his devotees perhaps had in common was the thought that religions had not worked to advance mankind to a more perfect world as God may have intended.

The widely held view that someday God, or a godly redeemer, would appear on Earth is not so farfetched. The Revelation of John 22:12, of the New English Bible, mentions a second coming of the Lord: "Yes, I am coming soon... I am the Alpha and the Omega." In the Judaic faith we see the longing for the coming of the Messiah as the redeemer. In Islam the waiting is for the Imam Mahdi, who will rid the world of wrongdoing, injustice and tyranny. In the *Bhagavad-Gita,* we read that during times of moral decline the Lord himself will come down to set the affairs of the world straight. All these scriptures hold a promise for the deliverance of human suffering by God himself or his special messenger. When Sai Baba in an interview with the authors Peggy Mason and Ron Laing confirmed that he was indeed the "Cosmic Christ," this seemed plausible in the light of the predictions in the Holy Scriptures.

But the question is, "How is God or a messiah-like figure to be found?" As Jesus was foremost known by miracles that drew people to him, the same could be said for Sai Baba, who already from an early age on was said to have performed amazing materializations, as recounted in many books. When we experience things "out of this world," they are often called miracles. A miracle is something that cannot be grasped with the normal mind. That God performs miracles, we can find in the Hebrew Bible, in the Old Testament as well as in the New Testament, and in the scriptures of other world religions. It is understandable that spiritual people are attracted to miracles, because they believe miracles happen where God's hand has visibly touched mankind. Miracles are divine calling cards all through the centuries.

It is not surprising that, when people heard about the Sai miracles, they flocked to his ashram. In the interview room, devotees witnessed materializations of sacred ash, rings, diamonds, *japamalas* (strings of prayer beads), watches, etc., as did I during my five interviews with him. It all seemed genuinely miraculous. As I carefully watched him during these manifestations, Sai Baba often reminded me of a magician pulling things out of a hat, and one who was enormously pleased with his own show. He undoubtedly wanted to convince the devotees that he had the power of the universe in his hands, as I heard him remark on several occasions. Devotees, in general, were extremely attached to the gift of special objects that had appeared by the motion of their Swami's hands. Receiving these materialized gifts set such a devotee immediately apart from the others and the devotee's status often depended on how many interviews he or she had, or on how many materialized gifts he or she had received. A noted pecking order existed amongst the devotees.

Aside from the so-called miracles of materialization there were presumed miracles of healings and spiritual experiences:

Healings:

Most devotees truly believed in the healing powers of Sai Baba. These powers had been extensively recorded in the many books written by devotees. As related in Part V, Chapter Thirty-nine, "Ashram Life," I remember that during my first year in the ashram, when I was sitting on the temple-grounds, an Italian woman with cancer ran towards Swami in an attempt to find healing. Instead of paying attention to this unfortunate young woman, Swami allowed his volunteers to grab, subdue and remove her from the ashram grounds. Afterwards, Swami came to us murmuring as if speaking to himself, "A crazy woman, a crazy woman, what can I do?" I was shocked to say the least and pondered why he would make such remarks, if he was the avatar (highest descending Consciousness on Earth). But the serene spiritual atmosphere of the ashram and the continuous stream of devotional tales of Sai miracles made me doubt my own critical analysis again and again.

I traveled to India eleven times, but never personally met any person who had experienced the miracle of a healing. Instead, my good friend Elly, who had breast cancer and trusted to receive healing from Sai Baba, died from her disease in India in May 2000. Later on, I became aware that many other western women had died of breast cancer after they had come to India in hopes of finding divine healing. I understand that I cannot claim they would not have died had they received prompt and proper medical attention.

For comparison I like to refer to a book by Ruth Cranston, *Miracle of Lourdes*, an in-depth narrative of the miracles that happen in Lourdes in southern France. Ruth describes how in

Lourdes, healings are not pronounced miracles until a group of doctors will confirm them as such. Patients are checked before and after the taking of the baths, located on the spot where the Virgin Mary appeared, to verify if they are truly cured from their disease. On top of that, there is a follow-up for years to see if the patient remains free from the former disease. When a patient is healed and remains so for many years, only then will a miracle be declared in Lourdes.

Unfortunately such scrutiny never took place in Baba's ashram. Devotees, hungry for miracles, made unsubstantiated hasty claims of Sai Baba's healings. Professors and students of the Sai Colleges often spoke of Swami's most recent miracles of healing during their introduction speeches prior to his acclaimed public discourses. I noted to my dismay how crowds of devotees enthusiastically applauded the mentioning of such miracles of healing. Even then, I thought, "God never needs such propaganda, and if Sai Baba is God, why would he allow such glorified talks? Was it to try to make the most out of people's psychological gullibility and spiritual openness?" The contents of Baba books were spiced with miraculous healings written by authors truly inspired by the stories they had heard, but who did not examine them in the same thorough manner as for example the Roman Catholic Church has regarding the miracles of Lourdes. I believe that physical healings can and perhaps may have occurred in Baba's ashram even though I am not aware of any. How these healings happen lies in the same category as the occurrences of spiritual experiences.

Spiritual Experiences:

During my time as a devotee I had spiritual experiences and attributed them as coming from Sai Baba. In his ashram, thousands of devotees waited patiently every day for God in *darshan*. The minds of all those people formed a positive force field when they collectively called out in prayer to the Divine. The force field amplified with Sai Baba's appearance when the longing for God reached its climax. In such intense moments miracles of change may take place in a person's heart and mind causing spiritual experiences and healing of the psyche or even physical healing. Even though Sai Baba was the catalyst, it did not prove he was God. What took place was powerful, but had little to do with the man Sai Baba, but much with the devotee's psychological and spiritual make-up and group consciousness.

I heard that the same type of experiences of a divine nature took place during Billy Graham's evangelical meetings in large stadiums, when he asked people to turn their heart to Jesus Christ as their personal savior.

Of course, spiritual experiences and healings are attainable for everyone in all religions through all forms, through no forms or through higher ideals, which all are part of the ONE Consciousness. Also know that when love is present, God is present. One can worship a stone, a river, nature, a statue of a Hindu God or one of the many Roman Catholic saints. That statue adored as God will speak to one's spiritual heart, because it too contains the invisible essence of God's formless presence. God uses even a person like Sai Baba to bring forth God's love, thereby accomplishing spiritual changes in the spiritual aspirant.

"One does not need to go to India to see God, feel God, or know God." Guruji always said, "Prince Gautama could have stayed home and become the realized Buddha in his own palace with his wife and young son. There is no need to go anywhere to find God or liberation. It is where you are, where God lives."

God, or the higher Consciousness, can be called upon through prayer and listened to through meditation anywhere. The more one focuses with all one's heart, mind and soul to a collective God concept or a personal one, HE will reveal himself. That is the truth.

Chapter Eighty-eight

Aftermath

After a fifteen-year focus on Sai Baba as the image of our higher selves, the shock of having been misled by Sai Baba and his organization at first caused a sense of sorrow and disorientation. It was a rude awakening out of a beautiful dream we had held for real. Jon and I sustained each other through the grieving period of the loss of this grand story, bringing us closer in spirit than ever before. Jon applauded me for making a stand against pedophilia as a voice for the abused and misused young males. He admired my dedication to work with ex-devotees around the globe to expose the "supposed avatar," which included many hours of unrelenting work.

On my spiritual path in the aftermath of the fall of Sai Baba, I continued traveling the pathway of *Kundalini* to reach the completeness of self-realization. The altered hard-to-live-through states belonged to the past and I began experiencing frequent states of infinite bliss. An enormous gratitude often wells from my heart to still have revelations of the luminous diamond-like white and blue lights, and the blue-purple colors, alive in my third eye (*trikuti*). I continue to grow in sensitivity toward others in the knowledge that I am the other also. Occasionally I see the auras of people, and objects that also carry divinity within and without as well. From these experiences I can truly state that divinity is in all things and that everything is alive. With that knowledge I also know that even though Sathya Sai Baba is seen by many as a pedophile, God as the higher Consciousness nevertheless spoke through him, when I showed him my manuscript, *Drawn to the Light,* and he said, "Not now," which certainly meant that the book was not ready for publishing at that time. Sai Baba spoke, like all of us can and occasionally do, from that higher cosmic perspective that lives in each of us. It was clear that the higher Consciousness knew that my book was not finished at that time, as Sai Baba's own "human downfall" had yet to be revealed and reported in my writings and given meaning.

Many devotees continue to believe in him, even after his death, as they embrace him as the representative of their higher Consciousness. I certainly cannot judge the path of another as all souls are undoubtedly guided by their own elevated soul-Self, also called the *Atman*, or divine Consciousness. Sri Ramakrishna, the saint from Bengal (1836–1886) who often lived completely absorbed in communion with God, was once quoted to have said that even the light that leads astray is the light of God. And how true this might be from that much higher perspective. An embodied spirit, called the *jiva* in Indian thought, sees only part of the total picture. Only in oneness with the ONE can the full picture of all that is happening on Earth be understood.

I also am sad to tell you that Amma or Amritanandamayi Ma, who I believed to be a true Indian saint (see Part VII, Chapter Seventy-four, "Meeting Ammachi," and Part VIII, Chapter Eighty-four, "Our Sai World Crashes"), has also been exposed as having a darker side. This can be read in Gail Tredwell's book published in 2013, called *Holy Hell*. Gail was Amma's personal attendant, devotee, and keeper of some devastating secrets for twenty years. I innocently introduced Amma as the representation of the divine Mother to my reader. I left the stories regarding her in my book unchanged, because my experiences with her were genuine as were the experiences with Sai Baba.

As I came to grapple with the downfall of two gurus I had revered as perfect masters, I finally came to the conclusion that these human gurus have a cosmic part by which a sincere devotee still can receive divine revelations, as had happened to me. If a seeker believes in an image, any image that to him or her depicts the divine, that image will or can reveal the higher truth to the believer. Nevertheless, I feel it is still preferable to choose a spiritual teacher or guru of the highest light to reach the ultimate goal of self-realization. I again urge spiritual seekers to make sure that their chosen guru is genuine by investigating what is happening with him or her and in the guru's inner circles. When we find more darkness than light it may signal that it is time to move on to other teachers that exude the vibrations of higher God Consciousness. Always keep in mind that there are human laws by which most civilizations live. Gurus that overstep such boundaries, because they are not as enlightened as claimed, still can fall prey to their own ego, which is not yet completely dissolved in the true knowing as to what God really is.

In an attempt to find a more balanced or even kinder approach to my writings about Sai Baba, I asked some important devotees still part of the flock to voice their opinions for inclusion in this book. Unfortunately they all declined my invitation. I have no qualms with the devotees that need to stay with the story of Sai Baba's divinity. Ultimately all is divine. My only hope is that they will find the spiritual strength to comprehend why so many loving and dedicated devotees left the Sai Baba path. The world or Earth plane is a place of "darkness and light," in which the light cannot be recognized without the darkness. Both are of God's creation. And we can be assured that the light will overcome the darkness when the mysteries of God are fully known. Then only light remains...

The loss of Sai Baba was another turning point in my life as well as for Jon as we needed to refocus our spiritual attention. Eventually we discovered that the break held its own treasures. There was a renewed sense of freedom to explore other realms of spirituality. We discovered works of highly evolved teachers that kept us on our pathway to God, the eternal Light without face or form. We hoped to spend many more years in the pursuit of a deeper understanding of the Divine. That yet a totally different spiritual challenge lay ahead soon became apparent when Jon's lung condition worsened, requiring our full attention.

Chapter Eighty-nine

Transition

Concerned with his rapid decline due to his illness, Jon and I visited his lung specialist for further advice. Dr. Ameen diagnosed him with interstitial pulmonary fibrosis and prescribed oxygen around the clock to keep Jon's heart and brain from deteriorating. Oxygen tubes were spread over every level of our house. Getting used to the new equipment was challenging, but soon we adapted. The huffing and puffing sounds of the oxygen machine constantly reminded us that the flow of oxygen to Jon's lungs might add another five to ten years to his life. With that sense of make-believe optimism, Jon went back to work to finish his music scores. "All is well," we thought; we just wanted to believe that.

January 22, 2004, came. I felt mentally numb, as we walked through the front door. I was in a state of shock and internally my heart wept. Jon and I had just come home from a second visit to his pulmonary specialist, who declared Jon's lung condition terminal. He wrote a prescription that Jon be placed under hospice care.

Downstairs Jon sat down with me on the lava-rock fireplace hearth and said, "Let us not think the worst now, but instead think that we still may have that five to ten years."

"Yes, why worry now when you are quite able to think, talk, walk, eat and work on your music composition," I whispered while holding my husband's hands.

During the following weeks, even though we resumed our normal routines, our attitude toward life shifted, as we knew that every moment was a precious gift that called for the deepest love.

But soon, a further decline in Jon's lung capacity set in, making it necessary for him to sleep in longer so as not to aggravate his lungs into devastating coughing spells. I began to take over all the household duties. During the years of our marriage,

Jon not only enjoyed cooking interesting meals, but also loved making the appearance on the plates a true piece of art. The time had come that I cook and serve the meals, and this role reversal was hugely painful for him. A hospital bed was also required, and when it came, I had it placed in my study, where large floor-to-ceiling windows overlooked a beautiful back yard. I will never forget the expression on Jon's face when he looked at me from his newly acquired bed with eyes fraught with anguish, calling out to me for help in his new uncertainty. It was in those eyes that I observed a spirit getting ready to transcend into the next stages of higher awareness. In that instant, my heart totally went out to him and an indescribable new deep spiritual connection was born between us, solid as a rock, and ready to endure all that lay ahead.

A hospice nurse came once a week to assess the situation. Jon, being the artist that he was, could not readily accept outside help. He had always been a self-made man, brilliant, as well as a true maverick. Anxiety attacks were occurring due to lack of oxygen, giving him the sensation of drowning. When I received his desperate anxiety calls on my cell phone while on the road, I sped home as if I had taken on wings. Jon's decline impacted me severely. My emotions often erupted in the car, where I cried uncontrollably, but at home the two of us kept on living in a kind of bubble, filled with endless love and sorrow, which no one else could even begin to understand.

At the end of January, our concerned daughter Femke appeared from California, followed by her husband, Ramon. I silently acknowledged that Jon's condition was deteriorating. He remained in bed most of the day and looked so fragile that we often thought he would not wake up again. Then Femke and Ramon announced the great news that Femke was pregnant. Jon and I were the first to know. Femke's own baby basinet, wrapped in plastic covers for thirty years, came down from the attic. Memories of Femke's birth and Harmen's catastrophic death flooded back to memory. Jon was super delighted with the news of the coming birth. He simply loved children. Ramon left for California to go back to work and Femke stayed on till David arrived from The Netherlands.

Jon's situation took another dive. With anguish, David and I frequently stood at his bedside looking at him asleep in his hospital bed breathing as if in labor. An incredible weakness set in close to David's departure and Jon remained bedridden full time. When awake, Jon – as impossible as this may seem – continued to be highly spirited and truthful to his promise not to let despair in, if at all possible. He helped us hold tightly to that sparkly creative notion that he was still going to live despite appearances that were telling a different story.

Jon had always been an eccentric, often exclaiming that he felt as if he had come from another planet. He had led a different and difficult life in his youth, which set the stage for the development of a unique personality. When Jon was three, his father abandoned the family, leaving his mother to care for her two sons. Denver, eleven years older, was soon to leave the family to be on his own, and Jon was left alone with a mother who had no child-rearing skills. She abused her child with a leather strap, beating him black and blue till the time came that he could run faster than she could. While trying to make a living, she often wanted to get rid of him and would unexpectedly abandon her son by leaving him on a farm or shipping him out to foster families.

As a young child, Jon often sat alone under the trees in contemplation, questioning what life was all about... His loneliness gave birth to a creative mind in which new worlds of possibilities opened. He found depth and meaning in the movies and adopted the stars as his companions. Ronald Colman, his favorite, acting in the roles of Smithy and Sir Charles Rainier in *Random Harvest,* became his father image, evoking characteristics of nobility. In later years he also based his life's philosophy on the well-known prayer of St. Francis of Assisi (see Part IX, Chapter Seventy-nine, "Mahashivaratri 2000") and on the ideals of Mahatma Gandhi and Dr. Martin Luther King, Jr. Jon truly tried to live up to these high ideals and make them his own. Yet the psychological scars of his childhood haunted him throughout his life. He often remarked, "I could so easily have gone the wrong way." Yet, his intellect and deep meditative sensitive nature kept him from such a disastrous outcome. Ultimately, the writing of music became his way to rise above his mental pain of abandonment and rejection. Music composition enabled him to connect with the higher octaves of his soul and make him free.

In May, Jon was no longer able to do the composition work he loved, which revealed that time was fleeting for him. He nevertheless still sought to personify his beloved actor Ronald Colman and emulated the dignity of that character. When I asked him, "How is it with you?" he answered like Smithy in *Random Harvest,* "I will be all right."

Life deepened for both of us and Jon and I became one in spirit. Night and day I sang Jon's favorite spiritual songs and read to him from the Psalms in the Old Testament. We immersed ourselves in the philosophies taught by mystical teachers. We especially enjoyed Baird T. Spalding's *Life and Teaching of the Masters of the Far East* and Eckhart Tolle's *Stillness Speaks.* These readings invoked experiences of expanded awareness in which we, at the same time, suddenly radiated with an abundance of divine light. The immense joy we both experienced at such moments was not of this world.

Our connectedness deepened still as time moved on. At night, I gained the ability to wake up well before Jon needed me, and I knew that some kind of an ethereal help-line had been installed between us, connecting our two souls. Jon could never speak about his own approaching death, but subtly showed me in a poem he presented to me for Mother's Day where he was in the process.

June came. On the fifth, President Ronald Reagan passed away after years of struggle with Alzheimer's disease. We watched the televised state funeral. How well I remember Nancy Reagan putting her head down on Ronnie's casket. I completely identified with her intense sorrow, which I suspected might be my own sorrow soon. Jon said absolutely nothing. When it came to talking about death, Jon's mind would turn it around much like Dylan Thomas's poem "Do Not Go Gentle Into That Good Night" when he suggests, "Rage, rage against the dying of the light." Jon was not ready to let go. His spirit was still high, but in contrast to Thomas's poem, he did not rage against the death of his physical self, but simply did not believe in it. He kept saying time and time again, "I will be all right."

I had to leave Jon for three days to be present in The Netherlands where David was to defend his PhD thesis. Femke graciously took time off to take care of her stepfather. Convinced he was in the best of hands with my daughter, an accomplished Intensive Care nurse, I nevertheless was well aware that he might die in my short absence.

David's defense in an old Amsterdam cathedral was an impressive event. I realized that I represented Harmen and Jon, who sadly missed the height of their son's academic achievement. David's promotion took place on his own birthday, which was also my wedding anniversary, and marked the beginning of my thirtieth year with Jon. In Amsterdam, we stayed in touch by cell phone. We talked as I walked by the seventeenth-century houses along the canals. One time his weakened voice whispered from the depth of his human desperation, "Please, *come back!*" ripping my heart to pieces. "Jon," I said, "already the day after tomorrow I will be home again."

As far as care was concerned, all had gone smoothly in Eugene. Upon my return home, I was intensely grateful to find Jon alive. Femke had to leave for her home in California. She was six months' pregnant, and had to say her final goodbye to the only father she had ever known.

Even though times of enormous physical decline followed, Jon's lively spirit remained intact. The management of Jon's illness was all consuming, and new learning was required of me to accommodate Jon's deteriorating condition. I was not only a wife and closest friend, but became Jon's counselor, minister, nurse and advocate twenty-four hours a day.

Physically and emotionally I was at the end of my rope. I took the opportunity of a five-day respite offered by hospice to have Jon cared for in a near-by nursing facility. Jon agreed wholeheartedly, thinking that he would have a ball with the staff of trained health workers. In the nursing home he received the best room, viewing a garden with flowering rosebushes. We were pleased and yet, Jon phoned me during his first overnight and anxiously let me know that he was in the wrong place. "I need to come home immediately!" he said. No one at the nursing home understood his special medical needs for morphine. It took too long for a nurse to appear, which put Jon in great agony and near death. It was a maddening situation.

I immediately made the arrangements to have a medical transport company take him back home the next Monday. Jon was eating less than ever before. He told me he had a plan, but did not clarify. In early August David arrived from The Netherlands and made his bed on the floor next to his stepfather's bed. During the night's emergencies David and I began working as a team. The extra pair of hands and the input of David's wonderful spirit were a tremendous help to Jon and me. Jon's spirit was still strong and he often joked with David as if nothing was happening. Even the hospice staff was amazed how Jon could live on, his eyes shining with light.

One day Jon decided that he did not want to be on oxygen. We took it away. David and I sat with him most of that day, as we feared that he would not last. Our friend Barbara came and we were all sitting around Jon's bed, when he awoke and said, "There are five people in the room, let me introduce you to..." In reality there were only the four of us. We were completely puzzled and wondered whom he was seeing that we could not see...

The next day Jon wanted his oxygen back. During this time he seldom ate and refused the tiny meals I brought in for him. His weight shrank down to around seventy pounds. The care for his emaciated body became intense. He had to sit up in bed to favor his lungs, but would slide down to the bottom of the bed under the force of gravity, and David and I had to pull him back up. David was needed at his job in The Hague and left, even though we wondered whether that was a wise decision.

Alone with Jon, I continued singing hymns read from the spiritual books he loved. Jon had no muscle tone left, but his spirit was radiant. One night I was standing at his bedside in my nightgown when Jon suddenly asked, "Tell me, who is that lady with the long blond hair walking in and out the door all the time?"

I felt cold chills running down my back. I was completely alone with him. I said, "Jon, there is no one here besides us." Then I asked, "What does she look like?"

"She is dressed in white robes." Overcoming my initial shock, I all of a sudden said, "It is all right! She must be your guardian angel helping us. This is simply wonderful." I relaxed and Jon was at peace with my remarks.

The next day the pastor of hospice appeared. Jon was asleep in his room and I invited her to sit with me on the deck. We got into a conversation about the scriptures when the pastor suddenly asked me out of the blue, "Is your husband seeing other people in his room whom you cannot see?" Taken aback, I told her that this had happened twice. The pastor said, "It is my experience as a hospice pastor that these appearances happen when a patient is close to crossing over. They already can see into the other dimensions." I was stunned and did not reply.

It was Wednesday night when I rushed down the stairs because Jon needed me. He had not eaten for several weeks and drank little. Again I sang the Lord's Prayer and quoted the 23rd Psalm. Jon looked at me quietly and said, "I want to go. I need to go. How do I do it?" He was ready to take the plunge and completely trusted me to guide him. I reminded him to look for the approaching light and said that I would go with him. All our prayers we had prayed till then suddenly came to a crashing halt. Unable to produce another prayer in desperation we both screamed for God to take him...

The next morning came. A hospice volunteer came to relieve me for an hour. I did not want to go. She insisted I go, while Jon was telling us that he wanted to let go of his oxygen. We took it away. I left, but returned within the hour. When I came into Jon's room, I was shocked to see water standing in the deep crevices of his neck. He had spat up water, as he no longer wanted to drink. Then it dawned on me what his plan had been all about, and I felt waves of chills running up and down my spine. I finally understood that Jon, after the nursing home experience, had consciously stopped eating and was now also refusing water and oxygen. He was ready to let go, knowing that his body had come to its finality. I was deeply moved.

The hospice nurse Nancy appeared and said that she had special medicine for Jon to help make his transition easier. She explained this to Jon and administered the medicine. Nancy then sat down in the living room with me and said, "Jon is actively dying and David should come back at once."

Unsure, I suggested that she make the call to David in The Netherlands. We both ended up speaking with David. Thoughts to the contrary were racing through my mind. "How could Nancy be so certain that Jon would die soon? How many times had we sat with him believing his end was near?"

Again Nancy said, "Your husband will not make it through the next weekend."

But as I wanted Jon's own input, I went to his room and said, "Jon, Nancy thinks that we need David back here. What do you think and what do *you* want?" Jon kept silent for a while and finally said, "Let him come back in September." It was Wednesday, August the eighteenth.

Jon's body was in agony and could hardly move or be moved. Nurse Nancy had to call for assistance and our friend Robin came to help. Later in the evening both Robin and her husband Jim appeared. They were Jon's oldest and most trusted friends.

Jim was a medical doctor and Jon had known him and his wife since high school. There was a special bond between Jon and Jim of an almost psychic nature. They understood each other without words. The administered medicine had a soporific effect on Jon and he no longer spoke. Jon was breathing with difficulty without the oxygen, but did not seem to be in discomfort. Jim and Robin stayed on for quite a while. It was already two in the morning when they left with a promise to come back later at five. I stayed with Jon for a while and spoke with him, but he no longer responded. It was two-thirty in the morning and I decided to try to sleep for a few hours before Jim and Robin would reappear.

I went upstairs to lie down. I asked in prayer to be woken up when needed. By the invisible thread that connected me to Jon, I experienced the beauty of oneness with his soul. In bed, I tried to settle down on my right side, and had my left hand lying flat on the left side of my body. While wondering if sleep would ever come, another hand appeared that in slow motion gently and lovingly caressed my left hand. The hand was not of this world. Too exhausted to give it much thought, I fell asleep maybe for a few seconds. In my sleep I felt my body sliding downward into an infinite dark abyss. Down, down and down I went. Suddenly, I was completely awake and my mind was crystal clear. The house was shrouded in endless silence. I knew for certain that I was not needed downstairs, but realized that I was awakened for a reason. I sat up in bed listening to the silence... Then I ran downstairs. Jon had stopped breathing. Something very deep broke inside me and I was no longer whole.

For the second time in my life I phoned to announce my husband's passing. Femke responded by heroically getting on the road with Ramon despite the fact that she was almost eight months' pregnant. They arrived in the early afternoon of Thursday, August the nineteenth. Ramon said, "I saw Jon in light-form standing on the deck welcoming us." Femke entered Jon's room with her arms filled with several bouquets of roses of all colors, tokens of her love.

Jim and Robin had the know-how to keep Jon's body home on ice till David could join us for a small ceremony after he came back to the United States on Saturday.

We said our goodbyes with only a few friends and family. The hospice minister prayed the prayer of Saint Francis. I sat in a complete daze next to Jon, who, surrounded by flowers, so peacefully lay there as if he were still with us. The funeral home director came to take the body away. How deeply it touched my soul that Femke had put on a CD with Mozart's *Ave Verum Corpus* when Jon's body was carried out of the house he had lived in for nearly thirty years. David and I sat down in the hearse to accompany Jon's remains to the funeral home. I felt totally lost but acted as if I was in charge and still taking care of Jon as if he were alive. Ramon and Femke followed the hearse in their own car.

In the days that followed, my mind kept filling with clouds and everything felt unreal. "Jon was no longer with us," and I could not wrap my mind around that. Ramon and Femke had to leave for California and David stayed on for ten more days.

Tuesday came, the day when David and I would send Jon's body off into the cremation fires. I wanted a pure white rose to go with him. No sooner had I thought of a white rose than a hospice volunteer appeared at the door handing me the exact rose I had in mind. It completely astounded me.

At the funeral home I removed the thorns of the rose and laid it on Jon's heart with an envelope with messages from both David and me to go with him. With unbearable pain in my own heart, David and I stood there as Jon's body disappeared into the large furnace. In utter silence we left. I remember driving up the McKenzie River and having breakfast at Jon's favorite restaurant in a total daze… Three hours later we drove back and picked up the ashes placed in a beautiful cloisonné urn with paintings of scenes of mountains, waterfalls and flowers.

I do not really know how we got home again. All I remember was that I held the box, which held the urn, tightly in my arms. I walked up the stairs to the master bedroom, the urn still in my loving and caring embrace, when halfway up the stairs, two brilliant lights suddenly appeared on my left side. They startled me and my whole body shook by the intensity of these lights. One light was white-diamond and the other diamond-blue... Again, I knew that:

life is love
and to love gives life,
but also that
love
never dies

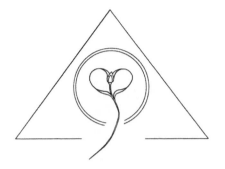

Epilogue

Chapter Ninety

Esoteric Knowledge

I often refer in my book to the seeing of the diamond-light. I wish to share with you the knowledge of two enlightened saints in India regarding these lights.

I. In the Shri Siddheswar Baba teachings, I found:

> When during the *Kundalini* process the upward flow begins
> to happen, he/she starts seeing different types of colors of
> light within and without him (her) self.

This seeing of colors within and without happens to me on a daily basis. When I stayed for the last time in Guruji's ashram, I remember meeting another student who advised, "Go inside." What she was trying to tell me is that inside is better than outside. "This is not true." A person who sees through the third eye also knows that inside is outside. Inside is where the light of God lives. By tuning in to this level of higher vibration, one can open the physical eyes and yet still see through the third eye that which is inside, on the outside. To give an example, "When I close my eyes during meditation, I see certain colors in my third eye, and when I open my eyes I continue to see what I saw inside, on the outside. The other way around is true as well. On the outside, I may experience seeing the light of God, but I know that this comes through the higher vibrations, inside."

I conclude that the outside world is but a reflection of our combined inner worlds, which is perhaps the same as the "collective unconscious" as Carl Jung coined it. Our world can only change by moving into the purity of our inner worlds and bringing the inner unconscious (in this book often referred to as higher Consciousness) to our outer awareness. Each of us has to find ways to embrace the true light of understanding within first. This will happen by going beyond the small and often busy ego-mind to become that which we are, pure light. The light then leads us to true clarity of thinking, no longer selfish, but in full embrace with all the forms and no-forms of creations. The more I connect with God, the more I become a knower, the more the presence of the light of God arises in me, spreading more light to everyone and everything.

Sadhana, or spiritual practice consists of:

1. Meditation (see Part VII, Chapter Sixty, "Meditation Camp in Bhigaan").
2. Reflection on the Self as the light.
3. Being the witness of the limited self (*see* your own short story).
4. Singing spiritually uplifting songs.
5. Reciting mantras.
6. Knowing that you and the other is the Self.

This practice helps in the process of becoming *That* (*Upanishads: Tat twam asi,* Thou art *That*). These exercises will bring the focus upwards, straight to the heart of God.

II. The second piece of knowledge I would like to share is from the writings of the Sri Aurobindo Ashram in Pondicherry, India: *The Mother with Letters on the Mother* in a chapter called the "Mother's Diamond Light":

(a) It [the diamond light] means the essential Force of the Mother.

(b) The diamond light proceeds from the heart of the Divine Consciousness and it brings the opening of the Divine Consciousness wherever it goes.

(c) The Mother's descent with the diamond light is the sanction of the Supreme Power to the movement in you.

(d) The Mother's diamond light is a light of absolute purity and power.

(e) The diamond light is the central consciousness and force of the Divine.

* * *

The diamond is the symbol of the Mother's light and energy – the diamond light is that of her consciousness at its most intense.

13-11-1936

Sri Aurobindo, *The Mother with Letters on the Mother and Translations of Prayers and Meditations*, SABCL Vol. 25, p. 86

I further read in the above-mentioned book:

The golden light is the light of the Divine Truth on the higher planes above the ordinary mind – a light supramental in origin. It is also the light of Mahakali above the mind. The golden light is also often seen emanating from the Mother like the white light.

17-9-1933
Ibid, p. 87

I have seen and see the diamond-light as well as the golden light. I also remember my vision of Shri Siddheswar Baba appearing in my room in a body of scintillating golden sparks.

After the passing of Shri Siddheswar I have seen the golden light around his tomb and around his chair in the old class-room. In Sai Baba's interview room I observed large bands of liquid molten gold moving in fan-like shapes around the room. I see light around spiritually focused people as an ethereal gold around and above their bodies.

The Mother book explains that the higher mind color is pale blue. Seeing these lights is one of the signs that the higher force is beginning to influence matter. I was aware of the ethereal color pale blue around the orange curtains in the *samadhi-temple* of my Guru. That same color surrounded my own body when I looked in the mirror of my hotel room in Whitefield, when I was pretending to be the *rishi* that Dr. Gupta said I had been in ancient India. Know that my seeing is not with the normal eye, but with the third eye, which corresponds with the normal eyes to register it to the senses.

Chapter Ninety-one

My Journey

Looking back on my life thus far, I know that it has been divinely pre-ordained as all life truly is. I am fulfilling my own blueprint, which in essence is my agreement with God before entering this world. My script has included many difficulties, but also many incredible experiences of deep-felt wonderment and joy. The deaths of Harmen and Jon shook me out of any complacency I may have had and deepened my awareness of the eternal love of the light that is God. Death showed me how my life is part of a wave in the ocean of God-consciousness. The waves swell and collide, roll in and out, but always remain a part of that total body of water, the unbound Consciousness.

Human beings can reach God by focusing on sacred images or sacred words. I already spoke of my revelations of God through the images of Krishna, Paramahansa Yogananda, the Buddha, Shirdi Sai Baba, and Sathya Sai Baba. Another transcendental experience happened through the Virgin Mary in the Abbey at Mount Angel in Oregon when I visited the monastery with Jon, who was going through a time of deep darkness and soul searching. While Jon was in the library I sat in the chapel praying for divine help while focusing on the statue of the Holy Mother. Suddenly the statue came to life and spoke from the higher levels of consciousness, bringing me for a moment to that higher place where my troubles seemed far away and of lesser importance. I could feel my soul singing with joy.

At a later time, I meditated on the well-known image of Our Lady of Guadalupe, another aspect of the divine Mother. She showed me that the diamond-light is hers when a sudden appearance of this illuminating light struck me. Our Lady of Guadalupe had appeared to Juan Diego in 1531, and her appearance facilitated a bridge between the old Aztec religions and that of the Catholic Spanish conquerors. I believe that God again is motivating us today to build bridges to other religions, to other cultures, and other ideologies, to build together rather than to destroy.

Through divine revelations, openings of the mystic veil happen whereby one passes from the third dimension into the next levels of consciousness. It is through these revelations that I can say that all holy images are in their pure essence always ONE.

My mother never forced me to embrace any particular spiritual belief system. She simply taught me, at age four, *het Onze Vader,* which is the Lord's Prayer. For a long time I did not know the importance of this prayer, nor that it was prayed the world over by believers of the Christian faith. I know now that within its essence, the prayer contains divine power that can heal or lift the veil between the earth plane and realms beyond. Other prayers, like the Hail Mary, have similar powers. During my Astarian days, when I prayed the Hail Mary, I saw my crystal rosary surrounded by the white light of the Christ. The power in these prayers comes from the same source, God. For the Jews it is in reciting the *Sh'ma Yisra'eil Adonai Eloheinu Adonai Echad* (Hear, Israel, the Lord is our God, the Lord is One). For the Muslims it is in speaking the *Allahu Akbar,* or God is the Greatest. The Hindus' mantras, *Om Namah Shivaya* (I bow to Shiva, the innermost Self) or *Rama Rama* (the Vishnu Avatar), just to name a few, lead a spiritual practitioner during *japa* (repetition of the mantra) into the world of God.

Another way of approaching the unfathomable unbound Eternal is by the simple teachings of my Sunday school teacher during WWII, when she remarked, "God is like the sun, always shining with a bright embracing light that warms the soul. Sometimes clouds appear and hide God from our sight. All you have to do is smile with all your heart and all your soul, and the clouds will evaporate. Then you see and know God."

I received an opening into the universal knowledge and became One with this knowledge at the age of twelve. Life after the experience was never quite the same. As I grew up, the God knowledge, even though part of me, became a bit shrouded so that I could live the short story of my life as a normal child. In other words that knowledge did not stay revealed in present awareness. But the depth of the knowledge still guided and nudged me to explore various pathways to seek that truth I had known.

Before I joined the Sai movement, I had mystical experiences. They never happened because of Sai Baba, but came from the living God within myself. My Sai involvement guided me to rediscover the ancient Indian scriptures, which I must have known in prior lives. I could have found those scriptures in the library of my own hometown, but would not ordinarily have looked for them there. I learned much through the course of traveling eleven times to India. The knowledge I gained led me slowly to the understanding that the true light ultimately cannot be contained in any form or name. I also learned that the Divine is everywhere and as higher Consciousness can speak through anyone.

Only in a land like India could I have found my true *Kundalini* Guru, Shri Siddheswar Baba, to help me with problems that arise during the *Kundalini* process and to help me understand the stages in that process towards enlightenment. It was Shri Guriji who ultimately made me free of all gurus when he taught me to know that the true Guru is, and always remains, within. Yet he also said to sit with a saint, who undoubtedly has more light to shed upon a student than any ordinary man. Despite his recommendation, I know for now that all I need to do is to fully surrender to the majesty of my revealed light from where my true guidance comes. This surrender leads to the inexpressible joy of being, and in such states I find my face turning into one beaming smile that lights up the world. To live in that formless pure ray of the ultimate sun is my soul's highway to my beloved other, also known as the Self.

When I see the various lights of God, I know I am receiving personal proof of the divine. This eternal star of illuminating light can take us into deep realms, even after the physical body has passed away.

For now, I travel with the light through my life's journey. This light is the eternal witness of all that I think, all that I speak and all that I do. Only God knows the time of my true uninterrupted awakening in his ultimate light. As long as I am not yet permanently one with that eternal light, I will be drawn to it.

Even though I write about this light through the limitation of mind expression, I can assure my reader that I know that when I am in that state of God awareness, I have realization and from that unbound experience I know that life is truly ONE.

My prayer for the world is that all may be drawn to the light and come home to *That* (*tat twam asi*), the understanding that there is only one Consciousness, called God, or Brahman in Indian terms.

Appendix

Checklist of Symptoms of Kundalini

- Altered states of consciousness
- Anxiety neurosis with reactive depression
- Arousal of Kundalini is sudden and frightening
- Auditory and visual perceptions beyond the third dimension
- Automatic body movements and postures
- Bliss, peace and stability

- Burning sensations along spine and the rest of the body
- Burning sensation in the eyes as if some magnetic pulls are taking place in them
- Confusion
- Cosmic sounds
- Delirium
- Digestive problems
- Dissociation with the world
- Distortion of though processes

- Dizziness
- Drowsy states
- Ecstasy
- Electrical current sensation in the spine
- Enlightenment experience, direct knowledge of the Real
- Extreme confusion and bewilderment
- Extreme emotions
- Extreme Sexual desires (often temporary)
- Fear
- Fear of death
- Fear of insanity
- Feelings of endless love and compassion
- Force going upward through the backbone
- Head shaking
- Headaches
- Heart palpitations
- Heat and cold experiences
- Heavy head
- Heightened awareness
- Increased creativity; music art poetry, writing
- Increased rate of breathing
- Increased rate of pulse beating
- Inner sounds
- Intercourse with the universe
- Involuntary weeping, laughing, screaming, whistling
- Involuntary movements of all kind
- Loss of confidence
- Loss of hunger
- Light experiences inside the head
- Magnetic pull to the crown chakra
- Mystical experiences
- Muscle twitches, cramps or spasms
- Nausea
- Nostrils are working almost equally at all the times
- Numbness or pain in limbs
- Opening of the third eye
- Orgasmic feelings
- Out of body experience
- Pain in heart area
- Pains and blockage anywhere, often in neck or back
- Pain in third eye when it is beginning to open
- Pain (sharp) in the big toes
- Paralysis (mostly temporary)

- Perfect knowledge
- Physical vibrations
- Pressure on the crown chakra
- Pressure on the nerves near the crown chakra
- Quick concentration at the mid-point between the eyebrows
- Red-aura spread throughout the brain seen through the third eye
- Restlessness
- Rolled up eyes toward the crown chakra
- Seeing auras
- Seeing beyond the normal
- Seeing the Light of God
- Sensations of ants crawling up the spine
- Sensations of fish, monkey, bird or snake going up the spine
- Shaking in various parts of the body
- Sleeplessness
- Sounds of flute, drum, waterfall, bird singing, bees buzzing
- Sounds roaring, whooshing or thunderous like ringing in the ears

- Spinal column movements (snakelike) inside sushumna
- Supernatural experiences
- Swings (frequent) between states of happiness and depression and suffering
- Thought processes slowing down or speeding up
- Tickling sensations
- Tongue is coated white with white thick saliva
- Trance states
- Transcendental awareness
- Understanding of spiritual truths
- Unusual breathing patterns
- Vibration in feet
- Vibration and spasms in spinal column
- Visions of the Divine
- Vision of the inner color purple blue
- Visions of golden light
- Waves moving up the backbone in a rhythmic fashion like the movements of a snake
- Witness of thought processes

Glossary

Amrita: Divine nectar.

Anitya: Constant changing/the world of illusion

Antakharana: Innermost heart. Bridge to the oversoul.

Arathi: The worship of God with the flame of camphor. The camphor burns and leaves no residue. Similarly, the flame of love of God must consume the ego, leaving no trace of I or mine.

Arjuna: White, pure, and unsullied. Arjuna was one of the Pandava brothers.

Ashram: Place of spiritual practices, usually headed by an enlightened master.

Avatar: The concept of God taking birth in human form to re-establish dharma and to do service to the world by putting righteousness into its high place.

Bhagavad-Gita: The song of God.

Bhajans: Singing hymns in God's glory with full devotion and rhythm.

Brahma-randhra: Gate to God located in the crown of the head

Brahmacharyas: Mostly understood to be individuals who remain celibate as part of their *sadhana*)

Brindavan: The forest of Brind. The pastoral lands, and forests, where Lord Krishna played in his childhood.

Chakra: Subtle centers of consciousness in the spine.

Darshan: Seeing a saint: to see the form of the Lord and receive his blessing.

Dharma: The dictates of God, the duty of man, morality, righteousness, virtue.

Dharma Ksetra: Field where Mahabharatar War took place.

Dhoti: Skirt worn by Indian men.

Dwesha: Dwesha and raga are the two nerves near the Brahma-randhra; dislocation of these two nerves happen when Kundalini is activated.

Ganesha: Elephant God, remover of obstacles.

Gayatri: Vedic mantra and universal prayer asking for illumination. That which saves when repeated.

Gnani/Jnani: Knower of wisdom, full of virtue. One who has attained self-realization.

Godman: An Avatar, Saint or Enlightened person.

Gokulam: Village of cowherdsmen.

Granti Lock: Locks on the first, fourth and sixth chakra.

Gunas: Human characteristics, qualities, attributes; satva: good noble; rajas: mere activity; thamas: darkness

Guru Poornima: The day set-aside for adoration of the Guru.

Iconoclast: Seeing divinity without images.

Ida: The major nerve in the backbone that runs on the left side of the sushumna.

Jiva: The embodied soul.

Kali Yuga: Last cycle of the four yugas or divisions of time. The age of iron.

Karma: Action.

Kosas: Sheaths covering the jiva.

Krishna: Avatar during the Mahabharata war.

Kriya Yoga: A yogi technique taught by Lahiri Mahasaya, whereby the sensory tumult is stilled, permitting man to achieve an everlasting identity with cosmic consciousness.

Kundalini: The creative force of the Universe also known as serpent power.

Kurukshetra: Field of action; camp of the wicked Kauravas.

Kwan Yin: Embodiment of the principle of divine love.

Lama yoga: Yoga practiced in Mystical School Astara.

Leela: Play, divine play, and divine activities, divine sport.

Lingam: The symbolic form of the Godhead.

Mahabarata: An ancient epic by sage Vyasa, relating the battle of Kuruk-shetra, between the Pandavas and Kauravas.

Mahasamadhi: Merging into the Godhead.

Mahashivaratri: Most auspicious time to transcend. The holiest of Hindu festivals.

Mandir: Temple

Mantra: Chants, sacred words or formulas.

Maya: World of illusion

Moksha: Liberation from the cycle of birth and death.

Mudras: Hand gestures by the deities having specific symbolic meanings.

Muladhara: Root chakra, where the Kundalini lies dormant.

Murali: Flute, the flute of Krishna.

Nagarsankirtan: Early morning singing of the glories of God in the streets.

Nishkamakarma: Action, karma, without any desire of the fruit thereof.

Nithya: Undergoing no change in past, present, and future

Om/Aum: The pranava, the original sound. Sound of the supreme universal reality, called Brahmam.

Omkar: The primal cosmic sound, which is the cause of the whole universe.

Om Namah Shivaya: The name of God is Shiva.

Padenamaskar: Touching the feet of a holy man or an elder with respect.

Paduka festival: Blessing of the Lords sandals.

Pandit: A learned person.

Parthi Sai: Sai Baba of Puttaparthi in southern India.

Pingala: The major nerve in the backbone that runs on the right side of the sushumna.

Prasad: Consecrated food blessed by God.

Puja: Hindu worship ritual to the deities.

Pranayama: Regulation of breath. The *sadhana* or practice by which you hold the prana of breath.

Punjabi: Indian suit consisting of a dress with puffy pants with shawl for ladies or pajama type suit for men.

Raga: Raga and dwesha are the two nerves near the Brahma-randra. Dislocation of these nerves happens when Kundalini is activated.

Ramayana: Epic about Lord Rama.

Ramesh Hall: Sai Baba's temple in Brindavan, Whitefield.

Renunciation: Non attachment.

Rishi: Realized saint in ancient India.

Root Chakra: Chakra at the base of the spine.

Sadhaka: Spiritual aspirant.

Sadhana: Spiritual practice.

Sai Ram: Greeting in Sai Baba's ashram, greeting to the God within; a mantra and a call to God.

Samadhi: A state of union with God.

Sambhaasham: Conversing with the Divine.

Sannyasis: Ascetics who have renounced the material world.

Sanskrit: Ancient language of Indian sacred works.

Sarva dharma symbol: Symbol of unity of all religions.

Sat Chit Ananda: Truth, awareness, bliss.

Satsang: Good and holy company.

Seva: Service as worship to the divine around you, adoration of the Lord.

Seva-dal: Volunteer at Sai Baba's ashrams.

Shakti: Kundalini power.

Shirdi Sai Baba: Sai Baba's said former birth.

Siddha loka: High place in Heaven where the saints dwell.

Siddheswar Baba: God realized saint.

Sohum: I am He, I am that.

Solar plexus: Third chakra in the spinal column.

Sparsanam: Touching the Divine.

Sushumna: The central yogic nerve in the backbone, which starts at the base of the spine and goes right up to Brahma-randra.

Tapas: Disciplined spiritual practice to control and coordinate the functions of the body. Austerities, the sacrifice and asceticism, that wins Gods grace, detachment.

Tat Twam Asi: Thou art that. That thou art.

Trikuti: Midpoint between the two eyebrows.

Upanishads: Ancient scripture of India. Study and practice of innate truth.

Vedic: Ancient times when the Vedic scriptures, containing divine knowledge were written.

Yogi/Yogini: Those who have achieved union with God; also referring to a person devoted to yoga.

Website: www.exbaba.nl (links to other websites to find more about the allegations against Sai Baba, deceased, 2011).

Bibliography

Aurobindo, Sri. *The Mother, with Letters on The Mother and Translations of Prayers and Meditations.* Pondicherry, India: Sri Aurobindo Ashram Publication Department, 1972.

Bhagavad Gita. Translated for the modern reader by Eknath Easwaran. Nilgiri Press, 1994.

BIBLE: *The New English Bible.* New York: Oxford University Press, 1971.

BIBLE: *The Holy Bible.* Revised Standard Version containing the Old and New Testaments. Grand Rapids, Michigan: Zondervan Publishing House, Old Testament Section, Copyright 1952, New Testament Section, First Edition, Copyright 1946. New Testament Section, Second Edition Copyright 1971 by Division of Christian Education of the National Council of Churches of Christ in the United States of America.

Brooke, Tal and Martha S. Serpas. *Avatar of Night.* End Run Publishing, 1999.

Chaney, Earlyne and William L. Messick. *Kundalini and the Third Eye.* Astara Library of Mystical Classics. 800 W. Arrow Highway, Upland, California 91786: Astara, 1980.

Colton, Ann Ree. *Kundalini West.* Glendale, California: ARC Publishing Company, 1982.

Cranston, Ruth. *The Miracle of Lourdes.* New York, London, Toronto, Sidney and Auckland: Image Book Doubleday, 1955.

De Jong, L. *De Bezetting* (The Occupation). Amsterdam: EM.Querido Uitgeversmaatschappij N.V., 1965.

Gersten, Dennis. *Are You Getting Enlightened or Losing Your Mind?* New York: Harmony Books, 1997.

Devi Mahatmyam, Glory of the Divine Mother: 700 mantras on Sri Durga. English translation by Swami Jagadiswa. Mylapore, Madras, India 600004: Sri Ramakrishna Math, 1953.

Gibran, Kahlil *The Prophet.* New York: Alfred A. Knopf, 1952.

Goel, B.S. *Third Eye and Kundalini.* Haryana, India: Third Eye Foundation of India, Shri Siddheswar Ashram, Bhigaan-131033, 1994.

Goel, B.S. *Psycho-Analysis and Meditation.* Haryana, India: Third Eye Foundation of India, Shri Siddheswar Ashram, Bhigaan-131033, 1997.

Goel, B.S. *Psycho-analysis and Meditation, Certain Related Essays.* Haryana, India: Third Eye Foundation of India, Shri Siddheswar Ashram, Bhigaan-131033, 1992.

Goel, B.S. *Shrimad Bhagavad Geeta. A Psychological Commentary for Spiritual Seekers and Psychic Sufferers.* Haryana, India: Third Eye Foundation of India, Shri Siddheswar Ashram, Bhigaan-131033, 1986.

Gospel, *The Gospel of Sri Ramakrishna*, Originally recorded in Bengali, in five volumes, by M., a disciple of the Master. Complete translation, with an Introduction, by Swami Nikhilananda. New York: Ramakrishna-Vivekanda Center, 2007.

Gunaji, Nagesh Vasudev. *Shri Sai Satcharita or the Wonderful Life and Teachings of Shri Sai Baba*, 15th Edition. Adapted from the original Marathi Book by Hemadpant. Bombay, India: Prof. Dr. Lekha Pathak Chairperson, Shri Sai Baba Sansthan, Shirdi 'Sai Niketan,' 804-B, Dr. Ambedkar Road, Dadar, 400 014, 1991.

Indian Culture and Spirituality. Haryana, India: Third Eye Foundation of India, Shri Siddheswar Ashram, Bhigaan-131033, 1995.

Joy, Brugh W. *Joy's Way. A Map for the Transformational Journey. An Introduction to the Potentials for Healing with Body Energies.* Los Angeles: J.P. Tarcher, Inc. 1979. Distributed by Houghton Mifflin Company, Boston.

Kasturi, N. *Prashanti: Pathway to Peace.* Prashanti Nilyam, India: Shri Sathya Sai Books & Publications Trust.

Krystal, Phyllis. *Sai Baba, The Ultimate Experience.* , Los Angeles: Aura Books, 1985.

Krishna, Gopi. *Living with Kundalini. The Autobiography of Gopi Krishna,* edited by Leslie Shepard. Boston & London: Shambala Publications Inc., 1993.

Larsson, Conny. *Behind the Mask of the Clown, Truths, Sex and Sects.* Podanur 641 023-Tamilnadu, India: I.B. Premanand Publisher, 2007.

Lumiere, Lynn Marie and John Lumiere Wins. *The Awakening West: evidence of spreading enlightenment.* Oakland, California: Clear Vision Publication, 2000.

Mason, Peggy and Ron Laing. *The Embodiment of Love,* third edition. Gateway Books, 1993.

Montgomery, Ruth. *The World Beyond.* New York, Toronto: A Fawcett Crest Book, 1972. Published by Ballantine Books, a Division of Random House, Inc., 1972.

Muktananda, Swami. *Play of Consciousness, Chitshati Vilas. A Spiritual Autobiography,* fourth edition. A Siddha Yoga Publication published by the Syda Foundation. Printed in the U.S.A., 1994.

Murphet, Howard. *Sai Baba Avatar. A New Journey into Power and Glory.* Published by Frederick Muller LTD, 1979.

Newton, Michael. *Destiny of Souls.* St. Paul, Minnesota: Llewllyn Publications, 2010.

Rama, Swami and Rudolph Ballentine, M.D. and Alan Hymes, M.D. *Science of Breath: a Practical Guide.* Honesdale, Pennsylvania: Himalayan International Institute of Yoga Science and Philosophy, 1981.

Sannella, Lee. *The Kundalini Experience.* Integral Publishing, 1992.

Spalding, Baird T. *Life and Teachings of the Masters of the Far East.* Volumes 1–5. DeVorss & Co., Publishers, 1924, 1937, 1944, 1972.

St. Teresa of Avila, The Collected Works of. Volume Two. *The Way of Perfection. Meditations on the Song of Songs. The Interior Castle.* Translated by Kieran Kavanaugh, O.C.D. and Otilio Rodriguez, O.C.D. Washington D.C.: ICS Publications, Institute of Carmelite Studies, 1980.

Taylor, Jill Bolte. *My Stroke of Insight: A Brain Scientist's Personal Journey.* London: First Plume Printing, 2009. Penguin Books Limited, Registered Offices: 80 Strand, London WC2R ORL, England.

The Mother. *Questions and Answers 1953.* Pondicherryy, India: Shri Aurobindo Ashram Trust, 1998. Published by Shri Aurobindo Ashram Publication Department.

The Mother. *With Letters on the Mother and Translations of Prayers and Meditations.* Pondicherry, India: Sri Aurobindo Ashram, first edition 1972. Eighth impression 2002.

The Teachings of Bhagavan Sri Ramana Maharshi in His Own Words. Edited by Arthur Osborne. Tiruvannamalai, South India: T.N. Venkata-raman, Sri Ramanasraman, 1977.

The Upanishads, translated for the modern reader by Eknath Easwaran. Nilgiri Press, 1995.

The Upanishads, a New Translation by Swami Nikhilananda. Volume I, sixth edition. New York: Ramakrishna Vivekananda Center, 2003.

Thijssen, Theo. *Het Grijze Kind.* Athenaeum-Polak & Van Gennep, September, 2006.

Tolle, Eckhart. *Stillness Speaks.* Vancouver, Canada: New World Library and Namaste Publishing, 2003.

Tredwell, Gail. *Holy Hell, A Memoir of Faith, Devotion, and Pure Madness.* Maui, Hawai'i: Wattle Tree Press, 2013.

Tweedie, Irena. *Chasm of Fire. A woman's experience of liberation through the teachings of a Sufi Master.* Element Books, 1979.

Twigg, Ena. *Ena Twigg: Medium.* New York: Hawthorn Books Inc. Publishers, 1972.

Verwaal, Ernst and Robert The Tjong Tjoe. *Kwan Yin: Over het hoger bewustzijn.* Uitgeverij Ankh-Hermes bv-Deventer, 1980.

Yogananda, Paramahansa, *Autobiography of a Yogi.* Los Angeles: Self-Realization Fellowship Publishers, 1979.

Website: www.exbaba.nl (links to other websites to find more about the allegations against Sai Baba, deceased 2011).